KU-073-220

Withdrawn

06 422 873 5

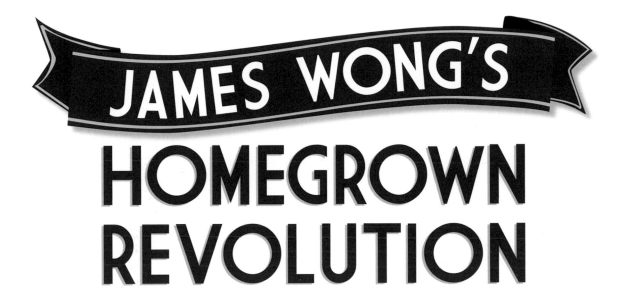

JAMES WONG'S
HOMEGROWN REVOLUTION

First published in Great Britain in 2012 by Weidenfeld & Nicolson

10 9 8 7 6 5 4 3 2 1

Text copyright © Suburban Shaman Enterprises Ltd
Design and layout © Weidenfeld & Nicolson 2012

Photography © Andrew Hayes-Watkins
with the exception of the following pages: 58, 89, 96, 173, 190 © iStock
229, 246 © Shutterstock
Design & art direction: obroberts
Illustrators: Fiona Osbaldstone & obroberts
Food stylist: Nico Ghirlando
Proofreader: Jolyon Goddard
Indexer: Rosemary Dear

All rights reserved. No part of this publication may be reproduced, stored in
a retrieval system, or transmitted, in any form or by any means, electronic,
mechanical, photocopying, recording or otherwise, without the prior permission
of both the copyright owner and the above publisher.

Note: While every effort has been made to ensure that the content of this book is
as technically, botanically accurate and as sound as possible, neither the author or
the publisher can accept responsibility for any injury or loss sustained as a result
of the use of this material.

The right of James Wong to be identified as the author of this work has been
asserted in accordance with the Copyright, Designs and Patents Act 1988.

A CIP catalogue record for this book is available from the British Library.

ISBN: 9780297867128

Printed and bound in Italy

The Orion Publishing Group's policy is to use papers that are natural, renewable
and recyclable products and made from wood grown in sustainable forests.
The logging and manufacturing processes are expected to conform to the
environmental regulations of the country of origin.

Weidenfeld & Nicolson
The Orion Publishing Group Ltd
Orion House
5 Upper St Martin's Lane
London WC2H 9EA

An Hachette UK company
www.orionbooks.co.uk

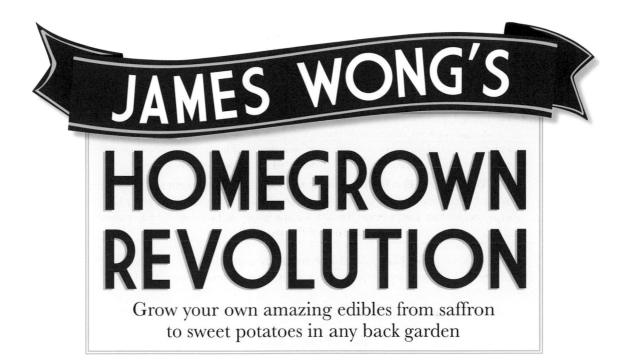

JAMES WONG'S

HOMEGROWN REVOLUTION

Grow your own amazing edibles from saffron
to sweet potatoes in any back garden

WEIDENFELD & NICOLSON

There is something innately generous about plant people. Wherever they are on earth or whatever their background, they can always be relied upon to be up for sharing the fruits of their labour, nifty growing tips or even old family recipes. It is only because of this enormous generosity that this book has been made possible, so right from the start I would like to extend a huge thank you to all the dozens of fellow plant geeks that helped in so many ways to make this project a reality.

CONTENTS

Introduction

Join the revolution!

So what's wrong with spuds, sprouts and swedes?

As every glossy magazine and middle-class dinner party conversation will tell you, we are living amid a great 'grow your own' revolution. What was once exclusively the preserve of the 'flat cap and whippet brigade' has now been opened up to a wider audience of young, urban foodies.

Yet, for some bizarre reason, if you sift through the hype and actually look at the beds and borders of the new generation of 'allotmenteers' fuelling this boom, the contents still look a whole lot more 'wartime ration book' than 'fancy fusion menu'. The whole concept of 'growing your own' has somehow got itself stuck in a weird 1940s time warp and most growers (newbies and veterans alike) appear unaware of options beyond spuds, sprouts and swedes – the allotment equivalent of powdered eggs and spam. But things simply don't have to be this way!

With well over 2,500 edible plant species – everything from kiwi fruit to sweet potatoes – perfectly happy to grow on our blustery North Atlantic island, it is crazy that pretty much every book on growing fruit and veg since the Second World War has drummed on about the same 20 or so crops, which represent less than 1 per cent of what we can actually grow. The fact is, the British diet has become infinitely more exciting and varied, drawing on ingredients and inspiration from all around the world in the last half century. Put simply, we don't eat the same stuff we did two generations ago, so why on earth should we be stuck growing it?

I believe we should stop growing crops that are cheap to buy, widely available and whose flavours differ little from the shrink-wrapped supermarket offerings. Let's take a look at the evidence: I recently phoned the upmarket London store Harrods and asked for its most expensive potato. I wanted it gift-wrapped and delivered to my door. It turns out that biodynamic, heritage spuds flown in from California are still cheaper gram for gram than if I were to buy one of those woven potato-growing barrel kits that are in all the catalogues. Planted in this way, it can make growing your own potatoes one of the single most expensive ways to get hold of them – and I guarantee you won't be able to taste the difference in a blindfold test. For someone like my grandad in the 1940s with no cut-price superstore five minutes down the road and acres of Welsh countryside to farm, growing potatoes made complete sense. For someone like me, in the 21st century, growing potatoes on my postage stamp-sized suburban patch just doesn't.

The fantastic news is that by simply swapping common, low-value crops for a range of easy-to-grow, genuinely productive cutting-edge ones, you can turn your yard veg patch back into a living larder of 'superfoods' and exotic delicacies. You just have to get out there and give them a go!

Learning from those adventurous Victorians

Despite today's global warming and the UK's ethnically diverse society, the Victorians and earlier generations of Brits were far more adventurous with food than we are. They grew everything from saffron (in huge plantations in places like Essex's Saffron Walden and London's Saffron Hill) and hardy Chilean guavas (reputedly Queen Victoria's favourite fruit) to Inca berries (for which the great Mrs Beeton developed a delicious jam recipe). In fact, the change in crops came with the First World War when the decisions about what was grown were taken out of the hands of thousands of tiny independent growers and instead put under the control of a few government officials. It was then that the more exotic yet surprisingly commonly grown crops were ditched in favour of staples such as cabbages and potatoes and a century later they have never really made a comeback.

My homegrown revolution promise

This book isn't about growing unconventional crops for the sake of it. It's about taking the plunge and growing delicious, high-yield foods that are expensive to buy, yet easy to grow. This idea, of course, does include many allotment favourites like strawberries, tomatoes and asparagus, but in this book I have focused on the plants that are not in your standard allotment starter kit and everything that's been selected has been tested twice by me.

To ensure the genuine 'garden worthiness' of the plants, I ran a 24-month trial growing more than 120 different edibles in my own garden to choose those crops that are objectively as high yielding, easy to source, low maintenance and, of course, good to eat as the much more conventional fruit and veg currently found in the average British backyard. My experiment ran over two of the poorest summers and coldest winters on record in Britain and used only crops and kit that I could source from an average garden centre (or order in five minutes online). No greenhouse, heated propagators or team of gardeners in sight, just me, a watering can and a whole lot of determination.

One of the things that I found most interesting was that many extremely common and widely recommended crops are actually far harder to grow than some of the truly weird and wonderful entries, despite enormous amounts of breeding and glowing supplier recommendations.

Five of the real stars

Some commonly recommended crops that didn't make it past my battery of tests include aubergines, patio peppers, cauliflowers, celery and soya. Among those that did pass with flying colours are the following five stars:

- **Tomatillos** – a lime-flavoured tomato-like fruit that sells for £2 each in fancy Mexican grocery stores. Each plant gave me an astonishing 10kg of fruit.

- **New Zealand spinach** – a thug that took over my garden, but gave me more spinach than I could eat from June to November and all from just a single sowing! Far tastier than your regular spinach.

- **Dahlia yams** – delicious tubers that are tastier and more productive than spuds, with the added bonus of a constant stream of huge florist-ready flowers from July onwards.

- **Alpine 'snow' strawberries** – a conveyor belt of almost artificially-flavoured mini strawberries from April to November that seemed invisible to birds and were avoided by slugs.

- **Asparagus peas** – foolproof to grow, covered in beautiful burgundy flowers and delivering finger-long 'peas' (more a bean really) that cost over £5 per 150g pack at my local Asian grocery store.

About this book

In this book, I've provided all the information anyone, from the complete novice to the skilled expert, needs to know to grow, cook and eat many exciting and often overlooked foodie treats. Before you dive on in, here are a few tips on how to navigate through its pages to become the ultimate urban farmer.

Common names

Although most crops have several common names, when it comes to more unusual fruit and veg, this number often spirals even higher, as the plants aren't mainstream enough (as yet) for us Brits to have decided on a universal label. When marketers wade in with a raft of snappy trade names this gets even more confusing – some species can be known by over a dozen different names, making it a headache when it comes to tracking them down.

In this book, I've made a deliberate decision to select one common name based on what I feel is most popular in the UK right now and what best describes the plant's edible use. For a species that is often known by an exotic-sounding name in another language I have opted for the English version instead. For example, 'New Zealand yam' is probably easier for us to remember than 'oca', the Andean Quichua dialect's name for the same crop. Where the crop is also a common garden plant that is only really known for its ornamental value in the UK, I have added specificity to highlight its edible nature – such as Hosta 'greens' or Dahlia 'yams'. Finally, if it has a handful of common names that are used pretty much interchangeably, I have highlighted its alter egos in the body of the text.

Scientific/Latin name

Although a little tricky to pronounce, scientific names are brilliant if you want to cut through the confusion, as each plant will have only one correct scientific name, despite potentially having a hoard of common ones. So if all else fails you can be sure that by going by the scientific name you will make a spot-on identification (it's like verifying someone using their passport number as opposed to their nickname). These scientific names are italicised next to the plant's common name at the beginning of each profile.

Photos and illustrations

The close-up images are designed to show the plant's structure and colour in full intricate detail, so you can be sure you have got their ID absolutely correct. Further assurance is provided by the full plant illustrations, which are also helpful for getting a clear picture of the ideal adult shape and stature of the plant – indispensable when planning your plot and anticipating how each plant will behave with its neighbours.

Key to symbols

As to how much light, moisture and space is required for each plant, as well as tolerance for frost, and the level of skill necessary for growing, just follow the quick symbols key below:

Light requirement

| Full sun | Partial shade | Light shade |

Water requirement

| High | Medium | Low |

Hardiness

| Full hardy | Half-hardy | Tender |
| -10°C | -5°C | 0°C |

Skill level

| Foolproof | Easy | Medium |

Spacing between plants

XX cm/m

My Ten Commandments

To the uninitiated gardening can sometimes seem complicated and confusing, full of rules that have to be memorised by heart before you can even approach a plant, but this simply isn't the case! Over millions of years plants have evolved to pretty much look after themselves. All gardeners really need to do is replicate the conditions of the habitats in which their plants thrive – with just a few tweaks to maximise harvests. Use my ten commandments and you'll get maximum yield with minimum work.

Let there be (loads of) light

It might be easy to take light for granted but it is arguably the single most important factor in plant growth. Yet frustratingly for home gardeners it can also be the trickiest to control. Get it right though and you can improve yields by up to an astonishing 50 per cent. Let me explain how ...

Catch the best rays

Plants' leaves are effectively living solar panels, designed to capture the maximum amount of energy from sunlight and use it to fuel their growth. This means that for the vast majority of crop plants, the more light you can give them the more vigorous their growth, and the higher your yields will be. But it doesn't stop there; for many crops, light intensity determines sugar content, especially with fruiting plants.

The effect of increasing the intensity and duration of light is so dramatic that commercial greenhouse growers often place their plants under specialised ultraviolet (UV) lamps at sunset, thereby tricking the plants into growing right through the night. While I'm not expecting any homegrowers to start stringing up lights over their vegetable patch, there are three simple tricks to give your crops as much light as possible.

1. Face south

The easiest way to ensure maximum light levels is choose the most southerly facing aspect of your plot for growing. This aspect receives the sun's rays for the longest period of the day, in addition they will also receive more warmth during the day. To figure out where south lies on your plot firstly make a note of where the sun rises (east) and sets (west) each day. Then stand with your left hand pointing east and right pointing west and you will then be facing south. For technology geeks an instant way to check is to use the compass function on your smartphone or look up an online map while standing in your garden.

2. Dodge the shade

Even if you don't have the luxury of having a south-facing plot there will be areas that are less eclipsed by shade than others. Look high – roof gardens, balconies, hanging baskets and pots and troughs attached to walls – as generally the further away from the ground you go the more sunlight will be available. Of course you could ditch the backyard altogether and start growing in your front garden – for so long just the preserve of the boring lawn but coincidentally almost always sunnier than the back garden.

3. Reflect light in

Cunning use of reflectors can bounce light into and around your garden. This trick is simply painting your walls and fences white or using a pale-coloured decking or gravel as ground cover. You can even use mirrors, such as the cheap, shatterproof acrylic types widely available from DIY stores or online that are pre-cut to size (up to 1.8m square). You can now buy flexible sheets of mirrored plastic on a sticky-back roll that can be hung like wallpaper on a north-facing wall.

In shady spaces using reflectors not only increases the net amount of light but also means that light comes from a variety of directions. These extra sources of light reduces the tendency of plants to arch dramatically towards a single light source, giving them a more balanced shape and improving productivity.

Crops for shade

If, despite your most valiant efforts, you still find yourself gardening in a rather gloomy site, there are a few crops you can get away with growing in shade. Some real exotics like wasabi, hosta greens, fiddlehead ferns and Japanese hardy ginger positively prefer shade. Here are just a few examples:

• **Fruit** – Alpine 'snow' strawberries, Chilean guavas, huckleberries and blue sausage fruits.

• **Veg** – mushrooms, New Zealand spinach, water-cress, bamboo shoots, squash flowers and leaves, fiddlehead ferns, wood sorrel, hosta greens, chop suey greens, borage, dahlias, Queensland arrow-root and Chinese chives.

• **Herbs and spices** – Tasmanian mountain pepper, Japanese hardy ginger, Vietnamese fish mint, meadowsweet, wintergreen, green tea, sweet cicely and wasabi.

The silver lining

While bright sunlight does indeed promote luxuriant growth and high sugar levels in most crop plants, it can also trigger the development of bitter or spicy chemicals and tough fibres in a few species of leaf and stem crops such as lettuce, rhubarb, borage, cardoons and dandelions. Growing these plants in shade will give you leaves that are larger, softer and paler, and that taste milder. Although not ideal from the plant's perspective, these leaves are far superior in flavour and texture for greedy gardeners.

You can capitalise on this phenomenon by deliberately excluding light to certain parts of a full-grown plant for a couple of weeks to sweeten it up before harvest. To plant geeks this process is known as 'blanching' and can be easily done by placing an upturned bucket over an adult plant or wrapping the base of a cardoon or borage plant in a 30cm-wide length of corrugated cardboard or hessian sacking. Leave in place for a couple of weeks and the plant's levels of bitter chemicals (which are only produced in the presence of direct sunlight) will naturally drop, turning the tissues a paler colour and elongating the stems, making these a whole lot tastier.

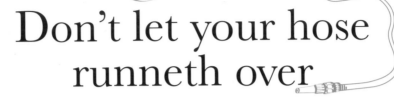

Don't let your hose runneth over

It's no surprise to anyone that water is fundamental for plant growth. Watering is easily the single most time-consuming chore in the garden but up to 50 per cent of the water used is wasted. Getting it right can save you hours of work, not to mention a hefty water bill.

My watering crash course

1. Little and often is NOT the way

Unless you're watering seedlings or extremely shallow-rooted species, the most common mistake among gardeners is to give their plots a daily 'once-over' sprinkling with a hose. This type of watering only really moistens the top few centimetres of the soil and doesn't reach the majority of the plants' roots. Within an hour or so this surface moisture is simply evaporated off by the sun.

Instead, give plants a proper soaking once or twice a week allowing water to permeate right down to the deepest roots and you will see two key benefits:

• The plants have an underground store of moisture to draw on over several days, giving them a more constant irrigation.

• The total amount of water used and your time spent watering will be greatly reduced.

2. Target water to where it's most needed

To get water to reach the parts of the plant that need it most (the roots) there is a simple Blue Peteresque device that can be knocked together from the contents of your recycling bin. This instant remedy is as simple as taking an old two-litre plastic milk or soda bottle and cutting the bottom two centimetres off with a serrated knife. Buried upside down with its open neck 15–25cm below ground level and its cut end sticking out of the ground, the bottle will act as a perfect sump (a pit or well that collects water) to store and direct water deep below ground. Make up a good few of these bottomless bottles and space them at 50cm intervals along your beds. Simply fill each of them to the brim with a hose or watering can once or twice a week. Apart from in the most scorching weather, that is all the watering you need to do.

For larger plants and shrubs, a mini-moat can be created by bulking up soil in a ring around the planting hole which will work in the same way, trapping water around the plant base and preventing it from running off.

3. Seal in moisture

Most of the moisture lost from watering is through evaporation; therefore sealing in this water with a layer of organic material such as chipped bark, leaf mould, compost and cocoa shells can help dramatically reduce the loss of moisture. This technique, known as mulching, has a variety of other benefits:

• It provides a barrier to any germinating weed seedlings from the soil below. These weeds cannot raise their heads, therefore cutting down the time you would spend removing these potential competitors.

• It creates a thick blanket to insulate the soil below, protecting delicate roots from biting frosts and scorching summer temperatures. As the mulch naturally breaks down over a season or two, it even helps enrich your soil.

Any fibrous, well-composted plant matter will do this job just brilliantly – spread it all around your plants in a layer about 5cm thick.

4. Water in the morning

Watering in the morning gives the soil time to absorb the moisture before the hot midday sun evaporates this off. Although there is no scientific basis behind the age-old gardening belief that watering at midday can scorch plants' leaves, the rapid evaporation (apart from being wasteful) can leave residues of salts, minerals and fertilisers that were dissolved in the water and which can damage plant cells.

Another good reason to water early in the day is that watering in the evening can leave plants sitting in cold water, which they cannot effectively take up and this can promote fungal diseases that thrive in cool, wet conditions. These conditions also provide slugs and snails with the perfect moist surface to travel over on their nocturnal raids. That said, if your plants are in a really desperate need of a drink in the middle of a dry summer, it is better to water them as soon as possible, whatever the time of day, rather than risking long-term drought damage.

Watering & flavour

Watering can have a big impact not only on crop yield, but also on taste. Generous regular soakings have the effect of pumping plant cells full of water. In general, a lot of water makes the resultant crop more tender and succulent but also dilutes the naturally occurring chemicals dissolved within them. In the case of leaf and root crops, plenty of water can prevent the build up of bitter or fiery flavours and stringy fibres, which suits most people's tastes. Regular soakings are great if you want a crisp, mild radish, but perhaps not so much if you like your rocket to have a really pungent kick.

With fruit, however, being too trigger happy with the hose during the ripening stage can result in a watery, insipid crop. The excessive moisture dilutes the sugars within the fruit cells, watering down the flavour. Abundant watering is often the reason why those giant supermarket strawberries usually lack that all-important strawberry flavour. Although you do get larger yields with liberal waterings, flavour almost always suffers.

In order to get the best of both worlds:

• Irrigate fruit crops generously throughout the whole growing season, especially during the key stage when the plants are in flower and the little green fruit are swelling.

• Reduce irrigation to a minimum when fruit reach their maximum size and start to change colour on their way to full ripeness.

This same process also works on leaf and veg crops. If you are keen on some really intense flavours, simply reduce watering a week or two so before you plan to harvest.

Drought-proof crops

If you live in one of the drier parts of the country, or just want to reduce your watering responsibilities to a bare minimum, there are a wide range of options for drought-tolerant edibles out there. Hailing from arid or semi-arid parts of the globe, many of these plants will usually only need watering when newly planted and once established they can pretty much take care of themselves. Here are some drought-proof crops that won't let you down:

• **Fruit** – olives, figs, huckleberries, Inca berries and pineapple guavas.

• **Veg** – artichoke, sea kale, purslane, asparagus peas, oyster leaves, red strawberry popcorn, fenugreek and tomatillos.

• **Herbs and spices** – lavender, society garlic, marigolds, eucalyptus, manuka, scented geraniums and saffron.

Crops for boggy areas

Most standard 'Dig for Victory' style texts suggest that a sodden, boggy patch of ground is useless for crop growing. However, the great thing about the crops featured in this book is that many are adapted to a wide range of habitats, including aquatic and near-aquatic environments. Some good examples are water celery, bamboo shoots, watercress (if the water is very clean), Queensland arrowroot, sweet galingale, wintergreen, hosta greens, fiddle-head ferns and wasabi.

3

Create the promised land
(i.e. the perfect soil)

There is an old-school adage that gardening is not the art of cultivating good plants but the art of cultivating good soil. As much as I cringe slightly at this hippy 'worship the earth mother' tone, I can't help but entirely agree with the idea behind this sentiment. Get your soil right and the plants will do the rest of the hard work for you.

An ideal growing mix

Although soil requirements differ from plant to plant, in my opinion the ideal formula for a growing mix for the majority of fruit and veg crops is:

• *Four* **parts loam** (i.e. regular garden soil).

• *Two* **parts organic compost** – any kind will do. You can often pick organic compost up at no cost at many council recycling centres, make your own from garden and kitchen waste or buy it in large bulk bags from builders' merchants (by far the cheapest way to buy it).

• *One* **part fine horticultural sand** – be careful not to use builders' sand (which can contain large amounts of lime) but sharp sand specifically sold for horticulture and available from builders' merchants.

Here, the compost acts like a sponge, helping improve water and nutrient retention in the mix. Additionally, sand helps improve drainage, especially in heavy clay soil, giving it a lighter, more friable texture to allow the roots of young plants to spread freely. If you are gardening on a free-draining soil with an already high sand content, simply reduce the amount of sand in the mix, and conversely add a couple of extra spadefuls of sand if you are gardening on particularly heavy clay soil.

In beds and borders
To create this mix in beds and borders simply:

• Place a good 15cm layer of compost and 8cm of sand over the surface of the soil and then dig in well with a spade or fork to a depth of at least 45cm. This digging might be a bit of a workout for an hour or two but once thoroughly incorporated you will almost certainly never need to do it again.

• To boost the mineral and nutrient content, sprinkle over pelleted chicken manure, horse manure or blood, fish and bone, which are all sold at most garden centres, according to the package directions and mix in well.

You should end up with an area of soil that has a light, airy texture (like the top of an apple crumble) that will be slightly raised above the surrounding soil level.

The 'no dig' method
Apart from this first thorough dig when setting up a bed, I prefer to leave nature to its own devices as frequent digging can destroy soil structure, encourage the germination of buried weed seeds and harm useful critters like earthworms and beneficial soil microorganisms (the horticultural equivalent of probiotic bacteria). Ditching the annual chore of digging, I opt for a technique known as the 'no dig' method. Simply, apply a thick mulch of well-rotted organic matter like compost, leaf mould or

manure over the whole site, once each year during spring, and plant your new crops directly into it. Worms will soon incorporate this top layer into the soil below, naturally creating a rich, crumbly, well-aerated texture. There is one caveat though: these beds are now a 'no stepping area', because walking over this area will instantly recompact the soil.

In tubs, troughs and pots

Despite the huge range of specialist composts for fruit and veg that are available in garden centres, I find that my growing mix works far better in tubs and planters than pure compost alone. Its high loam content means it retains moisture for far longer, contains a broad range of minerals, which help ensure healthy flavourful crops, and also gives plants a far stronger base in which to anchor themselves. Having such a complete mix also means nutrients do not get exhausted as quickly as pure compost, so you don't need to replace it every year as if you had used a shop-bought mix. Incidentally, because you can knock the formula together using low-cost (and often free) ingredients, you will pay a fraction of the price of those highly branded, quirkily packaged pre-formulated mixes.

Fertiliser for newbies

No matter how wonderful your soil, plants always benefit from a bit of a nutritional pick-me-up, which can dramatically improve overall health, raise their disease resistance and boost both their overall yield and flavour. Here are my top tips:

• Unlike watering – where the opposite is true – the 'little and often' approach ensures that the supply of minerals and nutrients is spread evenly throughout the crop's season. This approach also avoids the erratic bursts of soft, sappy disease-prone growth that excessive fertilising can cause.

• I like to use an all-purpose liquid feed mixed in the water that I use to irrigate. I apply it once a week right through the growing season from April to September. Don't be tempted to fertilise any later in the year because this can encourage the plant to burst into soft,

fresh growth that is prone to frost damage in the winter.

• There are many mixes available in garden centres but I prefer to make my own, which (depending on the size of your garden) can save you a good £100 throughout the season for very little effort. And the best thing is two key ingredients in my brew are common native weeds (see *Tips & tricks*, page 51).

• This same liquid feed, further diluted at half strength, can be sprayed as a foliar feed onto your crops' leaves to give them an extra nutritional boost.

Acid-loving plants

The only plants that I ever buy liquid fertiliser or specialist compost for are a small range of horticultural divas known as ericaceous plants. These species include green tea, cranberries, blueberries, gardenias and citrus. They hail from regions of the world with acidic soils and are so well adapted to these conditions that their health quickly suffers in alkaline environments like my chalky-soiled backyard. Symptoms include yellowing of veins in the leaves, leaf loss, delayed growth and severely impaired flowers and fruiting.

Of course, if you live in an area with acidic soil like most of Cornwall, Scotland and the Lake District these plants are a breeze to grow. However, if like me, you live in a hard water area (i.e. your kettle furs up) or your soil contains small white lumps of chalk or limestone, these plants will need some serious extra cosseting. To get around these problems I suggest the following:

• Grow these species in pots with a mix of neutral top soil (which you can pick up from garden centres or builders' merchants) and ericaceous compost (a slightly acidic growing medium sold by garden centres for plants like rhododendrons and camellias).

• Water with an organic ericaceous fertiliser, which helps keep acid-loving plants happy even when watered with hard tap water. Pretty clever stuff!

Pick the chosen ones

Once you've engineered the perfect growing conditions, now comes the exciting bit – a spot of botanical treasure hunting. A little planning at this stage of what you want to grow can make a massive difference to your success in the year ahead. So get a pen and paper and sketch out your ultimate wish list. My top three rules for helping you decide will ensure you don't waste your precious time.

Top three rules

Rule 1: grow veg you like to eat

I am always surprised by the number of people that dedicate huge amounts of time and effort cultivating the stuff they believe they should grow in a veg (or fruit) garden as opposed to what they actually like to eat. Just because a book, even this one, recommends a particular list of species, it doesn't mean you need to slavishly follow it – the best guide is always your taste buds.

Rule 2: plant at least six species

Even if you have only a small space to play with, don't be tempted to stick to only two or three crops. Planting a broad range of species on your plot means:

• You will never worry about having an enormous glut of any one crop, which can put anyone off a favourite fruit or veg.

• You reduce the risk of crop failure caused by the build-up of any one plant-specific pest or disease.

Rule 3: repeat performers make for an easy life

While most traditional crops are annual plants (species that are sown, harvested and die in the same year), perennial crops that come back year after year will provide you with a reliable annual harvest from just a single planting – so you do far less work for exactly the same reward. Many of the really expensive crops (think artichokes, asparagus and strawberries)

fall into this category, making growing them all the more logical. Fortunately, most of the crops in this book belong to this labour-saving group, making them the perfect slacker option for busy foodies.

Sourcing guide

Once you have completed your wish list, the next step is to get out and gather up what you need to get started. Other than the well-trodden route of garden centres (see *Supplier directory*, page 269), here are my hints for tracking down botanical treasure.

Seed swapaholics

Before you even reach for your wallet, there is a way to get your hands on some of the most rare and unusual varieties of heritage fruit and veg often without paying a penny – seed swapping.

Public seed swaps all over the country provide growers with a unique opportunity to exchange the seeds of weird and wonderful varieties with absolutely no money changing hands. I especially love 'Seedy Sunday' down in Brighton. This is held every February, with visitors asked either to swap seed packets or to make a donation of 50p per packet to cover the costs of organising the swap and is an absolute gold mine for one-of-a-kind plant finds.

Due to gardening trends and some confusing EU regulations that limit what seed companies can actually stock, many of the more unconventional fruit and veg varieties are becoming

increasingly tricky to find. Without seed swaps, hundreds of delicious varieties, which may have taken thousands of years to create, are in imminent danger of extinction. Can you think of a better excuse for a bit of freetail therapy?

Heritage Seed Library

Another amazing resource is Garden Organic's Heritage Seed Library, a unique botanical ark housing seeds from more than 800 endangered crop varieties. Garden Organic is steadily introducing a range of exciting exotics from British-grown seeds. Membership is open to anyone, and on joining you can access these crops free of charge. Volunteers called 'seed guardians' are responsible for growing these rare varieties in their own gardens to replenish the library's

stocks and keep these crops going. If you fancy doing your own bit of backyard conservation, get in touch with the library!

Mail order

Apart from seed swaps and the standard garden centre route, mail order is often overlooked as a means to seeking out botanical treasures. All the large seed companies and most tiny independent companies now sell online, meaning a previously unimaginable variety of species are just a few clicks away. Online auction sites like eBay make it possible to get live plants shipped from suppliers literally anywhere in the world (complete with official plant health certificates of course).

5
Spare the secateurs, spoil your harvest

When I was growing up I always thought pruning and training were ridiculous exercises: loads of convoluted techniques and confusing rules to remember, only to hack back perfectly healthy growth that surely was the whole point of gardening anyway? However, once you learn the effect just a snip or two can have, pruning and training suddenly goes from laborious chore to clever chemical engineering.

Removing a plant's leaves and branches can have a profound effect on its internal chemistry, triggering the production of various hormones, which in turn dictate how the plant grows. Although the exact method of pruning and training varies between crops (full information for each plant is detailed in its profile), the following is a general introduction.

Fruiting plants

Fruit-bearing crops can be chemically manipulated into producing far higher yields and better quality fruit than would occur in nature, simply through a little basic pruning and training.

Stimulating flower & fruit formation
Many fruiting plants produce hormones in their growing tips that inhibit flower formation further down the branch. Left to their own devices this would result in tall, upward-shooting growth, with relatively few fruit, far out of reach at the top of the plant. As a remedy, try:

• Pruning these growing tips out frees dormant flower buds lower down from this chemical control, resulting in the production of significantly more flowers and fruit all along the branches.

• Bending vertical boughs down at an angle (from anything to fully horizontal) and adding ties to keep them in place has the effect of slowing the flow of sap inside the branch. Similar to pruning, this 'training' of branches stifles the tree or bush's natural upward growth, releasing hormones that instead stimulate the formation of flowers and fruit.

• Thinning out clusters of newly formed fruit early in the season to leave just one or two mini fruits per bunch redirects all the plant's energies to these, resulting in fewer but much larger fruit come harvest time, instead of loads of tiny misshapen fruitlets.

By combining the above techniques for pruning and training you can significantly increase your total fruit yield while simultaneously improving its quality.

Improving fruit flavour
Removing dead, congested and crossing branches from the centre of a tree or bush allows sunlight into the centre of the canopy to its developing fruits. Exposure to light raises the sugar production and generation of various aromatic compounds in the fruits, resulting in a vastly improved flavour.

In order to achieve this effect all over a fruiting tree, you should aim to create an open, wine glass-shaped overall structure that is balanced on all sides.

All plants

For most crops only a minimal amount of pruning is required. This is largely either done to encourage fresh, healthy growth, restrict water loss when transplanting or to stave off infection.

Regenerative pruning

In most plants, the removal of leaves or branches sets off an internal chemical reaction, triggering the production of growth hormones that encourage the development of vigorous new shoots. Pruning takes advantage of this tendency and is particularly useful for plants that have become old and tired, producing with tough, woody, sparse growth.

A generous hacking back, followed by a good dose of water and fertiliser, can help rejuvenate your crops, quickly inducing a flush of fresh, green leaves. This pruning is usually done in spring and early summer. Any later in the year and this new tender growth may not have time to mature enough before winter sets in.

Restricting water loss

Water evaporates from little pores on the bottom surface of leaves in much the same way as sweat does from human skin. The vacuum created by the loss within the plant's vessels is what draws water up the stem from its roots. If these roots are damaged, for example by being dug up or transplanted, they may not be able to absorb enough water from the soil to replace the amount lost through its leaves.

Snipping off some of these leaves (or in some cases entire branches, depending on the size of the plant) helps redress this balance, ensuring that newly transplanted specimens don't suffer from drying out.

Staving off infections

Pruning off dense leaf growth from a congested canopy allows light and air into the centre of the plant, which helps reduce the chance of fungal infections that thrive in shady environments with poor airflow. This thinning is particularly effective for lush-leaved plants like courgettes, squash and tomatoes that are notoriously vulnerable to fungal attacks in humid summers, as well as tender plants like citrus trees when they are brought under cover in winter.

Unpruned: spindly, congested growth with all the fruit at the top

Pruned: open structure with loads more fruit along the branches

6
Love thy neighbour, nuke thy enemy

There is nothing more soul-destroying than having months of hard work fall prey to an army of marauding pests. Learn to spot the differences between your allies and enemies and you too can win the war on bugs.

Allies

Earthworms

If you like the idea of outsourcing hours of digging and fertilising to an army of assistants, then these little guys are without a doubt your best friends in the garden. Creating networks of thousands of tiny tunnels in your plot, earthworm activity functions like an air pump, drawing oxygen into the soil and helping release carbon dioxide. This aeration is vital for:

• Healthy root growth.

• Boosting the numbers of beneficial microbes that live in soil.

• Allowing water and nutrients to drain into the ground effectively for maximum absorption by your crops' roots.

Worm action can shift up to 150kg of soil per year in the average 4.5m x 4.5m small garden, helping draw up minerals from deep in the ground, while at the same time helping mix in organic material from the soil's surface. That's 150kg less soil per year that you need to dig to get the same result!

To keep the little guys happy:

• Provide a regular supply of organic mulch (like compost, leaf mould or finely chipped bark) layered over the surface of your beds.

• Avoid pesticide use at all costs.

Ladybirds

Capable of devouring as many as 5,000 plant-munching aphids in their lifetime, ladybirds are the perfect allies in the war on bugs. Attracting them into your garden depends on two key factors:

• Giving them enough aphids to eat (if your garden is anything like mine this factor won't be a problem).

• Providing them with a source of pollen, which is also an important part of their diet. Ideal sources for their pollen buffet include the blossom of chives, coriander, fennel, dill, calendula, marigolds and angelica.

Bees

Without a healthy number of bees buzzing around your garden, the yields of your fruit crops will be severely compromised. That's because bees are vital for successful pollination. With a global crisis in bee numbers, it's in the interest of all allotmenteers to encourage these little critters into our gardens. Here's how:

• Planting brightly coloured flowers among your fruit and veg will both attract bees and add to its aesthetic value.

• Pick up a bumblebee nesting box (available at most garden centres) to help lure a colony into taking up residence in your plot. These boxes mimic mouse and rodent burrows, which are the natural winter hibernation habitat for bumblebee queens. The best designs provide a dry, dark, ventilated cavity with a

small entrance hole that the bees can access at ground level.

• According to an entomologist buddy of mine, one top tip is to stuff the central nesting box chamber with leftover bedding from a pet hamster or mouse cage. The scent of the rodent pheromones apparently act like catnip to queen bumblebees.

Enemies

Slugs & snails

Very few pests can decimate a crop in a single night the same way slugs and snails can. But before you reach for the slug pellets, which apart from a raft of dodgy chemicals, also contain various substances that actually attract these pests into your garden, there are a range of truly effective natural alternatives out there.

Garlic spray

My weapon of choice for unwanted pests is a simple garlic spray. Particularly effective on slugs and snails and flying insects, it is simple to make:

• Blitz a bulb of garlic with a litre of water in a blender or pestle and mortar.

• Leave to stand for a couple of hours and strain out the particles.

• Spray all over your plants in the early evening when those slugs and snails are just getting set to make their night-time raids.

The sulphur-based compounds in garlic not only kill but deter these pests and unlike pellets will not be harmful to garden birds, swooping down to scoff their remains. Adding a handful of fragrant marigold leaves, which contain naturally occuring insecticidal chemicals, will make your garlic spray even more effective.

Aphids & whitefly

Just like slugs and snails, many flying insects are sensitive to the chemicals found in plants of the onion family, making my garlic spray (see above) a really effective way to limit their numbers. Neem oil-based insecticides (see *Tips & tricks*, page 51–52) will also stop them in their tracks. If you really want to wreak vengeance, why not mix up your very own deadly cocktail of neem oil and garlic spray for a real double whammy.

Mice & rabbits

All mammals, it seems (apart from humans), hate the taste of chilli. Making up a simple spray using chilli will coat your crops in a spicy film that will be effective against everything from mice and rabbits to squirrels and deer, deterring them without causing them any harm.

Another effective trick is to sprinkle black pepper generously over your seed beds or on the soil above newly planted bulbs.

Mildew & mould

All you need to do is give your diseased plants a quick douse in my chamomile and milk spray (see *Tips & tricks*, page 52). It might sound more like a cutesy scented hand soap than a deadly antifungal agent, but its range of naturally occurring antimicrobial chemicals are all but mild mannered for tackling mildew and other moulds.

Caterpillars

Apart from simply picking these off your plants and popping them on the bird table, the simplest way I know to control caterpillars is with a good spritz in homemade garlic spray.

7

United they stand, divided they fall

It may sound counterintuitive for those brought up on images of regimental rows of single veg varieties, but mixing and matching your crops to create little intermingled communities is the easiest way to reduce your work while boosting your yield. Practised by traditional cultures all over the world from the ancient Chinese to Native Americans, this agricultural matchmaking is known as 'polyculture' and exploits symbiotic relations between plants to improve their growth. Sound a little wishy-washy? Let's take a look at the evidence.

Polyculture: the benefits

They fertilise themselves
Plants in the bean and pea family possess a miraculous ability to increase the fertility of the soil by capturing nitrogen (a major plant nutrient vital for healthy leaf growth) that's floating around in the air and 'fixing' it in their roots. Any other nearby plants growing in the same soil will benefit from the increased richness, kicking out larger, stronger leaves. Species that will particularly benefit are leafy, salad-type crops like lettuce, rocket and so on.

Also, because different crops have different nutritional requirements, siting a mix of species in the same bed means that they can't all deplete the soil of one specific nutrient because each crop takes and gives back different elements to the soil.

They team up to deter pests
Many aromatic plants like tomatoes, marigolds, lavender and garlic have evolved a host of chemicals that repel and destroy pests, helping keep them safe from insect, bacterial and fungal attacks. In fact, this role is one of the key functions of aromatic chemicals in plants like herbs. While we humans love their smell, pests hate them. Deployed in a fragrant cloud around their leaves or roots, those chemicals give the same protection to any other plant growing nearby.

Some species go even further to repel their herbivorous enemies (like greenfly) by attracting the predators of these pests (like parasitic wasps), thereby recruiting their own deadly security force to keep themselves safe. As different plants have evolved different chemical cocktails to repel pests, the more variety of fragrant plants in a plot the greater the likelihood of cast-iron pest protection.

This muddled-up mix of smells can also work indirectly to confuse pests that locate plants based on their smell; throwing off the pests' olfactory sat-nav and sending them off on the wrong track. As gardeners, we can even hijack these chemicals to create our own natural, highly effective insecticides (see *Tips & tricks*, page 51). Even if they do make it past these defences (which a few inevitably will), the diverse mix of crops ensures that pests never get an endless supply of their favourite food, so there is far less chance of crop-specific baddies taking up permanent residence in your garden.

They attract pollinators
Flowering plants have evolved a range of ingen-ious strategies to attract beneficial pollinating insects like bees and butterflies by producing brightly-coloured 'billboard' petals and phe-romone-packed perfumes. Of course, the more flowers in your plot, the more chance it has of becoming perfect bee and butterfly bait, helping to increase your yields of fruit crops by ensuring

maximum pollination (the number of flowers that turn into fruit) while adding some serious kerb appeal.

Great edible crops for attracting pollinators include sunflowers, lavender, tomatillos, borage, marigolds and manuka.

They expand your growing area and squash weeds at the same time!

Okay, so they won't physically push back the boundaries of your plot, but growing a mixture of crops of different sizes and growth habits together can increase your total growing area by ensuring there is no wasted space in your plot. For example, tall skinny crops like corn planted on their own will result in a huge amount of empty floor space at ground level between plants. Left unattended, this bare soil will quickly become infested by weeds. By planting short, stubby crops like courgettes or squash under tall plants, you will suddenly double the amount of crops and leave little space for those pesky weeds. It is important to ensure that the crops you grow in the same plot are of different heights and sizes so they don't compete for space.

They provide an edible insurance policy

Finally and most simply, because different plants suffer from different afflictions, growing a range of species in the same space reduces the chances of a single factor (pest, disease or bad weather) wiping out your entire crop. Even if some horticultural catastrophe clobbers one or two of them, you are likely to be able to fall back on the other crops.

A horticultural three-way

Generally made up of a trio of crops, although they can include up to six species, polycultures employ a range of unrelated species that have non-competing sizes and habits. They include a 'canopy' layer of tall, skinny crops, followed by a medium section of stubby, rounded plants or climbing species that trail up the tall ones and then a final ground cover of pint-sized crops that suppress weeds.

There are only three things you have to bear in mind when doing your matchmaking:

1. Ensure that larger crops are planted a little further apart than if planted on their own to allow light and air to the lower levels. You can even pick off a few of their lower leaves if these are restricting the crops beneath them.

2. Ensure you pick crops that come into season at roughly the same time or can be harvested easily without damaging the others.

3. Avoid planting two root crops in the same plot, as they can compete for soil space and are unlikely to ever be harvested at exactly the same time.

Following the guidelines above, feel free to get experimenting from the list below:

• **Canopy layer** – corn, artichoke, cardoon, quinoa, fennel, sunflowers, Peruvian ground apple, dahlias, elephant garlic and borage.

• **Middle layer** – bush tomatoes, hyacinth beans, climbing beans, butterfly peas, cucamelons, peas and mangetout.

• **Ground cover layer** – wood sorrel, chillies, Chinese artichokes, sweet potatoes, saffron, electric daisies, wintergreen, Alpine 'snow' strawberries, ground cherries (sold as dwarf Inca berries like 'Little Lanterns'), courgettes, New Zealand yams and nasturtiums.

Combinations to try

I have tried planting a few combinations in my time and have found that particular blends work best. Give them a go and reap the benefits of matchmaking.

• **Persian trio** – bayberry bushes (with branches lower than 50cm removed) work great in a sunny spot underplanted with saffron corms, a ground cover of creeping chamomile 'Treneague' and a mulch of sharp grit. All three ingredients can be used to make a Persian-style rice pilaf that will knock Uncle Ben's socks off every time.

• **Three sisters, plus one** – practised by Native Americans, the 'three sisters' is arguably the most famous form of polyculture. Tall popcorn plants are used as the perfect support for trailing bean plants. The beans help fertilise the soil, by fixing nitrogen, and the large leaves of a ground cover of squash smother weeds and keep the soil cool. I have added a fourth sister, the towering Mexican mint marigold (*Tagetes minuta*), which helps repel pests and is so light and fluffy that it does not shade the corn. The trick to making this combination work is to wait until the corn is a good 30cm tall before planting the stay faithful to the original technique and use popcorn rather than its close relative sweetcorn because popcorn matures much later than sweetcorn, which can be a little tricky to harvest in the tangle of bean vines. By the time the popcorn is ripe, the vines will have stopped producing and can simply be cut down with the corn.

• **Double artichoke** – underplant regular globe artichokes with a weed suppressing mat of Chinese artichokes, for the ultimate in low-maintenance beds that will produce a supply of gourmet veg year after year.

8

As you sow, so shall you reap

It's not just about what you sow, but when and how you sow it. Getting this right saves money, avoids gluts and can even extend the season of your crops. One of the biggest errors rookie gardeners make when planting quick-maturing crops is to sow all the seeds in a packet at once. This common mistake results in an enormous glut of one crop coming into season at the same time and nothing for the rest of the year, not to mention the space that is taken up in your garden by just one species.

Successional sowing

If you sow the same packet of seeds in small batches, starting a new generation when the previous is just beginning to form small plants, you will have a constant supply over a far longer season. This technique is called successional sowing and works particularly well for microveg, baby salad crops, peas, asparagus and hyacinth beans, borage, chop suey greens and any other quick-maturing, short-lived species.

Catch cropping

Planting quick-growing veg in between slower-maturing species such as squash, tomatoes, dahlias and Peruvian ground apple, is a technique known as 'catch cropping' and gives you a fast return while you wait for the rest of your harvest. For more on quick-growing veg see *Express veg* on page 40.

Preserve their virtues

Coping with gluts is a surprisingly common problem for allotmenteers, especially considering how much time and effort we spend worrying about avoiding poor harvests. There is no point going to great lengths to ensure a bumper harvest only to find you have an enormous backlog of fruit and veg that goes off before you can eat it. So here's my 'in a nutshell' guide to making sure your harvest goes a long way.

Storage in the ground

One of the best (and laziest) ways of preserving all manner of hardy root crops is to leave them in the ground over winter, harvesting them only when needed. After all, these roots are designed to store the plant's energy reserves right through the coldest months. The low soil temperatures help slow bacterial growth, while relative moisture prevents crops from drying out. Surprisingly, this natural chilling works a lot better than any fridge around.

Freezing

Almost any crop, apart from those that are intended to be eaten raw such as salad plants, can be frozen. This is a quick and easy process that preserves flavour and nutritional value like no other by stopping bacterial growth in its tracks. Here's how:

• For berries, scatter these over a baking tray, making sure to leave a little space around each fruit so they are not touching and pop the tray into the freezer for a couple of hours. Once frozen solid, transfer the berries into ziplock plastic bags or Tupperware, seal tightly and store in the freezer – where they will keep for up to a year.

• For larger fruit, the process is almost the same, the only difference being that these should be sliced into chunks for easier thawing.

• For vegetables, peel and slice before popping them in a colander, which you then plunge into a pot of rapidly boiling water for about one minute. Lift the colander out and rinse the veg well with ice-cold water to halt the cooking process, and then continue as per fruit. This blanching process is necessary because it destroys the enzymes in the vegetables that can cause them to become soggy and lose colour upon thawing if put in the freezer in their raw state.

Drying

The process of drying food out removes the water that bacteria depend on to live, helping greatly extend the shelf life of any edible crop. This technique works best for crops with a relatively low water content like small-leaved herbs, popcorn and chillies, which can be dried by simply hanging them upside down in a dark, well-ventilated shed or garage for a week or two.

However, if treated right, pretty much anything that isn't a leafy salad-type crop can be successfully dried. Although in the UK, our damp and overcast climate rarely allows for Mediterranean-style sun drying, the same process can be replicated very effectively in a low oven. Simply:

• Thinly slice medium-sized fruit such as crystal pears, quince or kiwis.

• Arrange the fruit slices equally spaced on a grill tray and pop them into a low oven (set to 75°C) and leave to dry for six hours.

• As an optional extra you can dip the fruit slices in lemon juice or a syrup made of two parts honey and one part boiling water. This coating will help seal the fruit and prevent it from losing its colour.

Smaller fruit like berries can simply be scattered over the tray and dried in the same way. This same drying-out process also works brilliantly for vegetables like slices of sweet potatoes, peppers, squash, tomatoes and mushrooms.

Once dry, pop these in an air-tight Tupperware container and store in the fridge for up to six months.

Jams & jellies

It might sound a little 'WI', but making up a batch of homemade jam or jelly is really not much more complicated than preparing a packet of instant noodles (I promise!). Besides, it gives you a chance to experiment with all kinds of weird and wonderful flavour combinations you simply can't buy – think wintergreen and strawberry jelly or cocktail kiwi and elderflower jam. Trust me no farmer's market fare can match these in the snob-food stakes!

Here's how:

• Pour 500g of washed and chopped fruit in a saucepan, squeeze in the juice of half a lime, flick the heat on and simmer gently for 10 minutes. Meanwhile, put a small plate in the freezer to chill.

• Pour in 500g of jam sugar (this sits right next to the regular sugar in the supermarket) and boil for a further 10–15 minutes.

• Test the jam for setting: spoon a few drops onto the cold plate, leave it for a minute, and then push the jam with your finger. The surface should wrinkle; if not, cook it another 5 minutes and test again.

• Pour the hot mixture into sterilised jam jars (to sterilise the jars, run them through a dish-washer and then dry in an oven set at a low

temperature) and pop the lids on while still piping hot.

To make a jelly, the process is essentially the same, just strain out the chunks of fruit and fibre before adding the jam sugar.

> **Kitchen tip:** When making jam, adding a spoonful of butter will prevent any foam from forming during the cooking.

There is no reason why you need to make standard, single-fruit jams or jellies either. Try mixing and matching different fruit or adding in spices such as vanilla, chilli or cinnamon, or a shot of liqueur or white wine to cut through the sweetness.

Flavoured vodkas, liqueurs & vinegars

Despite costing a fortune in shops, all liqueurs are basically fruit and sugar steeped in alcohol – a great way to use up those leftover bottles in the booze cabinet. Here's how I make mine:

- Tip 250g of chopped fruit into a large jar with a couple of spices (like cinnamon sticks, cloves, star anise), mix in an equal weight of sugar and pour in about 425ml of strong spirit like vodka, brandy or rum.

- Cover and leave to steep in a cool, dark place for at least two months then strain the mix through a fine sieve.

- Once you've strained the liqueur it is ready to bottle up.

The leftover strained fruit makes a delicious, although rather deadly, accompaniment to ice creams, trifles, or creamy rice puddings.

My favourite candidates for transformation into liqueurs include pineapple guavas, Chilean guavas, quinces, calamondin limes, wintergreen berries (with a few leaves thrown in for good measure), lemongrass, mulberries, saffron and American cranberries.

To make a homemade vinegar, just swap the booze for a good quality cider, wine or sherry vinegar and you have a homemade salad dressing fit for even the fanciest restaurant.

Pickling

Making homemade pickles is surprisingly straightforward. All you need to do is follow the below simple steps:

- Slice your fruit and veg. Pop them into a sterilised jar and pour in boiling hot vinegar seasoned with sugar, salt and your chosen herbs and spices.

- If you are looking for a really crisp result, sprinkle the cut fruit and veg with plenty of salt and leave them for two hours to draw out much of the moisture. Just remember to rinse off all the salt very thoroughly before pickling.

- Screw the lid on and keep in the fridge for at least two weeks, after which your pickle is ready for a ploughman's.

Good options for pickling are – cucamelons (see *A recipe idea* on page 103), Chinese artichokes, fiddlehead ferns, hosta shoots, daylily buds, olives, bamboo shoots and elephant garlic.

> **Tip:** Adding an oak or grapevine leaf into the jar will help maintain the crunch, with the tannins in the leaves inhibiting the growth of enzymes that can cause the pickles to go soft.

Eat, drink and be merry

Raised on a diet of rigidly uniform fruit and veg sealed in little polystyrene containers, many first-time allotmenteers can't help but feel a little inferior when they compare their mere-mortal produce to plastic-perfect supermarket offerings. Doing this is like flicking through the airbrushed images of surgically enhanced supermodels and wondering why the reflection in your mirror isn't the same.

Sure your crops won't all be the exact same size and shape (neither are those of commer-cial growers until they are laboriously graded to size by hand in vast warehouses). They won't have layers of wax sprayed onto them to give them that glossy uniform sheen and they won't have been blasted with gas to ensure a flawlessly even coloration. What they will have though, is unparalleled freshness and truly superior flavour that will knock the socks off anything you can buy in the shops - not to mention the smug sense of achievement only munching of a fresh fig or pineapple guava still warm from the sun in your own back garden will give you.

My most important piece of advice to horticultural newbies is *don't expect perfection*. Just eat, drink and (especially if you try the 'Recipe pots' on page 44) be merry.

Tips & Tricks

borage

red radish 'sango'

Chinese chives

Express veg

'Growing your own' doesn't have to be all about patience and fortitude, simply pick the right crops and you can be munching on homegrown produce in less than a week. No kidding! Here are a few ideas for super-speedy veg to get you started, and they're ranked according to your patience level.

Ready to eat in about a week

Microveg

These are a new generation of sprouted salad leaves that are a far cry from the fodder that was found in 1970s health food stores. Coming in a range of vibrant colours and dynamic flavours (from fragrant Thai basil to green apple-flavoured sorrel), they are still just as easy to grow on your windowsill as cress.

To get started simply:

• Sprinkle the seeds over a seed tray of moist compost or across a quadruple layer of damp kitchen roll laid on a plate. You should aim for about the same coverage as sesame seeds on a burger bun.

• Place on a warm windowsill (a temperature of 18–22°C is ideal) and keep them moist, using a misting can once a day.

• Your 'microfield' will be ready for grazing on with a couple of snips of the scissors in just five to ten days.

A huge range of plants can be grown as microveg. In fact, pretty much anything with an edible leaf that sprouts quickly can be used.

Here are my favourites:

From the supermarket aisle

Try sprouting seeds that are available in huge packs for only a few pence in the spice or grain section of your supermarket. Here are just a handful of ideas grouped according to flavour: fenugreek and mustard (pungent and spicy); dill, fennel, caraway and coriander (fragrant and herbal); mung beans, dried peas and quinoa (fresh and green).

From the garden centre

Get over any sense of shame and rifle through the 'reduced to clear' bin at your local garden centre to find bargain-basement seed to start microfarming. Those half-empty packets that you have kicking around the house are also ideal candidates. Try any of these: purple basil, Thai basil (exotic and aromatic); leeks, onions, fennel, cress (pungent); lemon balm, sorrel (bright and citrusy); Swiss chard, kale, alfalfa, callaloo and radishes (rich and earthy).

callaloo

bean sprouts

pea shoots

Ready to eat in 4–8 weeks

Cut-and-come-again baby leaves

While microveg produce just one harvest, a tray of cut-and-come-again greens – as their name suggests – can produce up to three harvests of baby or 'teen' leaves from a single sowing. Fast growing and unfussy, if sowed at regular intervals from early spring to mid autumn, they will provide a supply of fresh, delicate salad and stir-fry leaves virtually all year round. Here's how:

• Sow the seeds slightly thinner than you would microveg and allow the young plants to grow to about 10–15cm high.

• Harvest the top two-thirds with scissors. Make sure to leave the smallest leaves of each plant intact so that they have a chance to recover.

• Store the tray in a bright warm site, water

well and you should be able to harvest again in 10–30 days.

Candidates for this treatment include – callaloo, chop suey greens, tree spinach, quinoa and mizuna.

Ready to eat in under 12 weeks

Check out what you could be eating in less time than it takes to get a new sofa delivered:

• **Leafy greens** – watercress, borage, New Zealand spinach, nasturtiums, purslane, mooli and water celery.

• **Vibrant herbs and spices** – saffron, Thai basil, electric daisies, Peruvian mint marigolds and eucalyptus.

• **Fruiting veg** – asparagus peas and oyster mushrooms.

No garden? No problem

You don't need a rolling country estate to get a piece of the good life. Pick the right plants and growing methods and even the most committed urban dweller can indulge in a spot of city-centre farming. The key here, when space is at a premium, is to grow fancy 'gourmet' crops that are small in stature but big on flavour.

Edible houseplants

There is a surprisingly large range of tropical crops that will feel perfectly at home on your average bedroom windowsill, from chillies and lemongrass to cardamom and even oyster mushrooms. In fact, many existing, standard DIY-superstore houseplants are actually major edible crops in their countries of origin. They include the zesty fruit of calamondin limes, the intensely aromatic flowers of gardenia (which add an uplifting fragrance to home-grown green tea) and the delicious leaves of scented geraniums (that come in every flavour from old-fashioned rose to Coca-Cola). This is all before we even get on to the tangy, apple-flavoured flowers of begonias, the jelly-like hearts of aloe vera leaves and of course ornamental chilli plants with multicoloured fruit and purple leaves.

Nowadays, a few innovative Dutch houseplant growers are adding even more exotic stuff like kaffir lime leaves, cardamom and vanilla grass (sold as 'Pandan' or *Pandanus*) to their ranges for their ability to put up with the low light levels and erratic watering they receive in the typical living room. Ask any good independent garden centre and they should be able to order these in for you within a fortnight. To help get you started with edible houseplants, here are some ideas:

• Keep a plant of aromatic curry leaves on your coffee table – its heady scent will transport you back to your last exotic holiday.

• Create a mini spice garden by planting lemongrass, Thai basil and fiery chillies in a small window box. Tex-Mex fans can swap the basil for coriander and the lemongrass for a little cucamelon vine, which can be trained up a tripod of sticks.

• Even Japanese hardy ginger and green tea will act like well-behaved houseguests if they are harvested regularly to keep their size in check.

• The new generations of micro tomatoes, like 'Tom Thumb' and 'Red Robin', tiny peppers like 'Mohawwk' and dwarf Inca berries like 'Little Lanterns' will grow no more than 30cm high, meaning they will thrive on a sunny kitchen work surface. Just remember to mist or tap their flowers to ensure good pollination in insect-free interiors.

• If you are as impatient as I am, trendy and oh-so-easy-to-grow microveg are a great solution for fresh, flavourful produce, fast (see page 40).

• Even if you have no light whatsoever, any empty kitchen cabinet can be used to grow a crop of fresh oyster mushrooms, astonishingly, on an old telephone book (see *Fruiting veg & grains*, page 117).

> **Safety note:** Sadly most houseplant growers still use synthetic pesticides on their plants so unless your plant is specifically labelled as 'grown for food use' (which increasing numbers are) it is probably best to leave it to 'detox' itself for six months or so before you get scoffing. ⚠

Window-box farming

Once your indoor space is filled, why not expand out onto your window ledges? Even a small window box 20cm high and 1m long can provide you with a couple of impressive harvests per year and look just as pretty as those boring busy Lizzies. The trick here is to

pick the tallest container possible (20–30cm high is ideal), as generally the deeper the bed, the denser you can plant – meaning you can eke out just that little bit more yield from the limited space.

Try any of the species just discussed in 'Edible houseplants', plus:

- **Fruit** – Alpine snow strawberries and fuchsia berries.

- **Veg** – cut-and-come-again salad crops, asparagus peas, mini tomatoes, dwarf daylilies, Chinese chives, dwarf courgette flowers (like 'Black Forest' and 'Midnight'), wintergreen, society garlic, red strawberry popcorn, chop suey greens, hostas, fiddlehead ferns, nasturtiums and fenugreek.

- **Herbs and spices** – herb marigolds, Vietnamese fish mint, electric daisies, Japanese beefsteak plant, lemon verbena, sugar leaves and saffron.

Mini roof terraces

Roof-top gardeners may dream of having a 'proper' garden one day, but look on the bright side – there's no lawn to mow, no hedges shading out your crops and of course no slugs and snails! Some of the latest plant breeding even means that you can now grow dwarf fruit trees like nectarines, quinces and apricots that grow no more than 1.8m high, allowing you to create a bonsai orchard on the 35th floor.

Try planting any of the plants listed in 'Window-box farming', plus:

- **Fruit** – Chilean guavas, melons, Inca berries, juneberries, Oregon grape, huckleberries and pineapple guavas. Also look out for dwarf or 'patio' fruit trees like quince 'Sibley's Patio Quince', peach 'Bonanza', nectarines 'Nectarella', figs (restrict their size by keeping these in a small container), apricots 'Apricompact', Asian pears and Japanese quinces.

- **Veg** – sweet potatoes, hyacinth beans, dwarf artichokes like 'Violetta di Chioggia', elephant garlic, tomatillos, dwarf pumpkins like 'Windsor', New Zealand yams, mashua, and Queensland arrowroot.

- **Herbs and spices** – borage, Sichuan peppers (if pruned to keep the plant small), Tasmanian mountain pepper, Japanese hardy ginger, manuka and green tea.

Recipe pots

I've been tinkering away in my horticultural kitchen to create simple recipe pots, for all manner of tasty planting combinations. Tried and tested in my own backyard, they cram in almost all you need to help create a sushi snack or to a blinding mojito into a single pot on your patio.

Cocktail buckets

• **Sugar leaf mojito** – a little calamondin lime tree underplanted with sugar leaves and mint will thrive on a sunny balcony. To get mixing, bash a handful of sliced green calamondin limes with loads of mint and sugar leaves, add ice, a splash of white rum and soda water and no one will care how bad you dance salsa. (NB: It's best to choose a mild-mannered variegated mint such as pineapple mint, as the regular stuff can be a bit of a thug and swamp its neighbours.)

• **Tomyumini** – lemongrass, dwarf chillies and fragrant Thai basil work just as well in a summer patio pot as they do in a chilled glass. Simply, slice a bit of each into a pitcher with a sprinkling of palm sugar, a few shots of Thai whisky and a refreshing twist of lime.

• **Electric lemonade** – the buzz of electric daisies makes them great underplanting to a canopy of sherbety lemon verbena and wood sorrel. Blitz a bottle of cloudy lemonade with a bunch of lemon verbena, apple-flavoured wood sorrel leaves, a good glug of gin and just four or five electric daisies. One pitcher of electric lemonade will be enough to hotwire even the dullest party.

• **Pimm's No. 2** – cucumber-flavoured borage is the perfect living trellis to train up tiny cucamelons. Underplant with fresh wild strawberries and mint to get your garden barbecue ready. Pop a little of each in a glass and muddle together with Pimm's, ginger beer and loads of ice.

• **Saffron and chamomile hot toddy** – The flowerless, carpet-forming chamomile 'Treneague' creates a fluffy, weed-suppressing lawn over dormant saffron crocus corms. Watch as each October they spring to life, delivering saffron, the world's most expensive spice right to your back garden. Simmer a little of each in some freshly brewed green tea (homegrown of course), add a twist of lime, a drizzle of golden syrup and finish with a shot of spiced rum. Totally worth getting ill for.

Edible micropond

As all 1990s garden makeover television shows have attested, no garden is complete without a water feature, but why not make one you can munch on?

Fill a half barrel or old zinc bath with water and plant it up by plunging in a few pots of sweet galingale reeds, watercress, water celery and wasabi. It is very important to wash and preferably cook any homegrown water plants (especially watercress) very thoroughly before eating as they can harbour dangerous bacteria and parasites.

Sushi bar

Take a trough and put in Japanese hardy ginger underplanted with wasabi and small-leaved hosta greens. Mulch with sharp gravel to deter slugs, place in a shady spot and get your chopsticks ready.

First-aid box

A crate planted up with aloe vera (great for cuts and burns), chamomile (for restful sleep and rashes) and creeping peppermint (for stomach upsets and colds) left by the kitchen door will cure all manner of ills.

Insect-repellent kit

Planting lemon verbena, lemongrass and lemon balm together will triple these plants' individual insect-repellent powers. In fact, just standing within two metres of this insecticidal threesome at your summer barbecue should be enough to fend off the worst of bugs. They're all effective against mozzies, gnats and wasps, for example, and you can even break a leaf off any of these plants and simply rub it onto your skin to add an extra layer of protection against these insects.

Undercover edibles

You might not know it, but lurking in your beds and borders there could already be a collection of exotic, gourmet fruit and veg that's ripe and ready for harvest right now. In fact, a huge proportion of our commonest garden plants, which we only value for their ornamental appeal, are mainstream edible crops in their countries of origin. Even pesky weeds often have a double life as highly prized delicacies in other parts of the world or were cherished in times goneby. Here is my guide to the undiscovered edible feast that could already be growing in your backyard.

Eat your weeds

Instead of chucking them on your compost heap, why not toss these weeds in your salad bowl, instead? This will give you a far greater incentive to weed – and provide a couple of edible side lines that are so easy to grow that they literally plant themselves.

- **Nettles** (*Urtica* spp.) can be harvested when young and tender and used just like spinach, although with a far fresher and more interesting flavour (don't worry, as their sting instantly disappears upon cooking!). They're wonderful added to creamy soups (just as you would watercress), quiches and even blanched and blended into pesto for a quirky twist on the more traditional basil.

- **Dandelions** (*Taraxacum officinale*) are a delicacy in northern France, where they are known as *pissenlit* (literally 'wet the bed') because of their diuretic properties. Covering the plants

with an upturned bucket two weeks prior to harvest will result in far milder tasting, elongated pale leaves that are very much like those of a delicate, tender leaf chicory. They are fantastic in salads with crisp fried bacon and croutons.

- **Shepherd's purse** (*Capsella bursa-pastoris*) is grown commercially on a huge scale in China for its spicy, watercress-flavoured leaves. It's fantastic scattered on winter salads or tossed into a stir-fry at the very end – not bad for a backyard weed.

- **Ground elder** (*Aegopodium podagraria*), despite being one of the hardest weeds on earth to eradicate, it was first introduced to Britain by the Romans as a popular vegetable and is lovely lightly steamed with grated nutmeg and a knob of butter.

- **Pineapple weed** (*Matricaria discoidea*), as the name suggests, has a tart tropical fruit-like flavour and goes brilliantly with its close relative, lawn daisy, which has a surprisingly tangy, piquant kick. Try them finely chopped in a raita, mixed into a Victoria sponge or scattered over a fruit salad.

Foraging your flower borders

Long before anyone thought they would make pretty outdoor ornaments, the following common garden plants were all valued edible crops. Give these forgotten flavours a go and your taste buds will thank you for it!

• **Dahlias** were introduced into Europe from Latin America alongside potatoes as a root vegetable for their sweet yam-like tubers. Despite being hugely productive and tasting great, this staple Aztec crop instead became popular for their blousy flowers.

• **Daylily flowers** aren't just stunningly tropical looking, they are also a delicious and incredibly popular ingredient in east Asian cooking. Generally called 'tiger lilies', they add a colourful, crunch to soups and stir-fries.

• **Sunflower buds** are steamed and eaten in Mexico just like artichokes, to which they are related. Pick a large flowered form like 'Full Sun' or 'Giant Yellow' and serve with lashings of melted butter.

• **Mahonias, fuchsias and barberries** are all grown commercially from Chile to Lebanon for their tangy, full-flavoured berries, yet despite fruiting prolifically in the UK, most of us Brits are completely unaware of their huge culinary value.

• **Marigold flowers and leaves** emit a powerfully sweet aroma of zesty citrus and mint. All over Latin America these parts are far better known for what they do in a fruit salad or spicy dipping sauce than in council bedding schemes.

• **Starry blue borage flowers** add a clean, cucumber-like edge to finger sandwiches.

• **Jasmine blossoms** can add a lingering fragrance to green teas and summer jellies.

• **Lavender** used sparingly, can transform a simple shortbread or fruit sorbet and can even be used to spice up a juicy, grilled steak. Don't go crazy with it though, because too much will leave you with a soapy aftertaste!

• **Nasturtium** aside from having peppery-flavoured leaves and flowers also produces seeds, which when pickled, are a convincing caper substitute.

Two crops for the price of one

A large array of conventional crop plants produces not just one, but two or more edible parts. Ironically, these less commonly eaten parts are the most interestingly flavoured and expensive to buy – yet most people simply throw them away.

• **Courgette plants** produce an abundance of crunchy, runner bean-flavoured male flowers throughout the summer. As only female flowers turn into courgettes, I think nothing of snipping them off to add to a quesadilla (**see page 70**) or stuffing them with ricotta and deep-frying them like the Italians do.

• **Grape and pumpkin leaves** can be blanched and used as a wrap for dolmas – those little Greek rice-filled rolls traditionally stuffed with lemon, mint and minced lamb. You could adapt these further by mixing and matching whatever fillings you fancy. My personal favourite, smoked salmon, cucumber and avocado, is a quirky take on California sushi rolls.

• **Garlic scapes** (the immature flower buds of 'Hard Neck' varieties of garlic) are probably my favourite vegetable. Prepared, cooked and served just like asparagus, but with a sweet and chive-like flavour, in my opinion they are more worthy of growing than the bulb itself.

• **Pea and broad bean plants** produce delicious young growth that adds a sweet, fresh pea flavour to salads and soups. Try wilting them down and mixing them with some fresh ricotta to fill your homemade ravioli or cannelloni. They will be the most light and delicate you've ever tasted.

Plants for free

Before you set off on a garden-centre shopping spree, why not try these simple tips, which prove that there is such a thing as a free lunch.

Saving your own seeds

By saving your own homegrown seeds and resowing them each year, not only will you have a perpetual source of free plants but, believe it or not, with each successive generation, your crops will slowly evolve to better suit your local growing conditions – eventually out performing anything you can buy. This won't take a millennium either, as within as little as two to three years you should already begin to see a real difference as you start to develop your very own unique varieties.

Collecting & storing

Collect seeds from the pods or fruit of your chosen crop, especially those of any plants that have proven particularly tasty or high-yielding. It is important that the fruit is fully ripe, which isn't necessarily the stage at which it is traditionally eaten. For example, with beans you have to wait for the fresh green pods to go dry, brown and brittle and with most fleshy fruit (like cucamelons and cucumbers) you need to wait for them to change colour and become soft. Some crops, particularly root and leafy greens, are usually gathered well before they have even had a chance to flower and fruit, so to save the seeds you will have to sacrifice a little of your harvest, letting a couple of plants grow to maturity and set seed.

Once you have removed the seeds:

• Wash off as much pulp or fibre as possible and spread the seeds evenly over a sheet of double-thickness kitchen roll to absorb any excess moisture.

• Place two more sheets of kitchen paper over the top of this to create a seed and paper sandwich and store in a cool, dry place for one week to dry the seeds out as much as possible.

• Tip the seeds into a paper (not plastic) envelope, label and store them in an airtight jar and then refrigerate.

Kept dry and cool, these seeds will stay fresh for several years (sometimes decades!) until you are ready to plant them out.

Sowing seeds

Growing from seeds is one of the most reliable and, certainly, the most common way to increase your stock of fruit and veg plants as all the germination process requires is water, warmth and light. Any packets from a reputable seed company will come with full instructions on how best to treat each variety. In fact, it is a good idea to keep the packet as a quick reference when sowing your homegrown seeds. However, even if you follow the packet instructions to the letter, here are a few simple tips for success that will allow you to sidestep common problems and get your little plants off to a flying start.

Light

Seedlings, sown on indoor windowsills early in the year, tend to arch toward the light, develop unevenly and become long and lanky. To help prevent this happening:

• Create your own mini reflector by wrapping a piece of cardboard in kitchen foil and positioning it behind the plants. This will bounce any light from your window onto the plants, ensuring a more even illumination from both sides.

• Rotate the trays occasionally to reduce any risk of weak, arched growth.

• If you don't have enough space by a sunny windowsill for your growing army of seedlings, consider investing in a basic grow lamp. Also known as a propagation lamp, it emits targeted wavelengths of light that specifically boost young plant growth. Quite pricey, but amazingly effective. In my book, it's the only gardeners' gadget worth forking out for.

Warmth

If you have an airing cupboard at home, this cosy nook can be used as a cost-free heated propagator for seeds sown indoors, adding that extra bit of warmth many exotic species like melons and tomatillos crave for optimal germination. All you need to do is:

• Sow a selection of pots or trays with seeds to the supplier's directions and water well. Place each pot or tray into a ziplock plastic bag (to help seal in moisture), seal and put it on the bottom rack of the cupboard.

• Check back every day or so, as seeds can emerge very quickly in the warmth.

• As soon as the seedlings break through the surface, remove the pots or trays and transfer them to a sunny windowsill to grow on.

Water

One of the key reasons for the failure of young seedlings is an affliction called 'damping off', a fungal infection that can cause young plants to rot at the base of their stem and subsequently collapse. A simple way to prevent damping off is to irrigate the plants with a homegrown anti-fungal solution each time you water. To make the solution, fill a spray can with cold chamomile tea (a natural anti-fungal agent) and spray the surface of the compost every few days to moisten it.

Home cloning

While the most common way of growing the majority of veg plants is by sowing seeds, home cloning (i.e. vegetative propagation) can be a far quicker and easier way to get your harvest. Before you don your white coat, cloning plants doesn't require a CSI-style lab, just a pair of secateurs or a spade and a little compost.

Taking cuttings

Cuttings are just small sections of stems, leaves or roots that are snipped off and encouraged to grow their own roots and leaves, and over time, become small plants of their own.

There is a huge variety of techniques to take cuttings, although for most of the plants in this book all you need to do is:

• Snip a short 5–10cm section from the tip of one of the plant's branches, cutting through a node (those little raised bumps along the stem from where leaves grow). Remove all the foliage from your cutting except two small leaves at the very tip.

• Dip the cut end in a hormone rooting powder and insert the shoot into a pot of loose, well-drained seed compost, to bury about half the stem. You can put various cuttings in each pot, spaced about 5cm apart.

• Water in well (using the cold chamomile tea idea to prevent fungal infection as outlined in 'sowing seeds' on page 48). Pop the pot inside a clear plastic ziplock bag, seal it and place on a bright windowsill.

Between two to three weeks later your little cuttings should have magically turned into small plants. They are now ready for transplanting into their own pots or outside into the garden.

Plants that are best propagated by this method include: watercress, purslane, tree chillies, tomatillos, goji berries, Peruvian ground apple, sweet potatoes, New Zealand yams, curry leaves, Tasmanian mountain peppers, electric daisies, Vietnamese fish mint, apple-flavoured begonias, Aztec sweet herb, fuchsias, dahlias and sugar leaves.

Dividing up mature plants

Another way to get more bang for your buck is to increase your stock by literally dividing up plants. Many species are clump-forming, which means that they develop lots of tiny offshoots around their base.

By digging up these plants in spring, when they are just beginning to shoot, and splitting the clumps into smaller plants, each mature plant can be turned into four to six smaller plants, which once planted out separately, will quickly grow into large, leafy specimens. This method might sound a tad brutal, but it can actually help revive congested masses, giving new life to established clumps. To get dividing, thrust two garden forks, back to back into the centre of a clump and pull the handles apart.

Plants that are best propagated by this method include: daylilies, society garlic, hosta greens, fiddlehead ferns, bananas, Alpine 'snow' strawberries, Japanese hardy ginger and winter-green.

Grow your own garden centre

Save yourself a fortune with my simple tips for growing everything from fertiliser to garden twine.

Fertiliser for free!

I must be one of the few gardeners who get excited to see a nettle or weedy comfrey plant pop up in a bed or border, as both these deep-rooted species draw nutrients from deep within the subsoil and concentrate them in their leaves – making these plants perfect for creating cost-free liquid fertiliser.

Comfrey (*Symphytum officinale*) leaves are specifically rich in potash, the key plant nutrient responsible for healthy fruit formation, while the humble nettle (*Urtica dioica*) contains high levels of nitrogen, which fuels lush leaf growth. To hijack these nutrient stores and deliver them to your precious crops do the following:

- Fill a large bucket with either roughly chopped nettle or comfrey leaves right up to the brim (or ideally two buckets, one with nettles and one with comfrey). Weigh them down with a brick and top the leaves up with just enough water to cover them. Cover with a secure lid.

- After two weeks, your mix will have fermented, releasing the nutrients from the leaves into the water to create a potent liquid fertiliser. It will stink (hence the lid), but it will work wonders on your plants.

- Dilute this 'tea', using nine parts water for every one part of the liquid, and you are good to go.

- For a general purpose blend combine equal quantities of the diluted nettle and comfrey liquid. For plants that need a boost in the fruit or flower department, extra comfrey works wonders, while leafy greens will be especially lush if given a couple doses of nettle tea in their water.

Nettles and comfrey are astonishingly fast growers. They can be cut right down to the ground up to five times a year and still provide you with a virtually endless source of free fertiliser for your plants.

Alternatively, if you live by the seaside you can use any kind of seaweed. These are particularly rich in a whole host of trace minerals. Just make sure to give it a good rinse with a hose beforehand to wash off any salt, as that can harm your plants.

For really lazy gardeners, you can just scatter the chopped-up leaves of any of these plants over the surface of the soil and lightly fork in. It's important to wilt any chopped-up comfrey by laying it in hot sun for a day or two before sprinkling it on your borders though. Because it is such a vigorous grower, freshly chopped stems and leaves can often take root.

Toxin-free bug spray

An all-natural, home-brewed bug spray might sound a little airy fairy, but I promise you that it is easy to make from cheap ingredients that are scientifically proven to repel or kill pests yet is 100 per cent safe to kids and pets.

The key ingredient you'll need for this spray is neem oil. Extracted from the nuts of a subtropical tree from India, it is a natural insecticide that is incredibly effective against aphids, whitefly and even headlice (it is the key ingredient in many over-the-counter headlice shampoos). Amazingly, it has the ability to tell the good guys from the bad as it specifically targets only those insects that ravage your crops, leaving beneficial species like butterflies and bees entirely unscathed. Neem oil can be bought in most health-food stores, larger pharmacies and, of course, online.

To make the toxin-free bug spray, simply:

- Boil 1 litre of water in a saucepan and add a handful of sliced, very spicy chillies or a tablespoon of chilli powder and simmer for 5–10 minutes. Capsaicin (the spicy chemical found in chillies) helps repel mammalian pests such as rodents and deer from your plants by coating their leaves in an unpleasant-tasting yet harmless substance.

- Turn off the heat and strain out the chillies. While the liquid is still hot, add a teaspoon of finely grated all-natural soap or eco-friendly washing-up liquid and stir in well to dissolve. This allows the neem oil and water to mix, while also being mildly insecticidal.

- Gradually add a teaspoon of neem oil while stirring vigorously to combine.

- Pour this mix into a spray can and mist affected plants once a day, ideally in the morning or evening. After about three applications, you will start to notice a difference.

Living pest control

Wage war on bugs with an arsenal of homegrown pest repellents cleverly disguised as mild-mannered garden plants.

- **Marigolds** – the fragrant chemicals in marigold leaves (*Tagetes* spp.) have insect repellent and insecticidal properties. Planting them next to other more vulnerable crops helps deter whitefly infestations.

- **Scaredy cat plant** – the spicy, herbal aroma of *Coleus canina*, marketed under a raft of colourful names, is said to deter both cats and dogs from digging up your beds.

- **Carnivorous plants** – a couple of cleverly placed carnivorous species in the greenhouse or indoor windowsill can help your plants strike back hard against insect invaders. Those innovative Victorians used butterworts (*Pinguicula grandiflora*) to control whitefly in their hothouses and the sticky tentacles of Cape sundew (*Drosera capensis*) that act like living fly-paper for fungus gnats. In return for all their efforts, all that these species require is a saucer of rainwater to stand in, the occasional misting and a brightly lit home in which the temperature doesn't fall below 5°C in winter.

Flower-based fungicide

Believe it or not, the aromatic chemicals in chamomile tea possess fungicidal effects, making it perfect to water young seedlings with to prevent fungal infections like damping off. Adding one roughly chopped clove of fresh garlic (which contains allicin, also a potent fungicide) or a splash of full-fat milk (which has a unique combination of mould-busting fatty acids) to a litre of chamomile tea gives it an extra fungicidal punch, making it a great spray-on treatment for mildew on courgette, squash and pumpkin plants.

Incidentally, if you fancy growing your own chamomile plants, a quick and cheap way to do this is to rip open a couple of unused chamomile tea bags and scatter the contents over soil. The dried flowers contain hundreds of tiny seeds that will begin to sprout in a matter of days.

Organic plant supports & twine

Why pay good money for imported bamboo canes that are shipped in from the other side of the world when you can grow your own? If kept wellwatered and fed, a mature bamboo (*Phyllostachys* spp.) plant can produce up to ten canes a year up to 3m long. By planting some dogwood (*Cornus* spp.) with brightly coloured stems, you can even produce multicoloured planting canes in every shade from lime green to lurid orange and bright scarlet.

For long-lasting, biodegradable garden twine, the fibrous leaves of New Zealand flax (*Phormium tenax*) and cabbage palm (*Cordyline* spp.) are indispensable. As its name suggests, New Zealand flax was once widely grown for its fibre, and used to make rigging for the Royal Navy. To extract flax fibre just snip off a leaf and slice off its pointy end. You will have a rectangle with long parallel veins running along its length. Pinch a section of these and pull them towards yourself, peeling away a thin strip of leaf as you go. This can be used just like regular garden twine.

Leaves & Greens

Bamboo shoots *Phyllostachys spp.*

The pandas are really on to a good thing

If your only experience of bamboo shoots is the soggy, ready-sliced ones from a can, crunching into a fresh green shoot from the bottom of your garden will be a true revelation. You won't need an enormous heated greenhouse either because the most sought-after shoots in Asia are not the huge tropical ones, but the blizzard-proof temperate types that thrive on near total neglect and are already an extremely common garden plant all over the UK.

Growing

If you choose the right variety, bamboo is possibly the easiest crop to grow in the UK. It puts up with drought and bone-chilling winter temperatures, suffers from few pests and diseases and being a long-lived perennial can reward you with a good 50 years of harvests in exchange for the 15 minutes it takes to plant. Flavour varies markedly between species, with *Phyllostachys dulcis* and *P. edulis* being sweet enough to eat fresh off the plant, while others such as *P. aurea* and *P. nigra* need to be cooked to reduce their slight bitterness.

Although bamboo puts up with a wide range of conditions, to ensure the tenderest, sweetest harvests I recommend the following:

- Plant bamboo 2m apart in a slightly shady location in deep, rich soil with plenty of organic matter mixed in.

- Generous watering and frequent high nitrogen liquid feeds (like nettle fertiliser on page 51) throughout the growing season. These actions will result in dramatically increased yields of particularly soft, young growth.

- To improve their flavour further, mulch the earth around the base of the plants with a good thick layer (20cm deep) of compost. This mulch helps conserve moisture *and* exclude light to new canes – making them longer, thinner and more succulent. Alternatively, cover newly emerging tips with an upturned bucket to get a similar result.

Harvesting & eating

Bamboo produces most of its shoots in spring, but if kept generously watered and fertilised it will send up a steady stream throughout summer. To harvest these shoots, slice them off with a pair of secateurs or a bread knife when they are about 7–10cm long, making the cut about 5cm below soil level. Once the shoots are over 30cm high, they will start to become tough and woody and are not worth harvesting, but as they are infamously quick growers it's worth doing a daily check to track their progress.

The plants can withstand having up to a third of their new shoots removed each season without damage to their overall vigour. In fact, because most gardening advice about bamboo

6m

2m

2m

is mainly on how to stop it taking over your garden, eating it is a great way to keep its plans for world domination in check.

Once harvested, slice the shoots in half lengthways and peel off the fibrous sheaths that protect the tender stalk at their heart, which looks like a knobbly, creamy-coloured asparagus spear. The species *Phyllostachys dulcis* and *P. edulis* are sweet enough to eat raw; however, most others contain bitter, mildly toxic compounds so they need to be thoroughly cooked to make them palatable and safe to eat. To do this, put the halved peeled shoots in salted water and simmer for 30 minutes. If they are still bitter, replace the water and simmer for a little longer until they are sweet and nutty to taste. Once this is done they are ready to eat.

I often add thinly sliced pre-cooked bamboo shoots to stir-fries and Asian-style soups where they add an interesting crunch and hazelnut flavour. Shredded into skinny matchsticks they are wonderful in veggie spring rolls with finely grated carrot, sliced shiitake mushrooms and lettuce. This same mix is fantastic as dumpling filling – simply fill wonton wrappers and fry or steam before serving with a sesame oil and soy dipping sauce.

Bamboo shoots don't strictly have to be cooked Asian-style. Try them sautéed with crispy bacon before tossing with chicory, croutons and a creamy garlic mayonnaise to make a stunning spring salad. I have a Swiss buddy who even adds sliced shards of bamboo shoots to potato and cheese rostis for added crunch. Get creative and the sky is the limit!

edible part at the heart

Chinese chives *Allium tuberosum*

Delicate, roasted garlic-flavoured blossoms and greens

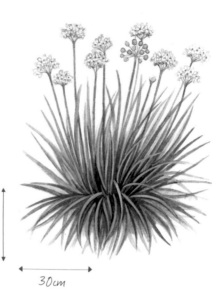

40cm

30cm

Meet the ultimate low-maintenance crop for slacker gardeners who are after loads of flavour for minimal labour. The young leaves and slender flower buds of Chinese chives are somewhere between a fresh cooking green and a delicate chive-like herb, with a sweet, roasted garlic flavour. Super long-loved and a cinch to grow, this plant will reward you with decades of gourmet veg harvests and has great ornamental appeal with its white star-shaped edible blossoms in summer. Also known as: garlic chives, Chinese leeks.

Growing

Chinese chives are extremely easy to grow from both seed and young plants, both of which can be found in the herb section of all good garden centres. To get growing, all you need to do is:

• Pick a bright, sunny position (although they can also cope well with light shade) and fork over the soil to a depth of at least 30cm with plenty of organic matter and grit to encourage these deep-rooted plants to settle in well.

30cm

- Plant them 30cm apart and water in well. Just six of these highly productive plants will provide more than enough flowers and leaves for the average family.

- Keep well watered and fertilised with a high-potash feed like comfrey liquid throughout the growing season and Bob's your uncle!

If you just can't get enough of their sweet, roasted garlic flavour, extend the harvest season right into late autumn (and kick start it several weeks earlier each spring) by laying cloches over plants. This will raise the temperature around the plants sufficiently to trick them into believing that your garden is actually a couple of hundred miles further south than it really is.

Harvesting & eating

The leaves can be harvested to within 3cm of the ground up to three times per year – four if using cloches. However, if the delicious flower buds are what you are after, only cut two harvests – one in early summer and one in late autumn so the plants have sufficient reserves to give a decent crop of both leaves and flowers. Like many flowering plants, the more blooms you pick the more they produce, so keep snipping throughout summer for maximum harvests.

Both the flower buds and leaves of Chinese chives can be used in the same way as regular chives, scattered in salads and stir-fries or mixed into quiches. Yet unlike your regular supermarket-bought chives, Chinese chives have a succulent, fleshy texture that adds a delicious slippery crunch to all manner of dishes.

The delicate, sweet flavour of Chinese chives has a particularly good affinity with both eggs and seafood. The three are teamed up in several east-Asian dishes such as in a Chinese version of a Spanish omelette that uses fistfuls of sautéed chopped leaves instead of potato and golden, seared scallops instead of chorizo. Add a couple of threads of saffron and you'll be in culinary ecstasy. The Japanese employ a similar combination in a savoury egg custard known as *chawanmushi* (basically a crustless quiche) consisting of sautéed leaves, prawns, sliced shiitake mushrooms, sweet rice wine and soy sauce in an egg custard.

The fully opened blossoms, which resemble constellations of tiny white stars, look fantastic served raw in salads (as do the leaves and buds). However, don't let their delicate appearance fool you – when raw, they usually have a far more spicy, garlic flavour than the leaves.

Society garlic

If you love the flavour of Chinese chives but are after something even more ornamental, why not go for the pretty pink flowers and the silver-edged leaves of the South African wild flower (and common UK garden plant) *Tulbaghia violacea*? Used by the Zulu as both a prized edible and key medicinal plant, its common name 'society garlic' was used by early Afrikaans settlers because of its ability to provide all the flavour of garlic without any after-effect on the breath. A perfect first-date garlic option!

Elephant garlic _Allium ampeloprasum var. ampeloprasum_

Fist-sized garlic bulbs with asparagus-flavoured flowers

Producing enormous bulbs, six times the size of regular garlic from the same amount of border space, this giant easy-to-grow variety is a must-try plant for any aspiring allotmenteer. With the added benefits of milder, sweeter cloves and spectacularly delicious edible flower buds, plant this and you will wonder why you ever wasted space with those puny, pungent supermarket types in the first place. Also known as: jumbo garlic, giant garlic.

Growing

Not a 'true' garlic at all but a rather unusual large-bulbed variety of leek, elephant garlic is virtually identical to its namesake in flavour, appearance and growing technique.

Planting should ideally be done between November and January, as after developing its first roots the plant needs to experience at least one month of temperatures below 10°C to produce a good head of cloves. Without this cold spell you will end up with a single smaller, onion-like bulb that is just as good to eat but a far more meagre crop. To get growing:

- Break open a bulb into individual cloves and discard any that are soft, bruised or spotty.

- Plant each of the remaining healthy cloves, pointy end up, at a spacing of 15–20cm in a sunny site in well-drained soil. The tip of each clove should be 3–5cm below the soil surface.

- Keep well watered and fertilised and you really won't have much else to do to ensure a bumper crop.

In May, the plant will produce its first crop of scapes, little marble-sized flower buds on thick stems. Snip these off before they open (even if you aren't interested in eating them) to redirect the plant's energies in producing the largest bulb possible.

Harvesting & eating

The scapes are ready for harvesting when the stems are no longer than 20cm because the little buds are at their most tender at this point. Then, in July as the leaves begin to yellow, reduce watering for a week or two to encourage the bulbs to fully mature. Harvest by loosening the bulb with a trowel. Shake off as much soil as possible and leave the whole bulb to dry in a warm, sunny spot for a few days prior to storing them in the fridge, where they will keep for up to three months.

Elephant garlic has the great benefit of producing two edible crops, bulbs and scapes, both of which are sold as gourmet veg in fancy farmers' markets and posh delis. The bulb itself can be used just like regular garlic and has a far milder, sweeter flavour (like a cross between a leek and regular garlic).

Try slicing off the top half of an entire bulb and roasting the bottom half in the oven with a generous drizzle of olive oil and loads of black pepper. Softening to a virtually spreadable consistency, it's the perfect accompaniment to roast chicken and can transform a boring ready-made bread sauce into a thing of true culinary beauty when mashed and stirred through. It's also great thinly sliced and added to salads just like onions; the milder taste provides all the flavour of garlic without being as overpowering.

The scapes' crisp heads combine the flavour of fresh asparagus and chives and the texture of crunchy, sprouting broccoli (yet somehow taste far better than any of these three). One of my top-ten favourite meals is finely sliced scapes, sautéed in a little butter, mixed into scrambled eggs and served on toasted soda bread. Alternatively, try them stir-fried, roasted, grilled or battered in tempura. Steamed and topped with hollandaise sauce, they knock the socks off of the most fancy asparagus and are a revelation blitzed into creamy soups.

20cm

30cm

1.2m

Daylilies *Hemerocallis spp.*

The exotic, oriental veg lurking secretly in your flower border

Most Westerners have a hard time seeing beyond the blousy, lily-like flowers on slender, graceful stalks of these common ornamental plants and accepting them as a 'proper' veg – that is of course until they taste them. A typical supermarket veg throughout east Asia, daylily flowers combine the flavours of fresh runner beans, nutty asparagus and delicate okra. Get ready to be stunned! Also known as: tiger lilies, golden needles, yellow flower vegetable.

Growing

Hailing from a climate remarkably similar to the UK, daylilies are so at home in our corner of Northern Europe that they often make a break for freedom, colonising land well outside of the cosy confines of suburban gardens. Their ability to fend for themselves in the wild, without so much as a glance from a gardener, demonstrates just how easy they are to grow. To get them off to a flying start:

• Plant out potted plants anytime between spring and early autumn in a sunny site in beds of fertile, well-drained soil. They will also grow well in light shade although their yields will not be as generous.

• Keep them well watered with a high-potash feed like comfrey liquid, spread a good thick layer of mulch around plants each spring to conserve moisture and you'll really have little else to do.

• Finally, once they are growing strong, increase your stock for free by lifting large clumps in spring or autumn and dividing them into smaller sections about 10cm wide. Replant these in the border up to 30cm apart.

Varieties to try

Astonishingly, there are over 60,000 varieties of daylilies to choose from. The most commonly cultivated by the Chinese as an edible crop are the orange and yellow varieties (hence its traditional name *jinzen*, meaning 'golden needles'). Good examples with a particularly long flowering season and excellent flavour include 'Happy Returns', 'Lemon Lollipop' and 'Stella D'Oro'.

Harvesting & eating

All parts of daylilies are edible, from their fresh leaf tips in spring to their fleshy tubers in autumn. However, as harvesting both of these parts damages the plant and therefore reduces flower yield, I generally stick to eating their flowers – by far the tastiest part for me.

Flowers can be harvested either in bud (picked off when they have begun to swell but before the petals start to separate), when fully open or even as spent (withering) blooms. At each of these stages, the texture and flavour vary so much that they should be cooked and prepared in totally different ways.

30cm

The buds can be added to stir-fries and treated as you would French beans or mangetout including one of my personal favourite childhood dishes, tigerlily prawns. In this, the fresh buds are tossed in a wok with a dash of sesame oil, a handful of king prawns, soy sauce and Chinese rice wine.

Adventurous Westerners usually eat daylilies once the flowers are fully open (which is uncommon in Asia) because the petals make a colourful addition to salads. At this stage, they have a satisfying crunch and an extra level of sweetness, provided by the nectar at the base of the petals. These can also be battered and deep fried in tempura or even sliced up and stirred into pancake mix with blueberries to make American-style hot cakes, drizzled with lashings of maple syrup. Yum.

Perhaps the most popular way to eat daylilies is as wilted blooms, which is fantastic as this means you won't ruin your floral display and you'll also have a brilliant excuse to tidy up the spent heads. Pick newly wilted flowers the day after flowering (each bloom generally only lasts 12 hours) and scatter them over a sunny windowsill for a few hours to go fully limp. These flowers can be used in any stir-fry, adding a chewier, savoury bite to an array of dishes. Fully dried, these are a staple ingredient in east Asia, used to thicken and add meaty texture to soups and stews, including shark's fin melon soup (see *A recipe idea*, page 106).

50cm–1m

50cm

Globe artichokes & cardoons

Cynara scolymus & C. cardunculus

The gourmet crops that grow on big, posh thistles

While globe artichokes are a well-known vegetable delicacy, their extremely close relative, cardoons, are still a well-kept secret. Their tender, cream-coloured stalks – like artichoke-flavoured celery sticks with a hint of lemon – were hugely popular in Britain right up until Victorian times. Indeed, they are still considered a gourmet veg in France, Spain and Italy, gracing many a continental Christmas table. Sophisticated, delicious and producing enormous mounds of arcing silvery fronds, it is high time this remarkable crop made its comeback.

Growing

Despite their reputation as 'gourmet' crops, both globe artichokes and cardoons are basically big, posh thistles and are just as easy to grow.

The key to success is to:

• Mimic their Mediterranean habitat, giving them the sunniest site possible in slightly acidic, free-draining soil.

• Plant out small plants (available from any garden centre) in early spring 75cm apart.

50cm–75cm

2–3m

• Keep them well watered while establishing and you won't need to do much else for them.

> **Tip:** For globe artichokes, trim away any flower buds from plants that appear in the first year to divert the plant's energies into properly establishing itself.

As both types of plants are so large and productive (artichokes throwing up as many as ten tender globes per plant) just a single plant may be more than enough if you only have a small plot.

Varieties to try

With artichokes, why not try growing one of those fancy purple-blushed varieties like 'Romanesco' or 'Violetta di Chioggia'? If you fancy growing cardoons but don't have room for a 3m monster, seek out the dwarf variety 'Cardy', which grows no taller than 1.2m.

Harvesting & eating

Artichokes
Pick the buds when they have swollen to their maximum size but before their scales start to open. From a single planting they will reward you with an annual harvest for years to come, requiring very little in return.

To prepare artichokes for cooking, slice about 3cm off the tip of the globe and steam the remainder over a large pan of simmering water containing a bay leaf, sliced garlic clove and a few peppercorns for 25–45 minutes or until the outer scales can be easily pulled off. Once cooked, serve them whole with melted butter or an aioli dip.

Eat by pulling out the 'petals' one at a time, dip the fleshy end of the petal into melted butter or aioli and bite off the soft base with your teeth.

After you have munched on these, scoop out the inedible fuzzy part called the 'choke' with a spoon and discard. The remaining base of the artichoke is known as the heart. Slice into pieces and dip into the sauce to polish this off.

Cardoons

For cardoons, the stems are what you are after, so if you snip off all the flowers as they appear they won't drain the plant's resources. In October through to mid November, bunch all the plants' leaves up towards its centre and tie this bundle up with string. Wrap this column of bunched leaves up in a couple of layers of sacking or corrugated cardboard (30–50cm wide) to create a cylindrical sleeve, leaving the top open. Then tie with string to keep in place. This process is called 'blanching', the aim of which is to exclude light to the leaf stems, making them more tender and sweet by eliminating the bitter compounds that make unblanched stems unpalatable.

After three weeks of this treatment, the cardoon stems will be ready to harvest. Just unwrap the cardboard and cut the plant down to near-ground level. Remove all leafy top growth from each stout, cream-coloured stem.

To prepare cardoons for cooking, top and tail and peel off any remaining leaves and stringy fibres from the stalks with a vegetable peeler. Cut them into 8cm pieces and soak them in a bowl of water with two tablespoons of white vinegar for 30 minutes (the vinegar helps reduce the bitter taste of cardoons and prevents discoloration). Plunge into simmering, salted water for 30 minutes or so until they are soft. They are then ready to use in any recipe.

Follow these steps for a tasty Italian-style treat. Dip cardoon pieces in beaten egg and then roll in polenta, seasoned with a few tablespoons of grated Parmesan cheese, salt and pepper, before frying in olive oil until crisp. Alternatively, serve them in a gratin by arranging sliced cardoon pieces in a baking dish, scattering over fried bacon, sliced onions and topping with cheese sauce and breadcrumbs. Bake in a medium oven until golden. Another delicious way to eat cardoons is to sauté with some golden, crispy garlic and smoked paprika – your one-way ticket to creamy vegetable heaven.

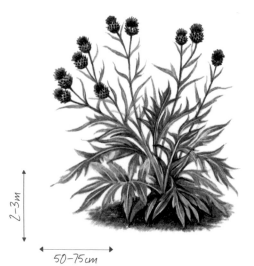

2–3m

50–75cm

Fenugreek *Trigonella foenum-graecum*

The curry-house green you can grow from seeds on your spice rack

Known in the UK mainly for its heady and spicy seeds, which form the basis of dozens of curry-powder blends, fenugreek has wonderfully fragrant leaves that are still a little under the foodie-radar. Also known as *Methi*.

Growing

Growing fenugreek for its hay-scented, pleasantly bitter greens could not be more straightforward. Simply:

• Pick up the seeds (often sold in little spice shakers) from your local supermarket or Asian grocery store.

• Scatter the seeds over well-prepared soil or pots of compost any time between April and September. The plants prefer full sun but can cope with a little light shade.

• Rake over the soil after sowing to lightly cover the seeds and water in well.

• Once plants are 5cm high, thin them out to a rough spacing of 10cm and remove any seed pods as they appear to ensure the most tender leaves.

• Keep sowing every two weeks and you will have a constant supply of fresh leaves right up until the first frosts.

As they belong to the bean family, the plants will fertilise themselves by fixing nitrogen in the soil (see *My ten commandments*, page 19).

Harvesting & eating

To harvest, simply get out there with your scissors and snip the top growth of the plants to within 10cm of the ground. This ensures that you harvest only the softest, newest leaves (not the old tough ones at the base) and that

the plants have a chance to recover, delivering a brand new harvest just a few weeks later.

If you ever need inspiration on how to cook fenugreek greens, just go to your local curry house and look for the word *methi* in the menu (the name for the plant in Urdu, Hindi and Nepali) and you will quickly see how versatile an ingredient it is – used in everything from curries to sauces and salads.

Chopped up, fenugreek can be used to replace spinach, mixed with spices and fried potatoes in a particularly flavourful Indian dish called *aloo methi*. Try it simply sautéed in a little chilli and garlic, ripped up and scattered over salad or on freshly baked naan bread.

10cm

60cm

30cm

Squash flowers & leaves

Cucurbita pepo (courgette) & C. maxima (pumpkin)

The forgotten harvest lying hidden in every allotment

90cm
(courgette)
1.8m
(pumpkin)

If you've ever grown squash before and only eaten its fruit, you will have inadvertently wasted two-thirds of your harvest. Easily as delicious as the squash themselves, the flowers and young shoots of many squash plants are eaten as conventional vegetables in every country from Argentina to Zimbabwe. In the UK, the blossoms often cost over four times the price of squash sold at fancy farmers' markets and upmarket delis. So why has it taken us Brits so long to realise that it's cheaper to grow them ourselves? Also known as pumpkins, courgettes, winter squash, summer squash.

Growing

Squash are four closely related species from the cucumber family, including courgettes, pumpkins, marrows and butternut squash. Vigorous and extremely productive, both courgettes and pumpkins are easy to grow but can take up a lot of space. However, they really will earn their keep because you will need only a maximum of two plants to keep the average family in fruit, flowers and shoots. They can even be perfectly happy stuck in a growbag and left to go mad. Here are my growing tips:

• As squash flowers and leaves need a long growing season, plant them indoors in April on a sunny windowsill in small individual pots of compost. Insert the seeds 2.5cm deep into the compost on their sides to help ensure good drainage and prevent them from getting fungal infections.

• When little white roots start to emerge from the holes in the bottom of the pots, transplant the squash plants to a slightly larger pot (12.5cm is ideal).

• To save time and windowsill space, you could buy young squash plants from any garden centre in spring. Whichever option you go for, the plants will be ready to bed out in the sunniest site possible in a rich, well-drained soil at the end of May.

• Space the courgettes, which generally form neat rosettes, about 90cm apart. The sprawling vines of pumpkins will require a 1.8m gap between plants. If space is limited pick a dwarf variety of courgette like 'Patio Star' or 'Buckingham' or adorable mini-pumpkin plants like 'Windsor'.

Squash are generally quite tough, but without enough water around their roots they can quickly become susceptible to 'powdery mildew' – a fungal infection that rapidly smothers leaves in a dusting of white blotches and can really knock yields for six. So to keep them in tip-top condition, give the plants a good weekly soak with a dilute, high-potash liquid feed and mulch the soil around them with a moisture-sealing layer of organic matter.

40cm

trailing to 2.5m

Harvesting & eating

While I probably don't need to tell you how to eat courgettes and pumpkins, the floral and foliar delicacies the plants offer might need a little more introduction.

The tender tips and soft young leaves on the ends of the trailing stems of pumpkin plants can be snipped off after three or four baby fruits have formed. Cook them just like any other leafy green. The little prickles on the leaves disappear quickly after a few seconds in the pan.

In the Congo and Zimbabwe, the leaves are chopped up and fried in a little oil and garlic, a flavour that is an exotic cross between broccoli, green beans and spinach. In Korea, the leaves are first steamed and then sprinkled with sesame oil, puréed chillies and a hint of mustard. In Thailand, they are simmered gently in coconut milk, and served as a creamy, veggie side dish.

The flowers of all squash plants can be eaten. They have a delicate eggy flavour reminiscent of yellow courgettes. There are two types of squash flowers: female and male. Female flowers have swollen immature fruit where the petals meet the stem and male ones that look almost identical apart from the missing fruit. Although both are delicious, the male ones are the better ones to go for as picking the females results in sacrificing your fruit harvest. Pick when fully open, but do leave a few male flowers so that insects can pollinate the fruit-bearing female flowers.

In Italy, the flowers are stuffed with ricotta, lemon zest and pine nuts, dipped in a light beer-batter and deep-fried. You can always tie the open end shut with a chive leaf to avoid losing any filling. Served crisp and drizzled with honey, these delicious options alone are more than enough reason to grow squash.

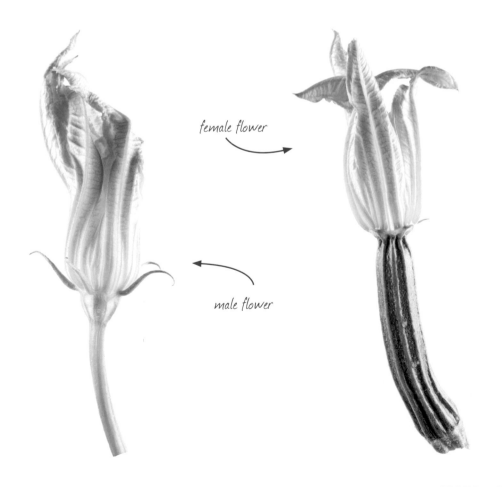

female flower

male flower

a recipe idea

Squash flowers &
red pepper quesadillas

Wilted squash flowers between crisp tortillas and melting mozzarella cheese make these quesadillas enough to win round the most die-hard edible flower sceptic.

Serves 2

Ingredients
1 red pepper, finely sliced
olive oil, for frying
1 garlic clove, finely chopped
salt and pepper
5 fresh squash flowers
100g mozzarella cheese, sliced
4 flour tortillas (20cm)
2 jalapeños, sliced
small handful of parsley, finely chopped

Fry the red pepper in a little of the olive oil over a medium heat until the slices are soft and beginning to char. Sprinkle over the chopped garlic, season well with salt and pepper, stir and leave to cook for a further 2 minutes.

Prepare the squash flowers by removing and discarding the hard parts from the inside of the flowers and any bits of stem still attached to their bases. Set aside.

Lay half of the mozzarella cheese over a couple of tortillas and then top with the squash flowers, red peppers, jalapeños and parsley. Finish by adding the remaining cheese and top with another tortilla to create a pair of tortilla sandwiches.

Heat some more olive oil in a frying pan over a medium heat and fry each quesadilla, flipping once. When the quesadilla begins to turn golden brown and the mozzarella cheese starts to ooze out, it is ready. Serve with a simple tomato salsa.

Fiddlehead fern *Matteuccia struthiopteris*

Little green spirals of springtime deliciousness

With their fresh, nutty crunch and woodsy 'green' flavour, the young unfurling fronds of fiddlehead ferns are fast becoming the trendiest 'wild food' ingredient among stateside foodies. Eating these little spirals, which somehow meld the flavours of asparagus, mustard greens and french beans has been described as being like 'an early morning in wet woods'. Also known as: ostrich ferns, shuttlecock ferns, *kogomi*.

Growing

Although there are dozens of fern species known as 'fiddleheads' eaten around the world, I would stick to the common 'ostrich fern' (*Matteuccia struthiopteris*), as it is both the most flavourful and widely eaten. Officially the state vegetable of Vermont in the US, the plant's stunning shuttlecocks of ostrich feather-like fronds have also made them a popular garden plant that can be picked up in any good nursery.

Originating in the moist forests of North America, where they grow in large colonies on the edges of streams, ostrich ferns thrive in cool, wet environments, where pretty much no other vegetable can grow – making them perfect for a damp, dark corner of your yard. To get growing:

• Plant the ferns out in naturalistic groups in a shady site in rich, moist (or even wet) soil, at a spacing of about 45cm between plants. Planting can be at any time of year, as long as the soil is workable.

• Keep them well watered, soaking the ferns two to three times a week to keep the soil constantly moist, because if the soil dries out, they will wilt and start to loose their leaves.

• A thick layer of mulch up to 5cm deep scattered around the plants will help trap moisture (pine needles and leaf litter are perfect for this), as will digging into the soil large amounts of moisture-retaining organic matter.

• Give your plants a boost once a year in spring, ideally just after harvesting, by showering them with a diluted liquid feed high in nitrogen such as nettle tea.

The best shoots come from plants that are at least five years old because until then, they can be too fiddly to prepare. You will also need quite a few plants to produce a good harvest, as only about a third of each plant's young leaves should be harvested each year to allow it to recover. However, as the ferns will thrive in areas where no other veg will grow, they won't be competing with other crops for space while you wait for your gourmet harvest.

Harvesting & eating

Harvest fiddlehead ferns when they emerge in mid spring, by snipping them off with scissors. You are looking for fronds that are still tightly

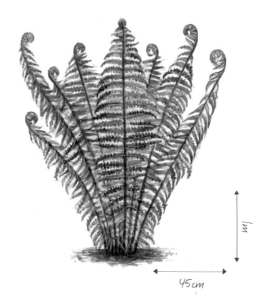

45cm

rolled, with just 3–5cm of stem beyond the coil, known as croziers. At this stage they will usually come enveloped in a thin layer of papery-brown fuzz that needs to be removed before cooking because it has an unpleasant, bitter taste. Simply rub it off with your fingers. Wash the de-fuzzed ferns thoroughly to remove any extra traces of the fuzz and tip the croziers into a pan of rapidly simmering water for a minute or two.

Parboiling will ensure even cooking and help retain their colour, but most importantly it will help remove any further bitter compounds that can sometimes be found in new leaves making them safe and palatable to eat. Take them out when they have turned bright green but are still al dente, or as the Americans would say 'tender-crisp', and they are ready to use in any recipe of your choice.

Once prepared as above, fiddleheads can be cooked in pretty much the same way as you would asparagus. They are wonderful sautéed with olive oil, garlic and pancetta, and then sprinkled with freshly grated Parmesan cheese.

Try them smothered with hollandaise sauce, as an unexpected pizza topping or even stirred into a creamy pasta sauce, sprinkled with a little tarragon and finely chopped sweet, red onion just before serving.

A huge hit in Japan, where they are called *kogomi*, fiddlehead ferns add an incredible nutty, broccoli-like taste to stir-fries, soups and also work as tempura.

Pickled in a sweet, herbed vinegar, the little croziers make a zippy condiment for cheese, cold meats or on a ploughman's lunch, adding a rich-woodsy flavour to even the most simple dishes.

Hosta greens *Hosta montana, H. sieboldii & H. fluctuans*

The Japanese sushi delicacy anyone can grow

Crisp, succulent and slightly salty, the young growing tips of hostas are far better known in Japan as *urui,* **a springtime delicacy, than merely as slug fodder in suburban beds and borders. Because they are not readily available in UK supermarkets, in springtime you will often find Japanese students foraging in the grounds of London parks in search of their leaves! Also known as: plantain lily,** *giboshi, urui, oobagibooshi.*

Growing

Hailing from the damp woodland of northern East Asia, hostas are resilient and extremely popular garden plants that are as attractive as they are easy to grow. All they need to thrive are three basic conditions that mimic their forest homes in the highlands of Japan and Korea: a shady site, moist soil and protection from their arch-enemies (slugs and snails). All you need to do is:

- Plant hostas out at any time of year, incorporating a large amount of organic matter into the soil and a good thick mulch of sharp gravel, which will seal in moisture around the plants' roots and provide a protective spiky barrier to deter slugs and snails.

- Double up your security system by spraying the plants regularly with a garlic spray (see *My ten commandments,* page 28), especially in spring and autumn when slugs and snails are most active.

- Hostas thrive best in the shade where they produce the tenderest, full-flavoured leaves but they will also do well in full sun as long as they are kept well watered.

- To propagate plants, lift and divide established clumps in early spring into smaller offsets and plant these out individually, spacing between 45cm–1m apart depending on the variety.

Varieties to try

Although there are hundreds of varieties and numerous species to pick from, the most widely eaten ones in Japan are *Hosta montana, H. sieboldii* and *H. fluctuans* as they are the tenderest and least bitter of all types.

The most esteemed is probably the *H. fluctuans* cultivar known as 'Sagae', with its creamy variegated striations, which was developed specifically as an edible variety.

Harvesting & eating

As much as a third of the newly grown shoots can be harvested each spring without affecting the plant's overall health or productivity. These can be snipped off either when the new green shoots reach about 10–20cm high, but are still tightly rolled up in little upside-down cones, or when they have just begun to unfurl.

For the finest flavour, cover the newly emerging shoot tips in spring, when they are just beginning to poke through the surface of the soil with a 10–20cm layer of straw. Harvest these shoots once the leaves are sticking out above the straw and starting to unfurl. This

45cm–1m

no standard width

will force plants to elongate their petioles (leaf stems) and become more tender and sweet. However, I would not do this every year as this process can weaken plants.

Hosta shoots have a fresh, nutty flavour that is reminiscent of asparagus and salty sea greens like samphire and nori (the seaweed wrap used in sushi) and can be used in a huge variety of ways. They are lovely blanched and laid over watercress salad with goat's cheese, crispy fried onions, capers, croutons and a handful of raisins thrown in for sweetness.

As tightly rolled young shoots, the growing tips of the large-leaved *H. montana* can be blanched in chicken stock and eaten much like asparagus. Simmered in stock and sprinkled with sliced red Japanese beefsteak plant leaves, sesame seeds, pickled ginger and sesame oil, they can be rolled with vinegared rice into fantastic homemade veggie sushi. When the shoots begin to unfurl, the same leaves are also delicious battered and fried as tempura.

In Hokkaido, the long leaves of *H. sieboldii* are most commonly harvested when they are about to unfurl. Leaf stems from the centre of the plant are harvested in spring (particularly in the morning when their moisture content is at its highest) and added to miso soup with sliced shiitake mushrooms and diced tofu. Sliced into sections they are great in omelettes with snipped chives and even work wonders stirred into risottos or a simple leek and potato soup.

The very best shoots to use for the recipe opposite are those that are still young (no more than 20cm in height), which are sweet and picked first thing in the morning, as this is when they are at their most soft and tender. Some growers will even give them a dousing of water the day before to insure they are at their most plump and succulent on the morning of harvest. It sounds fussy, but honestly does make a huge difference.

Pasta primavera with hosta greens, asparagus & hazelnuts

This might not be the traditional way of eating hosta greens, a prized Japanese spring vegetable, but boy does it work well. For this recipe, you want to harvest the tightly rolled 'spears' of hosta greens in mid spring.

Serves 4

Ingredients
500ml good-quality chicken stock
200g asparagus spears
100g young hosta shoots
 knob of butter
1 tbsp olive oil
1 garlic clove, crushed
1 small bunch of spring onions, finely chopped
100g fresh peas, podded
100g baby broad beans
450g tagliatelle, cooked
zest and juice of ½ a lemon
small handful of freshly grated Parmesan cheese
fresh nutmeg, grated
2 tbsp of chopped hazelnuts
salt and freshly ground black pepper
a large handful of mint, parsley, chives and dill, chopped
extra virgin olive oil

In a large saucepan, bring the chicken stock to boil. Add the asparagus and hosta shoots, blanching for 1–2 minutes, drain and submerge in ice-cold water, keeping aside a ladleful of the stock.

In a heavy-based saucepan, heat the butter and olive oil over a gentle heat. Add the garlic and spring onions and sweat over a low heat until the spring onions are sweet. Turn the heat up to medium and add the peas, baby broad beans, asparagus and hosta shoots. Sauté for another 1–2 minutes or until the peas and beans are just tender.

Add the tagliatelle, ladleful of chicken stock, lemon zest and juice, Parmesan cheese, nutmeg, hazelnuts and toss thoroughly to combine.

Season to taste with salt and black pepper, scatter over the chopped herbs and drizzle over a little extra virgin olive oil.

Callaloo *Amaranthus spp.*

The Caribbean 'spinach' that comes in every colour of the rainbow

Central to any good West Indian feast, the delicious spinach-like leaves of this super fast growing plant come in every conceivable psychedelic shade, from acid green and highlighter orange to the deepest blood red. Also known as: love lies bleeding, amaranth.

Growing

Callaloo is an easy-to-grow common garden plant and its seeds are available from any standard catalogue in a multitude of colours and forms. These, rather confusingly, will be sold and labelled as the garden plant *Amaranthus*. All species are edible, so pick any that take your fancy. It is a very close relative of quinoa (*Chenopodium quinoa*), which can be planted and eaten in exactly the same way – simply using the grains from a supermarket packet.

Here are my tricks of the trade for growing callaloo:

• Spark plants into growth by sowing the seeds directly into a finely raked, moist soil in a sheltered sunny position anytime from late May to early August.

• Although quite unfussy, the plants respond especially well to well-drained soil so add a couple of spadefuls of grit in order to fuel the most rapid growth.

• Within a fortnight you should have a carpet of infant plants. Thin these out to a spacing of at least 15cm apart. The thinnings make a great microveg for spring salads.

• If kept well watered, with an occasional dose of liquid feed, the plants should be ready for you to start cropping in as little as six weeks.

Tip: Because callaloo seeds are only tiny specks no bigger than that of a full stop on this page, a whole packet of hundreds of potential plants may only contain a pinch or so of seeds. It can be tricky to scatter over a bed, so try mixing the seeds with a tablespoon of fine sand before scattering the whole blend over the soil.

Harvesting & eating

To harvest, just snip off the fresh new growth with scissors. The young greens have a rich, earthy, broccoli-like flavour and are eaten all over the Caribbean, India, Africa and South-East Asia in much the same way as Europeans would eat spinach.

Callaloo is wonderful added to salads, soups, dals or curries. In India, the leaves are fried with garlic and chillies, or steamed and seasoned with salt, cumin and red chillies before being simmered in coconut cream, turmeric and garam marsala. They are also delicious in homemade bhajis – my favourite is a mix of onion, cauliflower and red callaloo.

In the Caribbean, the leaves often feature in pepperpot soup, a kind of stew made with beef, kidney beans, pumpkins and yams, simmered with thyme, onions and tomatoes.

Whereas in Greece, the leaves are lightly blanched, drizzled with olive oil and lemon juice and served with fried fish. If you blanch any of the coloured-leaf varieties, in particular the deep-red ones, you will find that the pigment quickly stains the water a brilliant hue. Try cooking white rice or quinoa in this tinted water to give it a rich, vibrant E-number-free shade.

50cm–2m

30cm

Sea kale *Crambe maritima*

The Victorians couldn't get enough of this creamy sea asparagus

75cm

Along with watercress and perhaps leeks, sea kale is one of the few truly native UK vegetables and was once found on coasts all over the country. The greedy Victorians loved its delicate, nutty flavour so much that they pushed it to the brink of extinction in the wild. Today, sea kale is a protected species and the only way to get hold of its delicate ivory stems legally is to grow it yourself.

Growing

A 'captive grown' sea kale in a small pot plant can be picked up in the herbaceous perennials section of pretty much any garden centre. Its silvery blue foliage and frothy white billowy flowers make it a common garden species. Here are my tips on establishing these plants:

• With its coastal origins, sea kale enjoys a site with particularly well-drained soil in full sun.

• Dig a good couple of spadefuls of grit into the soil prior to planting and keep well watered while the plants establish themselves.

• Apart from the above, the plants only need a hard pruning in late autumn, when you should cut them down to ground level.

Harvesting & eating

Sea kale must be blanched (grown in exclusion of light) before harvesting in March because the plain green shoots can be bitter and stringy. Simply pop an upside-down bucket over the plant just as it comes into growth in spring with a brick on top to steady it against wind. A large flowerpot with the drainage holes taped closed works just as well. After about three weeks, the leaves will be elongated, white and far better to eat. Snip these off when they reach about 30cm long and they are ready to use.

Although, in theory, sea kale can be used in all the same ways as white asparagus, it is the one vegetable I am a real purist about. Sea kale has such a delicate, creamy maritime flavour that I feel it is a shame to corrupt it by introducing too many other competing ingredients.

Steam the velvety stalks lightly for five minutes, then add a drizzle of extra virgin olive oil, dusting of flaky sea salt and smoked paprika and serve with a really fresh loaf of crusty bread. Alternatively, dish up with a homemade aioli or hollandaise sauce, with a squeeze of lemon and a sprinkling of chopped tarragon for a truly sophisticated treat.

75cm

50cm

Water celery *Oenanthe javanica 'Flamingo'*

The technicoloured, super-low maintenance 'celery'

If you love celery, but long for something that isn't so infernally difficult to grow, the pink and white blushed leaves of exotic, water celery are a heaven-sent option. With all the flavour of your typical celery, mixed with carrot, coriander and parsley-like notes, this aquatic veg from the paddy fields of South-East Asia will grow like a weed in virtually any site. Also known as: Chinese Water celery, Japanese celery, paddy field celery.

Growing

Native to riversides, paddy fields and pools in South-East Asia (hence its species name *javanica*), water celery is a vigorous, creeping plant, which despite its origins have a remarkable cold tolerance, right down to −10°C. Here's what you need to know:

- Plant young plants (available in the aquatic section of your local garden centre) in your patio pond or damp border soil, in full sun or partial shade at any time from spring to autumn.

- The brighter the location, the more intense the leaf's colour, so if you are going for a real 'wow factor' in appearance, pick the sunniest possible location.

- Planted in or around the edge of a pond or other waterlogged site, you will never have to water these plants, but if planted in a regular flower border it is important to ensure the soil never dries out.

Varieties to try

In Asia, it is usually the plain green form that is used, but I prefer the vibrant-leaved cultivar 'Flamingo' because, although it has an identical flavour, it looks far more exciting, is the most widely sold in the UK and is slightly less vigorous than the ordinary form, which can swallow up a border in a single season.

30cm

Safety note: Although *Oenanthe javanica* is extremely commonly eaten throughout east Asia and recognised as 100 per cent safe to eat, there are many members of the same Oenanthe genus that are extremely toxic, so double check to be absolutely sure that the plants you buy come clearly labelled with the correct Latin name. The brilliant pink leaves are a pretty good giveaway though.

Harvesting & eating

Simply snip off the leaves at the base of the plant with a pair of secateurs or scissors, wash thoroughly and you are ready to go. The leafy plumes are eaten throughout east Asia, from Japan to Java, either raw, mixed into leafy salads or as a pretty garnish much like parsley.

The whole of the young stem and leaves are snipped up and scattered over curries, soups and fried rices. They are also used in stir-fries with prawns or chopped and boiled as you would spinach. The older the leaf, the stronger and spicier the flavour, so in general young emerging tips are used raw like a herb, while mature leaves are treated more like any cooked vegetable.

Its celery-like flavour works well as a colourful imposter in Waldorf salad, Coronation chicken, sandwiches, soups or stuffings.

30cm

no standard width

Wood sorrel *Oxalis tetraphylla, O. triangularlis, O. hedysaroides*

Tropical shamrocks that taste like sour apple candy

Like oversized clover leaves painted pink and purple, the vibrantly coloured leaves of these ornamental *Oxalis* species betray their exotic Latin American origins. The leaves of these common garden and houseplants have the refreshing, tangy flavour of sour apple candy. As if that wasn't enough – their pink and yellow flowers are edible too. Also known as: iron cross plant, false shamrock, sourgrass.

Growing

Ornamental wood sorrels are a snip to grow from dry bulbs or young plants picked up from garden centres. Simply:

- Plant them out in a site with full sun in a well-drained soil, with plenty of grit incorporated to mimic the dry, Mediterranean climate of their home range.

- In milder areas of the UK, treat them as perennial outdoor plants because, despite their exotic origins, many of these species will handle a certain degree of frost (as low as −5°C).

- Alternatively, lift the plants and treat them as colourful, munchable houseplants over the winter.

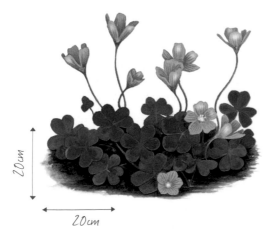

Varieties to try

My favourite varieties are:

- *Oxalis tetraphylla* '**Iron Cross**' from Mexico with deep burgundy leaf hearts and pretty pink flowers.

- *O. triangularis* from Brazil with Cadbury wrapper-coloured foliage that comes with hues of electric pink.

- *O. hedysaroides*, from the Caribbean with hundreds of small, sulphur-yellow flowers and burgundy leaves on long trailing stems – perfect for hanging baskets.

Harvesting & eating

Gather wood sorrel throughout summer by snipping off handfuls of leaves with a pair of scissors. Because wood sorrel grows so vigorously, you can harvest up to a third of the leaves every month or so throughout the growing season, and the plants will spring back as if nothing happened.

Wood sorrel can be used in your kitchen just as you would regular sorrel. With its fresh lemony flavour, wood sorrel pairs well with all seafood. Try it stirred through a white wine sauce served with scallops, sprinkled over clam chowder and moules marinere or add to a tartare sauce just before serving. It is also a particularly fun garnish to anything eaten on St Patrick's Day. I also love it stirred into a simple omelette with sautéed spring onions. Finely chop sorrel with parsley and dill and then stir into cream cheese for an easy dip. You can even enjoy wood sorrel in a dessert teamed up with elderflower to make a cool, clean sorbet.

Kitchen tip: Don't overcook the leaves, as you'll quickly lose the tangy flavour and bright colour with prolonged or excessive cooking.

Watercress *Nasturtium officinale*

The 'superfood' salad anyone can grow – no chalk stream necessary

This aquatic member of the cabbage family might be trendy to eat and expensive to buy, but it is also one of the most nutritious, delicious and fast growing of all salad crops. You don't need a crystal-clear Hampshire chalk stream at the bottom of the garden to grow it either. All you really need is a pot of compost and saucer of water.

Growing

Watercress can easily be grown from either packets of seeds or cuttings from sprigs fished out of supermarket salad bags. Both the green and fancy new red-leaved varieties are just as easy to grow, with some sprigs already coming with little white roots attached. Here's what you need to do to grow watercress from cuttings:

50cm

30cm

5cm

- Tip the contents of the bag onto a table and pick out the largest, healthiest-looking sprigs.

- Pop a small bunch of these in a glass of water placed on a sunny windowsill (just as you would a vase of flowers) and in a matter of days you will start to see roots emerging from submerged sections.

- Once the roots are at least 3cm long, plant the sprouting sprigs about 5cm apart in a shallow, wide-brimmed pot of compost, and sit the pot in a high-rimmed saucer filled with up to 5cm of water or a patio pond.

- Place outdoors and keep the level of water constantly topped up and the springs will quickly form a lush head of leaves.

Harvesting & eating

Traditionally only harvested in months with an 'r' in them, watercress provides a delicious source of fresh greens right into the darkest days of winter when little else is around. Give it a break to flower over the summer months though, when this happens their leaves can become a little pungent and fibrous.

Once large enough, the plants can be harvested with a quick snip of the scissors every couple of weeks virtually all year round, apart from when there is a hard frost on the ground. Remember to leave at least 3cm on the base of each plant for recovery between harvests. Two pots the size of washing-up bowls of these peppery leaves will be more than the average family can eat. Watercress adds a peppery twist to salads and is also delicious in soups, blended into creamy sauces, chopped and mixed into a potato salad and even whizzed into pesto.

Safety note: Avoid eating watercress from bodies of water that are home to water snails, as these can carry a particularly dangerous pathogen. Growing it yourself at home in a pot of clean, fresh tap water ensures snail-free, safe leaves. ⚠️

New Zealand spinach *Tetragonia tetragonioides*

The exotic, bolt-free spinach that grows like a jungle vine

The first Westerners to discover New Zealand spinach, eaten for centuries by the indigenous peoples of Australia and New Zealand, were the sailors on Captain Cook's voyage who ate it to stave off scurvy. Delicious, versatile and so rampant that you'll virtually need to hack it back with a machete to keep its megalomanic tendencies in check, this is hands down the easiest and most productive leafy green you can grow in the UK. Also known as: warrigal greens, *kokihi*, Botany Bay spinach, Cook's cabbage.

Growing

Anyone who has cultivated regular spinach will know it can be a pain to grow: bolting into flower and keeling over if the weather is too warm or too dry, victim to quite a few pests and needing continuous sowing throughout summer. Swap your regular spinach for New Zealand spinach and you wipe out all these problems in one fell swoop. To get planting:

• Start plants off in late May after any risk of frost has passed by soaking the large, knobbly seeds overnight in a glass of water (this hastens the germination process by ensuring the seeds are well hydrated).

• Sow the soaked seeds directly outdoors in a well-prepared bed, in full sun to light shade. I usually pop two to three seeds in each hole, spacing the holes about 30cm apart.

• After about a fortnight, thin out the weakest seedlings, to leave only the healthiest plants.

• Keep well watered and fertilised and the plants will quickly grow until the first very hard frost, spreading out in all directions with branches up to 1.5m long.

Apart from a frequent trim (see 'Harvesting & eating' right), the plants need little in the way of maintenance, being ignored by pests and diseases and tolerant of even quite extreme droughts. As a naturally coastal species, they can even tolerate the salt spray and impoverished soils in seaside gardens.

They will often self-seed themselves in many areas, with new plants popping up late in the following spring of their own accord. Although a perennial species in all but the mildest parts of the UK, this plant should be treated as an annual because the first hard frost will turn its leaves to mush.

Harvesting & eating

The young tips of the branches, which produce the tenderest leaves, should be harvested by snipping them off with a pair of scissors. This coincidentally encourages dense, bushy growth. Harvest at least once a week in high summer because the plants are notoriously thuggish.

As its name suggests, New Zealand spinach can be eaten in pretty much all the same ways as regular spinach. Try it blanched, steamed, boiled or fried in butter or olive oil. Add the chopped leaves to omelettes, cream sauces and casseroles or blitz them up into a pesto. To do this simply dry-fry a large handful of leaves until they have wilted right down. In a food processor, blitz the spinach with a couple tablespoons each of cashew nuts and Parmesan cheese and a clove of garlic. Drizzle in 125ml of olive oil and you're done. Homemade pesto in less than 10 minutes!

The key difference between this plant and your regular spinach in the kitchen is that it won't wilt down into nothing when cooked and it retains its colour far better, remaining vibrant green instead of khaki-coloured mush. Make space for this mega-crop and the days of regular spinach in your allotment will be numbered.

30cm

trailing to 1.5m

1.5 cm

Chop suey greens *Chrysanthemum coronarium*

The oriental chrysanthemum that's ready to eat in six weeks flat

Although you're more likely to find the seeds of this plant in the flower section rather than alongside trendy oriental veg like pak choi, the leaves of this pretty chrysanthemum are easily the most delicious traditional Chinese green that can be grown in the UK. With super fast-growing leaves and aromatic, sunny yellow flowers, there is so much more to this plant than just an eye-catching window-box decoration. Also known as: garland chrysanthemum, *shungiku*, *tong ho*.

Growing

Chop suey greens are an absolute doddle to grow, but to ensure great flavour there is one golden rule you absolutely must bear in mind:

• Do not sow your seeds on the hottest days of midsummer, especially in full sun, as excess heat will trigger these plants to flower far too early. If allowed to flower prematurely, this will radically change their internal chemistry causing the flavour of the leaves to suddenly turn from sweet and herbal to bitter with an unpleasant fibrous texture.

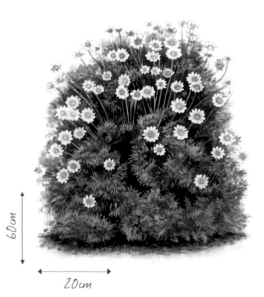

60cm

20cm

The following tips will ensure success:

• Sprinkle seeds outdoors over prepared soil between either April to May or September to October. Cover with a very light layer of soil. For extra-early crops the plants can be started off in March and transplanted outdoors after the risk of the hardest frosts has passed.

• You can sow two to three batches at two-weekly intervals thinning these to 10cm apart and keeping them well watered. You should then have a constant supply of fresh green harvests right into early winter.

• Plants are adaptable to any site and soil, but to err on the side of caution I would usually plant summer sowings in shady sites to help delay flowering.

Harvesting & eating

Your chop suey greens should be ready to harvest after six to eight weeks, when the plants have reached a height of 15–30cm, and before they have flowered. Snip off the young, tender top growth, but remember to leave at least 5cm of the plant intact at the base to give it a chance to recover. Harvested plants bounce back quickly, so you should be able to get a second and sometimes third crop from the same plant after leaving them to re-grow for just a few weeks.

As the flowers are beautiful and have an interesting flavour of their own, I normally leave a couple of the plants unharvested to provide a delicious edible sideline in the ornamental veg garden.

Chop suey greens taste mildly herbal and savoury, blending the nuttiness of broccoli, the herbal scent of garden chrysanthemum leaves (that's what they pretty much are) and a slight hint of the marine saltiness of samphire. A cross between a herb and a leafy vegetable, chop suey greens are a bit like rocket in their ability to straddle the culinary boundary between being a central part of a meal or a flavouring agent sprinkled on at the end – which makes them extremely versatile.

In Japan and China, chop suey greens are eaten raw or lightly cooked in much the same way as watercress or spinach. However, unlike these two, chop suey greens are more robust and do not lose their shape to become a mush when cooked. Their pretty, fern-shaped leaves makes them a decorative addition, floating in clear broths or miso soups, tossed raw into mixed leaf salads or as a straightforward garnish that is far less 80s than the usual ruffle of curly parsley.

As the name suggests, chop suey greens are a key ingredient in an authentic chop suey (see *A recipe idea,* overleaf). Literally meaning 'bits and pieces' in Mandarin, you really can serve whatever you fancy in this dish.

Prolonged cooking makes chop suey greens lose their unique flavour and vibrant green, so a quick blanch in boiling water for one minute or flash in the wok for no more than five minutes is all that is needed.

Their sunny flowers have a very similar flavour to the leaves, albeit far more intense and pungent. They are great tossed into salads and add a rich herbal scent and golden hue to homemade flavoured vinegars.

a recipe idea

Crab chop suey

If you don't fancy crab, just swap it for cooked, shredded chicken, king prawns or toasted cashew nuts. Chop suey does mean 'bits and pieces' afterall. In any case, you will have deliciousness on a plate in a matter of minutes.

Serves 4 as a side dish

Ingredients
200g chop suey greens
2 tbsp olive oil
100g white crabmeat
1 red chilli, sliced into shreds
3 spring onions, sliced into shreds
2.5cm piece of ginger, sliced into shreds
2 cloves of garlic, sliced into shreds
½ tsp chicken stock powder
1 tbsp chop suey flower petals (plucked from 4 flowers heads)
1 tbsp toasted sesame seeds
2 tsp sesame oil

Half-fill a small saucepan with salted water and bring to a rolling boil. Add the chop suey greens and blanch quickly for 30 seconds to 1 minute – just enough for them to go limp and turn bright green. Drain the greens through a colander and blast them in ice water to stop further cooking.

Pour the olive oil into a wok and heat on high until smoking, then tip in the crabmeat, chilli, spring onions, ginger and garlic. Sprinkle over the chicken stock powder. Stir-fry for 2 minutes or so until the garlic begins to turn crisp and golden (be careful not to burn the garlic, which can happen in a matter of seconds).

Tip the blanched chop suey greens into the wok, toss to incorporate and heat through (which should take only a minute or so over the high heat). Remove from the pan.

To serve, transfer to a warm plate and sprinkle with chop suey petals and sesame seeds. Drizzle over the sesame oil and serve immediately with steamed rice and a cold bottle of beer.

Purslane *Portulaca oleracea*

A succulent creeper with leaves that taste like mangetout and Bramleys

Once a hugely popular salad vegetable in Tudor England, the ancient herb purslane is still a foodie staple all over the Mediterranean. Its small, fleshy leaves and stems are filled with a crisp, succulent gel that has an unusual and refreshing flavour of mangetout and sour green apples. The best thing? It's a weed that will thrive on any patch of dry, dusty ground. Also known as summer purslane.

Growing

Considered a weed in the US and Australia, this low-growing creeper is absolutely foolproof to grow if you give it just three things: full sun, well-drained soil and protection from frost in the growing season. My tips are:

• Sow purslane seeds any time between May and August directly into beds with plenty of grit incorporated in the sunniest site possible.

• Once they have sprouted into small plants, thin them out to leave about 10cm between plants. Don't throw the thinnings away as they make great microveg for spring salads.

• Although these plants will cope with near desert-like conditions, regular watering will greatly improve the quality and succulence of your crop.

30cm

30cm

Harvesting & eating

The acid level of purslane (provided by malic acid, the same stuff that makes green apples taste sour) fluctuates wildly over the course of each day, making them up to ten times more sour when picked first thing in the morning than late in the afternoon. So select a time of day to pick your purslane according to how much tang you fancy. The plants will provide continuous harvests until they are cut down by the first frosts.

Purslane is most popular as a salad ingredient in France, where whole sprigs are tossed in olive oil and fresh rocket. The French also add sprigs to tangy sorrel soup; their fleshy leaves have a delicious slippery texture. They are also often pickled in sweet, herby vinegar and then served with cold roast pork.

In Turkey, purslane as a central ingredient in a rustic salad called fattoush, in which crispy-fried shards of pitta bread are tossed with olives, purslane, onion, mint, tomato, feta and cucumber and served dressed with sumac (see page 168), olive oil and lemon juice. Also rich in vitamin C and apparently the highest green vegetable source of omega-3 fatty acids, this herb is as good for you as it is delicious and much easier to grow than boring old spinach.

Borage *Borago officinalis*

Starry blue flowers and cucumber-flavoured leaves

In Britain, borage's cucumber-flavoured leaves and starry blue flowers are usually confined to the herb gardens of stuffy stately homes or the pages of heritage seed catalogues, yet on the continent borage's fresh, delicate taste with hints of green melon has made it a common supermarket vegetable from central Germany to Crete. Delicious, easy to grow and stunningly ornamental, borage is the ideal multi-tasker's veg for gardeners who want it all. Also known as: starflower, *borraja* (Spain).

Growing

The first thing to know about growing borage is to ignore all the standard gardening advice written about it in every textbook. You know … full sun, sow it in spring, potash-rich fertiliser, etc. Following this advice will encourage huge masses of blue flowers and stunted, dry leaves covered in irritating prickles (the key edible bit). Grown this way, it's no wonder none of us Brits think they taste any good.

60cm

60cm

Although the flowers are tasty and make a beautiful garnish, it is really the leaves that are the most delicious. To encourage long, lush, tender foliage, you need to prevent the plants from bolting (i.e. flowering prematurely), which can be done by following just a few crafty tips I learned while working with commercial borage growers in Navarra, Spain, to grow the ideal edible plants:

• Plant the seeds in late August and September (NB: not spring as commercial seed packets say) in fertile, well-drained soil in a shaded, sheltered site.

• Choose a white-flowered variety, as these are a little slower to flower and have a denser, leafier appearance.

• Thin them out to a maximum of 20cm apart. This very close spacing will encourage plants to shade each other out, forcing them to grow longer, sweeter leaves.

• Keep the plants very well watered with a dilute nitrogen-rich fertiliser, such as nettle liquid, once a week. Do not use a potash-rich fertiliser (like comfrey liquid) as this will give you flowers at the expense of leaves.

Follow the above simple tips and you should have lush, leafy plants with long, strappy, almost fuzz-free leaves in about eight-weeks' time.

Harvesting & eating

Borage greens can be harvested by slicing the whole plant down to the ground before it starts to flower. So if you are keen on muching on the blossom too, it is a good idea to plant one or two extra specimens on a sunnier site and grow these just for their flowers. Alternatively, you can put off harvesting one of your main batches until a flower stalk eventually erupts from the centre.

Borage is prepared in all manner of ways across Europe, from a Ligurian cannelloni filling mixed with ricotta, nutmeg, Parmesan cheese and garlic, and served with walnut pesto, to the Bavarian *Grüne Soße*, a kind of herby mayonnaise that blends hard-boiled eggs with sour cream, a dash of vinegar and a good fistful of finely chopped herbs (borage, sorrel, chives, parsley, cress) and is served over potatoes.

With their clean, cucumber and melon flavour, the tender, young borage stems and leaves are fantastic added to salads or creamy dips. Try them stirred through leek and potato soup, and served cold as vichyssoise, sautéed with peas and bacon or popped into crustless sandwiches instead of cucumber for high tea. The most common way to consume borage in the UK is in the classic summer drink Pimm's along with mint, strawberries and sliced oranges. Some people substitute it with cucumber slices which are more readily available though.

The stunning blue, star-shaped flowers make a beautiful garnish on whatever you fancy. Try them frozen in ice cubes for summer cocktails or crystalise to decorate cakes.

Kitchen tip: The key to preparing borage in the kitchen is to lightly blanch the leaves first in a large pot of simmering salted water for a minute or two, or chop them up extremely finely to break down any tiny fuzzy hairs that may be attached to the leaves.

Fruiting Veg
& Grains

Hyacyinth beans *Lablab purpureus 'Ruby Moon'*

Chestnut-flavoured, fluorescent purple mangetout-style pods

Bright pink clusters of flowers and stunning purple mangetout-style pods make this scrambling bean from South-East Asia a fetching addition to your vegetable plot. The beans are eaten throughout India, southern China and Malaysia. In the UK, the plants are still good croppers, rewarding you with chestnutty sugar snaps after a summer of fuchsia–pink flowers. Also known as lablab.

Growing

Hyacinth beans require a long growing season to successfully fruit, so give them a head start by sowing them indoors in March and April. When choosing which kind to grow, I usually go for the pretty, fluorescent, purple-podded variety known as 'Ruby Moon', which is sold in the ornamental seed section of gardening catalogues. To begin planting:

• Sow the seeds in little 9cm pots of seed compost, allowing two to three seeds per pot and pop them in an airing cupboard or propagator at 20–25°C to ensure the best germination.

1.5m

20cm

• After about five to ten days, the shoots will start to appear. Transfer the plants to a sunny windowsill, potting them on as need be. Keep on top of this as plants that become root-bound at this stage often remain stunted for life.

• Plant them outdoors in late May or after all risk of frost has passed in the sunniest site available, at 20cm apart in a ring.

• Create a quick wigwam of bamboo canes (homegrown, if possible) tied together with a piece of twine to give young plants a support. They can reach up to 1.5m high by the end of the season. If you have greenhouse space available, try planting them under glass, which will result in larger crops.

• Keep well watered and fed with a high-potash fertiliser throughout the growing season and the bean plants will reward you with plenty of purple pods from midsummer onwards.

Harvesting & eating

As with most beans, the more you pick the more will grow, but try to pick them when they are nice and small (just like sugar snaps), as older, fully mature pods can be rather stringy.

With their floury, chestnut-like flavour and vibrant colour, young hyacinth bean pods can be served and eaten just like regular mangetout. Stick a handful in a stir-fry or flash-boil them for a minute or two before using in salads or shred raw into a colourful coleslaw. To help preserve their intense colour, cook them only very briefly on a high heat, preferably with a splash of lemon juice. The citric-acid content of the lemon helps protect the bean's bright purple pigments from being broken down.

Chickpea edamame *Cicer arietinum*

Little packets of sugary, soy-free 'edamame'

Twenty years of intense breeding work still hasn't given us a soybean that will produce a reliable crop in the UK (well, for me at least). But edamame fans need not despair, as fresh, green chickpeas are the new, improved soy. It really is a wonder why this sweeter, tastier and way easier-to-grow crop has taken so long to reach British allotments. Also known as: garbanzo, Indian pea, Bengal gram, ceci bean.

Growing

Drought tolerant, impervious to most pests and capable of withstanding several degrees of light frost, chickpeas can even fertilise themselves *and* the plants around them. Talk about the ultimate low-effort crop. To get growing:

• Sow seeds directly outdoors anytime from late March to early June.

• Choose a sunny site, burying each seed about 2cm deep and 10–15cm apart in pots or beds of very well-drained soil with loads of extra grit dug in. Encouraging fast drainage prevents the fungal infections that chickpeas can be susceptible to if left to sit in cold, wet soil.

• Sprinkle the planting hole with a generous amount of ground pepper or chilli powder. Both of which deter mice or squirrels from digging your chickpeas up and scoffing them.

• Skimp on feeding as chickpeas are capable of producing their own fertiliser (a soil that is too rich will encourage leafy growth at the expense of pods).

Chickpeas are rapid growers and will start to flower and fruit in as little as eight weeks after sowing. They produce little inflated pods containing just one to two peas each in quick succession, if regularly harvested, right up until the first hard frosts. Once plants are up and growing they will require very little from you, apart from the occasional watering and weeding around the base of the plants.

Harvesting & eating

Harvest the pods as soon as they have filled out while they are still fresh and green. It is a good idea to wear gloves as their leaves are covered in fine, rusty 'dew' in hot weather that can irritate sensitive skin.

Drop whole pods into briskly simmering salted water for two or three minutes to produce a stunning edamame substitute. They are perfect served with a sprinkling of flaky sea salt and sesame oil. Alternatively, you can pan roast the whole pods by tossing them into a cast-iron skillet with a tablespoon of olive oil over a fierce heat, allowing them to char for a minute or two. Serve tossed in sea salt, smoked paprika and a drizzle of olive oil. Whichever way you decide to cook them, eating them is as simple as squeezing the sweet little peas out of their pods with your fingers and scoffing them.

60cm

20cm

10cm

Asparagus peas *Lotus tetragonolobus*

Star-shaped runner beans with the nutty crunch of asparagus

Now here's a plant that really lives up to its name, a perfect combination of fresh garden peas and nutty asparagus in tiny, curiously-shaped pods. With frilly wings running along their length, the pea pods are enormously popular throughout southern Asia but cost a fortune in the small handful of oriental supermarkets that stock them here in the UK. Also known as: winged pea, winged bean, four-angled bean.

Growing

The asparagus pea plant is one of the most ornamental veg you can grow. It has little trailing branches that radiate out from a central point, giving the plant a snowflake-like appearance when viewed from above. Its pretty, rusty red flowers adorn the growing tips.

Delicious, **ornamental** and easy to grow, this plant really is the perfect horticultural multitasker.

To get growing:

• Sow the seeds at weekly intervals between early April and late May in small pots of gritty compost and pop them on a sunny windowsill.

• Be careful not to overwater young plants and ensure good ventilation, as they can be prone to fungal infections if kept too damp.

• From early June onwards, plant them out in the garden in a warm sunny site in well-drained soil about 20cm apart.

• Keep in mind that their compact growth and trailing appearance makes the peas look wonderful in pots and hanging baskets as a stunning edible bedding plant.

• Asparagus peas are a perfect crop to plant as ground cover under taller edibles like fennel, young fruit trees or quinoa. Their nitrogen-fixing roots work dually to improve soil fertility and also acts as a weed-smothering carpet.

• Keep the plants well irrigated throughout the summer, especially as they start to flower. The peas suffer from few pests and diseases and will reward you with a continuing harvest of little pods.

• After the first flush of beans, the plants can become quite weak and straggly. To kickstart them back into growth, cut the plants back by about half and give them a couple of generous liquid feeds. This can often trigger a second crop in autumn.

> **Tip:** The more pods you pick, the more that will grow, so keep on nibbling to maximise your yield.

20cm

20cm

20cm

Harvesting & eating

In the UK, the pods often have a totally undeserved reputation for being rather stringy and fibrous. I firmly believe that this is simply because there is a lack of knowledge on how to properly harvest and prepare them. Follow these two simple, but crucial, rules and I guarantee a crisp, fibre-free harvest.

1. The pods should always be harvested young, when they are no more than 3cm long, as the fibres in the pod toughen as they mature.

2. The pods should always be prepared sliced extremely fine (a few millimetres thick). This splits any fine fibres into such short strands that they are no longer noticeable and transforms dense pods into shards of X-shaped confetti.

Once sliced, the pods can then be served in a huge variety of delicious ways. In Indonesia and Malaysia, they are often sautéed over a fierce heat with a ground paste made from shallots, ginger, garlic, shrimp paste (anchovies would be a good substitute) and chilli.

In China, they are stir-fried with garlic, chicken stock, soy sauce and Chinese rice wine, along with a handful of king prawns.

Try them blanched or steamed and served with butter or even added to a pasta primavera to really celebrate their asparagus and pea flavour.

The best way I've found to eat them is in a salad of finely sliced vegetables, either raw or lightly blanched. This makes the most of their delicious crunch. Asparagus peas also go particularly well with a fresh, spicy dressing like the asparagus pea, peanut and prawn salad recipe opposite.

a recipe idea

Asparagus pea, peanut & prawn salad

This simple salad combining crisp, sliced asparagus peas with aromatic herbs, coconut and roast peanuts transports me back to being six years old in my grandma's backyard in Borneo.

Serves 4 as a side dish

Ingredients
2 tbsp finely chopped roasted peanuts
20g desiccated coconut
2 tbsp shallots, finely sliced
2 tbsp coconut or other vegetable oil
200g asparagus pods, sliced as finely as possible
2 red chillies, finely sliced
½ red onion, finely sliced
100g king prawns, shelled and cooked
150g pomegranate seeds (½ a pomegranate)
2 tsp roughly chopped fresh mint
2 tsp roughly chopped Thai basil (or regular basil)

For the dressing
120ml coconut milk
juice of 1 lime
2 tbsp tamarind pulp
2 tsp fish sauce
1 tsp soft brown sugar

Scatter the peanuts and coconut into a hot saucepan and dry-fry over a medium heat, stirring occasionally until lightly toasted. Tip into a salad bowl and set aside.

In the same saucepan, fry the shallots in the oil over a medium heat, until they look crisp and golden brown. Put the shallots into the salad bowl along with the toasted peanuts and coconut.

Add the asparagus pods, chillies, red onions, prawns, pomegranate seeds, mint and basil to the bowl and give it all a thorough mix.

Whisk the salad dressing ingredients together and drizzle generously over the bowl and serve immediately.

Cucamelons *Melothria scabra*

Tiny grape-sized watermelons that taste of cucumber and lime

These tiny watermelon lookalikes from Central America are small enough to fit into a teaspoon. Bite into one and the flavour is cucumber with a fresh tinge of lime. Cucamelons' rampant trailing vines produce a constant stream of fruit throughout summer. Despite their exotic origins, they are much easier to grow than regular cucumbers and perfectly happy outdoors in the UK, given a sheltered sunny site. Also known as: Mexican sour gherkin, mouse melon, *sandia de raton*.

Growing

Cucamelon require pretty much the same conditions as your standard outdoor cucumber. However, they are far easier to grow. Simply:

• Sow the seeds indoors from April to May in pots of gritty compost. Using a propagator on a sunny windowsill at this stage will give them an ideal head start.

• Plant them out in a sunny, sheltered position after all risk of frost has passed, in growbags, tubs or directly into the ground, spacing them about 30cm apart.

• Cucamelons are a little more cold tolerant than outdoor cucumbers, which can be a lifesaver in areas prone to late cold snaps. Coddle them in a greenhouse however, and they will be even more productive.

• Provide a tall support for these vigorous scrambling vines to clamber up. A cage of chicken wire would be perfect.

• Water regularly and feed with a high-potash fertiliser like comfrey liquid to encourage maximum fruiting.

• Once the main growing shoot of each plant reaches 2.5m, pinch it out to restrict the plant's size. Also trim the lateral side shoots

(branches that grow out from the central stem) once they get to 40cm long to keep these rampant growers in check. The plants will fruit from late July, right up until the first hard frosts.

Unlike cucumbers, cucamelons can also be treated as a perennial, providing you with handfuls of tiny fruit year after year from a single sowing. As the vines mature, they begin to produce a swollen radish-like root, which can be lifted in late autumn and stored in barely moist compost in a cool garage or shed over winter.

In early April, encourage them back into growth by transplanting them to a pot of moist compost placed by a sunny window. Planted out after the last frost, these second-year plants will start to fruit much earlier, making a far longer season of harvests and larger yields.

In very mild regions, the roots can even be left in the ground. Cover with a thick layer of straw mulch to provide insulation against the worst of the cold and they should be able to

trailing to 2.5m

30cm

shrug off chills down to −5°C. To increase your chances of success, incorporate plenty of sand or grit into the compost when you first plant the cucamelons, to ensure the roots do not succumb to rot over the damp, cold winter months.

Harvesting & eating

Cucamelons are ready to harvest when they have swollen to the size of olives or small grapes and are still firm to the touch. Leaving them any longer can result in a slightly bitter flavour and soggy texture (just like regular cucumbers). Just snip the cucamelons off the vine and store them in the fridge, where they will keep for up to ten days.

Cucamelons can be eaten in exactly the same way as traditional cucumbers – sliced into salads, chopped into salsas or pickled whole like cornichons. Mix whole cucamelons (fresh, blanched or pickled) into a bowl of olives and serve with drinks, or spear them with toothpicks and pop them in a Martini.

Pickled cucamelons with dill & mint

A brilliant way to make these crisp summer fruit last well into the depths of winter, home pickling is far easier than you would ever think.

Makes enough to fill a 500ml jar

Ingredients
375ml white vinegar (such as distilled malt or
  white wine)
1 tsp salt
4 tbsp caster sugar
1 tbsp chopped dill
1 tbsp chopped mint
1 tsp coriander seeds (or Tasmanian peppercorns)
250g cucamelons
1 fresh grape leaf or oak leaf

Pour the vinegar into a bowl and add the salt and sugar. Whisk until the salt and sugar have completely dissolved. Stir in the dill, mint and coriandar seeds (or Tasmanian peppercorns if using).

Wash the cucamelons in water and pour them into a sterilised jar. (See *My ten commandments*, page 35.)

Scrunch up the grape (or oak) leaf and place it on top of the cucamelons. The tannins in the leaf will slowly disperse outwards and help keep the fruit crisp.

Pour the seasoned vinegar into the jar and seal tightly.

Refrigerate for 2 weeks, at which time the pickled cucamelons will be ready to eat. Once opened, store in the refrigerator where it will keep for up to 3 months.

Shark's fin melon *Cucurbita ficifolia*

The essential ingredient for a sharkless shark's fin soup

Plant one of these green monsters in your backyard and stand well back. Sprawling out in all directions, this jungle vine is capable of delivering over 10 kilos of great, white-striped melons in a single season. The fruit are highly prized all over Asia as a veggie, shark-friendly alternative to the world-renowned shark's fin soup. Plant a seed, save a shark – it's not often you get to say that now is it? Also known as: Siam pumpkin, *cabello de angel*, *chilacayote*.

Growing

Shark's fin melons grow on rampant, trailing vines and can be reared in exactly the same way as a regular pumpkin:

• Sow the seeds indoors in April, in little individual pots. Use good-quality seed compost and insert each seed vertically to a depth of 2.5cm. Place the pots on a sunny windowsill.

• When little white roots start to emerge from the drainage holes underneath, transplant them to slightly larger pots (12.5cm is ideal) and continue to grow indoors until the end of May.

• When the risk of frost has passed, they should be transplanted outside into a rich, well-drained soil in a sunny site, positioned about 1.5m apart.

• Water well throughout summer, as this will stave off powdery mildew attacks that can afflict water-stressed plants.

• Go easy on the fertiliser because plants overwhelmed with large amounts of fertiliser can turn into botanical megalomaniacs – sprawling out in all directions. These inquisitive new shoots make a delicious crop too (see *Leaves & greens*, page 68) so don't feel bad about nipping these off if they start to get out of control.

Shark's fin melon plants are so large and productive that I wouldn't advise growing more than two, unless you are planning on stocking your local Chinatown or have hectares of space. Each plant is capable of producing around five large rugby ball-sized melons, weighing in at 3 kilos per fruit in the early autumn.

The plants are generally much more resistant to many key afflictions that affect other members of the squash family. In fact, despite their exotic name, they are the most cold-tolerant variety, even producing a good crop in the most miserable of summers.

Harvesting & eating

The melons are ready to harvest once they reach the size of a rugby-ball (about 30com long), at which point they can be simply snipped off with a whip of the secateurs. The whole fruit

1.5m

30cm

2.5m

will keep fresh for ages (from several months to supposedly up to two years) in a cool, dry garage or shed over winter.

These cucumber and green melon-flavoured fruit have broken out of their native Mexico, where the fruit is called *chilacayote*, to become a popular ingredient in cuisines of countries like Argentina and Vietnam, where they play a central role in both sweet and savoury recipes. Once cooked, the delicate flesh of shark's fin melon magically separates out into filament-like strands. Slightly gelatinous in texture, the strands have an amazing ability to take on any surrounding flavours you pair them with like a culinary sponge.

In Central America, the melons are snipped off the vines when they reach the size of a small marrow and are used just like courgettes. Throughout Latin America and Spain, candied ripe shark's fin melon is a popular dessert flavouring, simmered with lemon zest and a sprinkling of cinnamon into a jam known as *cabello de angel* or 'angels' hair' because of the masses of glistening golden threads. Just one melon makes about five jam jars worth of sticky, amber deliciousness. Angel's hair is surprisingly versatile and you can stuff it into pastries, tarts, cake fillings or just spread it thickly on hot buttered toast. Pure heaven.

My favourite recipe for the melon is in a shark-friendly version of a Chinese New Year speciality, shark's fin soup. When simmered in the traditional stock and spices, the melon's taste virtually identical to shark's fin. This might seem unfathomable but anyone who has tried real shark's fin soup knows that shark's fins have almost no flavour, just a soft gelatinous strand-like texture. In fact, shark's fin melons have been used for hundreds of years in China as a vegetarian alternative in a poor man's versions of this ultra-expensive delicacy. They are gaining a huge following from younger generations of Chinese people, myself included, as an eco- (and pocket) friendly treat on any oriental banquet table.

Shark's fin melon soup

A sharkless 'shark's fin' soup, perfect for any oriental banquet.

Serves 4 as a starter

Ingredients
500g shark's fin melon
1 tbsp goji berries
4 dried shiitake mushrooms
1 head of fresh shimeji mushrooms
1 whole garlic bulb
2.5cm piece of ginger
2 tsp salt
½ tsp ground white pepper
1.5 litres good-quality chicken, fish or vegetable stock
1 tbsp cornflour
2 tbsp water
5 spring onions, finely sliced
100g cooked white crabmeat
2 tbsp Chinese rice wine (Shaoxing wine)
1 tsp sesame oil
a small handful of chopped coriander or chop suey green leaves
Chinese black vinegar (or balsamic vinegar)

Slice the melon in half and remove all the seeds. Chop into 1–2cm sized chunks. Trim off the skin from each piece.

Place the melon chunks in a large saucepan with the goji berries, shiitake mushrooms, shimeji mushrooms, garlic, ginger, salt and white pepper. Pour in the stock and simmer gently for 40 minutes to 1 hour over a low heat. The goal is to cook the melon for long enough so that it separates into strands, but not so far as disintegrating.

About 5 minutes before serving, take the pan off the heat. In a small bowl, mix the cornflour with a little water until smooth. Gradually whisk the cornflour and water mix into the soup until thoroughly combined, ensuring there are no lumps, along with the spring onions, crabmeat, Chinese rice wine, sesame oil and coriander (or chop suey greens). Cover and leave to stand for 5 minutes.

Serve piping hot in warmed bowls with extra white pepper and Chinese black vinegar on the side to be added to taste.

Tomatillos *Physalis philadelphica*

Lime-flavoured 'tomatoes' that have their own Chinese lanterns

Sealed snug inside their own little papery envelopes, these round, green tomato-like fruit have a refreshing fruitiness that tastes like a cross between a lime and a beefsteak tomato. An indispensable ingredient for any true Mexican cook, tomatillos are far easier to grow and immeasurably more productive than the lowly tomato. Also known as: Mexican green tomato, husk tomato, *tomates verdes*.

Growing

Closely related to Inca berries, these plants can be treated in virtually the exact same way as you would a tomato. So all you fajita fans need to do to get started is:

• Sow the seeds in shallow trays of compost in a propagator or on a sunny windowsill in April; transfer them into small pots when they get to about 5cm high.

• In late May, transplant the little bushes into their growing positions outdoors.

• As vigorous growers, they will do best in full sun in a warm, sheltered position. Set 1m apart, allowing enough space for them to branch out.

• You will probably need only two plants for the average family, as they are extremely high-yielding. Do not plant just one tomatillo bush, however, because it will need a friend nearby to ensure effective pollination.

• Unlike Inca berries, tomatillos respond well to a high-potash feed like comfrey liquid, producing even higher yields of fruit.

Although it can be very tempting, do not try to stake your young tomatillos. Losing their neat upright shape when they reach about 30cm tall is a natural phase of their development, in which the central stem flops down in contact with the soil and sends out loads of lateral roots, followed by shoots that produce much heavier yields. For this reason, I would also strongly recommend growing the plants in open ground rather than in pots, to allow them space to spread out over the ground.

Harvesting & eating

Tomatillos are ready to harvest at any stage between walnut and medium-tomato size – when they start to split their lantern-like casings but are still green. They are ridiculously productive when well grown, with each plant capable of kicking out up to an astonishing 10 kilos of fruit per plant before the first frosts – that has to be some kind of a record for an outdoor annual fruit crop in the UK.

Although there are many colourful fruited varieties of tomatillos from deep purple to pale yellow, in Mexico most tomatillos are traditionally harvested green. They lose their fresh

1m

1m

acidity and crispness when ripe, becoming sweeter and softer but with a curious slightly unpleasant flavour a bit like the scent of wet tobacco.

Tomatillos are incredibly versatile and can be used in similar ways to regular tomatoes, but do bear in mind that tomatillos are slightly tarter and do not contain as much sugar.

Probably the most popular way of serving tomatillos in Mexico is in *salsa verde* (literally meaning 'green sauce'), which is used as a condiment on everything from quesadillas to fried chicken, just like ketchup is used by us Brits, only far more fresh and zingy. To make salsa verde, the tomatillos are first either boiled whole or sliced in half then seared in a hot pan

until their skin blackens. They are then peeled and the smoky flesh is whizzed up with green chillies, raw onions, a twist of lime, a pinch of salt and lashings of fresh coriander. This exact same mix can double up as a mouth-watering marinade fit for any barbecue. Just smother it over grilled fish, prawns or chicken with a good glug of olive oil and leave it overnight to mingle. Slices of grilled tomatillos, charred in a searing, hot saucepan are wonderful chopped into cubes and stirred into guacamole instead of tomatoes to give it a citrusy lift. But perhaps the most exciting way I have served them is as fried green tomatillos (see *A recipe idea* on the opposite page), more inspired by a cheesy 90s film than authentic Mexican streetfood culture, but are nevertheless absolutely delicious. My Mexican buddies have yet to complain …

Fried green tomatillos with aioli & chilli honey

More inspired by a cheesy 90s film than authentic Mexican street food culture, these crisp golden discs are pure bliss with a bottle or three of cold Corona.

Serves 4 as a starter or side

Ingredients
6 large tomatillos, sliced
2 tsp salt
¼ tsp ground cayenne
½ tsp garlic powder
2 tbsp plain flour
1 egg, beaten
2 tbsp polenta
4 tbsp olive oil

For the chilli honey
½ a small green chilli, finely chopped
2 tbsp honey

For the aioli
½ clove of garlic, very finely chopped
3 tbsp good-quality or homemade mayonnaise
salt and pepper

Select your tomatillos – unripe green tomatillos will give you a tart, fresh flavour, whereas ripe yellow or purple ones will give you a sweet, fruity tang. Remove the casings from the tomatillos, wash and cut them into 0.5cm-thick slices.

Place the slices on a chopping board, sprinkle generously with salt and leave to stand for 10–15 minutes. The salt will draw out the excess water, ensuring the tomatillos are crisp instead of soggy when fried. Rinse and pat the slices dry with kitchen towel.

Mix the cayenne, garlic powder and flour together on a plate. Lightly dust a dry tomatillo slice in the flour mix, then dip into the beaten egg and finally dip into the polenta. Repeat with the rest of the slices.

Heat the olive oil in a large frying pan until smoking. To test when the oil is hot enough, dip in the tip of a wooden spatula and if it hisses with bubbles the oil is hot enough. Fry the tomatillo slices until golden brown. This can be surprisingly quick, taking only a minute or two each side.

Meanwhile, prepare the chilli honey by mixing the chopped chilli with the honey in a small bowl. For the aioli, simply mix the garlic into the mayonnaise and season well. Serve the fried tomatillos with the chilli honey and aioli on the side.

Tree chillies *Capsicum pubescens*

The world's hardiest chilli that grows on 'trees' up to 4m high

They might look like cute, little bonsai-sized red peppers, but don't let that deceive you because tree chillies are anything but mild-mannered midgets. A completely different species from any of the regular supermarket types, these ultra-fiery spice bombs grow on bushy 'trees' up to 4m high and live for up to an astonishing 15 years. Also known as: *rocoto* or *manzano*.

Growing

Hailing from the cool highlands of Bolivia, the plants have a built-in cold tolerance that most of this tropical family sadly lack. Given the right protection, an outdoor chilli 'tree' could well be an option for those lucky enough to live in milder areas. Here's how:

• Start the plants off between February and April, by sowing seeds in a 10cm pot of good quality seed compost.

• Place the pot either in a heated propagator or simply cover it with an upturned clear plastic bag, held in place with a rubber band to create the warm cosy environment essential for good germination of chillies.

• Once the seedlings pop up and reach 2.5cm tall, prick them out and transfer each to its own little pot on a sunny windowsill and allow to grow on until planting them out after the last frost in late May.

• Choose the sunniest, most sheltered position you can find such as against a south-facing wall or tucked in a corner by a conservatory.

• Keep them well watered with a high-potash fertiliser, like comfrey liquid, throughout the summer.

You should start seeing your first crops by late August in the first year, and early July each year after that.

Tree chillies make perfect pot plants on the patio that can be brought safely undercover and treated as houseplants over winter before the hardest frosts hit in November. Keep indoor plants on the dry side over winter because if left to sit in cold, wet soil they can succumb to root rot.

Alternatively, if you have a perfect, protected spot in mind and live in a milder area of the country, it might just be worth a gamble to plant it in the ground all year. Mine have managed to pull through some pretty horrendous winters in suburban London with a little protection. If you are up to the challenge:

• Pick larger plants that are in their second year (let them have at least have one winter of indoor spoiling before subjecting them to the elements).

• Mulch the ground around them with a thick layer of straw, trim back the bushes to the main stems and wrap the whole plant in a few layers of horticultural fleece, stuffing any extra gaps with straw to create a sort of straw woolly jumper. This protection can

1.5m

be removed in April the next year, after the worst of the cold weather is over.

The bushes both inside and out will lose their leaves over winter. This is a perfectly natural response to low light levels and if undamaged by excessive cold, they should leaf out again next spring.

Harvesting & eating

Tree chillies can be picked either when they are still green or once they mature to a full red, yellow or purple (the mature colour depends on the variety), just as you would with sweet peppers.

Being atrociously spicy (easily as hot as a habanero and with a similar fruity tang), tree chillies are a perfect candidate for a near nuclear strength homemade chilli sauce. Just whizz half a cupful of chopped tree chillies with one chopped fried onion, three cloves of garlic, half a teaspoon of mixed spice and a teaspoonful of salt until you get a smooth paste. Thin the mixture down with a about 250ml of vinegar and give a final blitz to combine. This can be bottled up and will last for well over a year in the fridge. I have a friend from Bermuda who swaps the vinegar for sweet sherry to make a unique condiment that packs a double whammy of booze and chilli that lasts virtually indefinitely in or out of the fridge. Trust me, no bacteria will dare grow on that concoction!

Try adding finely sliced tree chillies to curries, or sprinkle them sparingly over tacos, enchiladas or quesadillas. When pickled, they make a super-strength jalapeño substitute.

In Peru and Bolivia, tree chillies are traditionally stuffed with curd cheese, herbs and breadcrumbs then baked in the oven to make *rocotos rellenos*, meaning 'stuffed tree chillies'. Although I must confess that those hardy Andinos must be made out of stronger stuff than me, as despite several valiant attempts, even my chilli-hardened Malaysian palate remains well and truly defeated by this dish.

Goji berries *Lycium barbarum*

The eastern 'superfood' that's easier to grow than a stinging nettle

Splashed across the pages of glossy magazines for their sky-high antioxidant levels and with a dedicated celebrity following, the exotic Himalayan goji berry, you might be surprised to learn, lives a secret double life as a common, and quite often very invasive, weed throughout much of the UK. Also known as: wolfberry, boxthorn, duke of argyll's tea plant.

Growing

Native to large swathes of Asia, where it crops up on disturbed ground, roadsides and wasteland areas, the goji berry is both a tough weed species and a highly prized medicinal plant. Introduced to Britain in the 1730s, the plant has an adaptable, rugged constitution and quickly escaped into the wild. It has been a common weed species in much of southern Britain ever since, colonising itself freely in hedgerows, sandy banks, coastal dunes and railway lines.

If taken out of these harsh environments however, and brought into the five-star luxury of a cosy suburban garden with rich soil, generous watering and fertiliser applications, these plants will quickly start to misbehave. In fact, the healthiest, most productive goji berry plant I have ever seen was growing out of a crack in a platform at White City Tube station – so covered in oval red berries that it looked as though it was strung with tiny red Christmas lights.

Spoilt specimens react by producing masses of soft floppy branches, which are prone to fungal infections like mildew, and bear next to no berries. Gardeners also tend to enthusiastically prune these plants, cutting away the one-year-old branches on which the flowers and fruit are produced. The combination of this cosseting, however well intentioned, means that many growers will see almost no fruit, despite years of loving care.

Goji berry plants are triggered into producing flowers and fruit when they are under stress and therefore require:

• Poor, well-drained soil in a sunny situation.

• Almost no feeding or watering once established.

It really is a case of 'treat 'em mean keep them keen'. To get started:

• Plants can be grown from seeds extracted from a dried, supermarket berry sown in spring, or stem cuttings taken in summer

• These young saplings will need protection through their first winter though so pop them in a glazed porch, greenhouse or windowsill to give them the best start. You should then plant them out the following year.

• Alternatively, young plants that you can plant out straight away are also available from an increasing range of suppliers.

3m

3m

1.5m

Harvesting & eating

Plants begin to fruit after about two years, producing masses of drop-shaped berries in succession from late summer until the first frosts. Only fully ripe fruit are edible, so the redder the better. At this stage, they are very easily squished and can turn black when handled, which is why they are almost always sold dried.

> **Tip:** To avoid being covered in juice when harvesting goji berries, lay a tarpaulin or large mixing bowl beneath the branch and give it a gentle shake to remove the berries.

Think you don't like goji berries? Well think again. Goji berries are absolutely delicious *if* they are prepared properly, but it is a pretty big 'if' – the difference between exotic delicacy and hippy-food nightmare all depends on how you use them.

Since they first hit the shelves of our health-food stores in the early noughties, goji berries have sadly become a chronically misunderstood ingredient by us Brits. Perhaps the reason for this is because they are called 'berries', which has led to goji berries being most commonly added to sweet dishes like smoothies, muesli mixes and cereal bars. Goji berries in fact have a relatively low sugar content and a mild, more savoury flavour. The Chinese have been eating the berries for about 5,000 years and find the way they are eaten in the west totally bizarre.

In the Far East, they are treated a bit like a tomato (which is also a berry and a close botanical cousin) to add a savoury and mildly sweet depth to stir-fries, soups and stews. They are particularly delicious in a fiery homemade chilli sauce. Try them savoury and I promise you will never look back.

a recipe idea

Pork, prawn & goji berry steamed dumplings

Super-easy dim sum treats enriched with the fruitiness of homegrown goji.

Serves 4 as a starter or side

Ingredients
100g minced pork
18 raw king prawns, shelled (pre-prepared)
2.5cm piece of ginger, peeled and finely grated
2 spring onions, finely sliced
4 cloves of garlic, finely chopped
65g fresh goji berries
2 tbsp light soy sauce
1 tsp sesame oil
2 tsp Chinese rice wine (or mirin)
1 tsp sugar
2 tsp cornflour
20 wonton wrappers

Start by pulsing the pork and prawns in a food processor for about 1 minute or until the mixture looks roughly chopped and well combined. Aim for a chunky texture a bit like minced beef.

Tip the mixture into a mixing bowl and squeeze in the juice from the grated ginger, discarding the fibre. Add the spring onion, garlic, goji berries (keep a handful back for decoration), soy sauce, sesame oil and rice wine. Sprinkle in the sugar and cornflour and then roll up your sleeves and mix well with your fingertips to combine.

Brush around the edges of each wonton wrapper with a few drops of water (use a brush or your fingers). Dollop a tablespoon of the mixture in the centre, lifting up the edges of the wrapper around the filling, creating pleated folds (almost like a mini pork pie without the lid).

Top each dumpling with a fresh goji berry and steam on a high heat for 10–15 minutes.

Serve with soy sauce as a starter, or for the true domestic gods or goddesses among you, with several other plates of freshly made dim sum.

Oyster mushrooms *Pleurotus ostreatus, P. citrinopileatus, P. djamor*

The gourmet mushrooms you can even grow on old telephone books!

By far the easiest edible fungus that can be grown at home (well, next to bread yeast at least), these exotic mushrooms with delicate coral-like frills are as delicious as they are curiously beautiful. While these might be sold for handsome prices in fancy foodie shops, anyone with a few handfuls of sawdust, a spray can, a bright windowsill and a plastic bag can start their own indoor fungi farm, harvesting a constant supply of these little beauties all year round.

Growing

Although quite a few edible mushroom species can be successfully grown in the UK, from rich morels to smoky shiitake, many of these species can be horticultural divas that require special growing conditions, including freshly cut logs from specific tree species, laborious drilling with fancy power tools and even misting almost every hour.

Oyster mushrooms however, are nowhere near as fussy and really do require minimum attention – making them the perfect rookie's introduction to 'fungiculture'. My first piece of advice is avoid buying one of those trendy mushroom-growing kits that are cropping up in garden centres and catalogues all over the place. Although they are the ultimate slacker option and generally work very well, the majority of these will cost many times more to buy than the value of the harvest they produce. You will be left wondering why you didn't just get the mushrooms from your local supermarket in the first place.

Instead, I would go direct and buy the mushroom spawn (live culture) from one of the many

wonderful online suppliers and make up my own kit at home in just a few minutes. This live spawn takes only a couple of days to arrive by post and produces many times the harvest of a kit for an absolute fraction of the price in just three easy steps (see below), but first let me describe some of my favourite types.

Varieties to try

The easiest of all oyster mushrooms is the **blue-grey coloured** (*Pleurotus ostreatus*), which hails from alpine regions and will fruit at a wide range of temperatures, from 12–25°C.

The **yellow form** (*P. citrinopileatus*) has the tenderest flesh, and along with the white form is a very close runner-up in terms of easy cultivation.

The tropical **flamingo-pink form** (*P. djamor*) is the strongest-flavoured of the genus and rightly so as it is slightly more demanding, requiring temperatures of about 22°C to produce the best crops.

Step one: Prepare your growing medium

While most mushroom species demand to be grown on freshly cut timber logs, the voracious oyster mushroom is greedy enough to devour pretty much any organic material that is rich in carbon, from spent coffee grounds, shredded newspapers and sawdust to strips of worn-out cotton clothes, old telephone books (talk about the ultimate in recycling) and whole loo rolls. Here's how to prepare your growing medium:

- Mix and match the ingredients that you have on hand, as long as they are free of synthetic chemicals. I usually grow mine in a mix made up of 50 per cent coffee grounds and 50 per cent shredded cardboard, straw or sawdust, wetted down with a few splashes of water. The goal is to thoroughly moisten this without making it soaking wet. The aim is to produce about 3kg worth of damp, fibrous growing material.

Bung this moistened mix into a large microwave-proof bowl, cover the top with a plate and microwave on high for four to five minutes to help sterilise the mix, knocking out any existing fungal spores that might compete with your crop.

- Take the bowl out of the oven and leave it to cool, still covered, for a couple of hours until it gets to room temperature and you will be ready to get growing.

- If using telephone books or whole loo rolls (i.e. tissue and cardboard roll), you can mimic the procedure by placing these in a roasting tray and pouring over a litre or two of boiling water. Let this stand for ten minutes to soak right through, then fish them out and place on a plate to drain off excess water and allow to cool.

Step two: 'Sowing' the spawn

Once your growing mix has completely cooled:

- Crumble up the contents of the packet of mushroom spawn and sprinkle this over your cooled growing material. Stir the whole mix together with a clean metal spoon until thoroughly combined. As a general guide, you need to use about 60g of spawn per 3kg of moist growing material. Please don't be tempted to add the spawn while the medium is still warm (above 35°C) though, because this can kill the fungi and ruin your harvest.

- Tip the mixture into a large ziplock plastic bag, fill right to the top and seal to close. Poke a few small 'breathing holes' with a pencil or skewer down the sides of the bag to give the fungi a little air and pop the whole bag in a dark, warm place (ideally between 20–25°C) for a few weeks to allow the spawn to colonise the fibre mix.

- If using telephone books, the procedure is pretty much the same, except the spawn should be sprinkled evenly between the damp sheets – every 50 pages or so. The whole book should then be popped into a sealed plastic bag with a couple of holes poked in it.

- For the loo-paper option, I would just sit the whole roll on a plate, fill the cardboard tube with the spawn and place an upturned plastic bag over the top.

- Check back on the spawn every couple of days, giving the growing medium a quick spritz of water from a spray can every now and them to keep it moist.

Within just a few days, you will start to see little white dots appearing over the medium which will quickly turn into a mass of white 'roots' that will cover the entire surface in a snowy down.

Step three: Trigger fruiting

After a few weeks, your growing medium will be fully colonised in white fuzz, at which point it can then be triggered into fruiting. To do this:

- Take the bag out of its warm, dark position and place it in a light, airy spot ideally at a slightly cooler temperature of about 18–22°C. Close to a bright windowsill would be perfect.

- If using the ziplock bag method, make about half a dozen 3cm slits around the bag to allow further oxygen to reach the fungi which, alongside plenty of light triggers them into fruiting. In fact, the mushrooms almost always form exactly at these slits, poking out like little ears from the bag.

- If using the telephone-book or loo-roll method, remove or simply pull back the bag to allow air in.

Little pinheads will start to form within a matter of days, swelling into colourful frills and fans at what seems like lightening speed. It is crucial at this stage not to let the growing material dry out as the fungi can abort their fruiting if they're not kept constantly moist. Keep a misting can next to the bag and give it a spray or two each time you walk past.

Harvesting & eating

Simply snip the fungi off with scissors or give each cluster a gentle tug. Fungi fruit in flushes, so if kept nice and moist through regular spraying, you will get two or even three harvests from the same block of substrate until the colony has exhausted all the available food.

Oyster mushrooms have a delicate, almost dairy-like flavour and work wonderfully in risottos, soups and creamy pasta sauces. Try dusting them in seasoned flour and frying in searing hot oil where they will crisp up and turn golden. A perfect accompaniment to a posh fry-up or scattered over an autumnal salad.

Future batches

Just like with sourdough yeast, once you have got your hands on some of the live, healthy culture, you can keep seeding this into fresh batches of new growing material pretty much indefinitely – providing you with years of harvests from a single Internet order. Just make sure to start off new colonies before the older ones have completely exhausted their substrate to ensure you are starting off with vigorous, live culture.

5cm

no standard width

Red strawberry popcorn

Zea mays var. everta

Grow your own edible explosives

As tasty as it is ornamental, red strawberry popcorn is the one sure-fire way to get kids to eat their veg. Particularly when they get to see the whole ear somersaulting in the microwave, spitting out little white clouds of deliciousness. Why this isn't a compulsory crop to grow in school science programmes I will never know!

Growing

Red strawberry popcorn is just as easy to cultivate as regular sweetcorn and can essentially be treated in the same way. The only major difference between the two is that popcorn requires a slightly longer growing season to allow its kernels to fully ripen, unlike sweetcorn, which is harvested when its ears are still immature.

Here are some essentials to get you started:

• Start your plants a little earlier in the year than you would sweetcorn, sowing the seeds in late April or early May in little fibre or paper pots filled with compost and place them on a sunny windowsill. Using biodegradable pots will mean the little seedlings can then be planted out pot-and-all, greatly reducing the risk of root disturbance which corn is notoriously fussy about.

• In late May or early June your little seedlings will be ready to plant out in a sheltered, sunny spot in rich, well-drained soil.

• Instead of planting these in single-file rows, you should set them out in a block-like grid, at least three rows deep with about 30cm between plants. Grouped together like this, there is a greater chance that the tiny flowers of each plant will get a thorough dusting of wind-blown pollen from its neighbours, thereby creating densely packed 'ears' of grains.

• It is important to situate them well away from other types of corn to avoid cross-pollination, which can result in cobs of weird genetically mixed-up kernels, and they won't pop half as well.

• As your plants grow, mulch them with a nice thick layer of organic matter, which can even be mounded up around their roots (about 10cm is ideal) to give these tall plants an extra bit of stability against high winds.

• Keep them well watered in dry weather, particularly when the female flowers are out (i.e. when little tassels of silk appear halfway down the stem).

> **Tip:** Something definitely worth doing to encourage pollination is tapping the tops of the plants when the male flowers appear (brown antennae that stick out the top of the plant).

1.2m

50cm

30cm

Varieties to try

There are loads of other popcorn varieties to choose from if you tire of the red strawberry kind. Check out:

• **'Brit pop'**, which as its name suggests was specifically developed for our temperamental climate.

• **'Calico'**, disco-coloured with each kernel being a different radiant hue, ranging from red, white, yellow and blue, all on the same cob!

• **'Tom thumb'**, a mini variety with tiny cobs that will fit in the palm of your hand.

Harvesting & eating

Popcorn is ready to pick when the husks surrounding each ear become dry and papery – usually in late autumn. I like to leave mine on for as long as possible to ensure the ears are as mature and full flavoured as possible. Harvesting is simply a question of grabbing each ear and yanking it down firmly, and twisting the cob as you do this.

Peel the husks on each ear back to reveal the stunning strawberry-shaped, red cobs then leave them to dry for a few weeks in a well-ventilated place. This process reduces the water content of the kernels, which is essential for ensuring a perfect 'pop'. To guarantee every last bit of moisture is removed, you can seal the air-dried cobs in a plastic bag and bung them into the freezer for a couple of days before returning them to a cool, dry place. Frosty temperatures force any remaining water out of the cells in this simple homespun form of freeze-drying. Once fully dry the cobs will last well over a year if kept in an airtight container.

For a healthy snack, simply pop a whole cob into a paper bag, tie it closed with a little string and microwave the bag on high for two to three minutes (or until there are about two seconds between pops). For the insatiably sweet-toothed, try brushing the cob with melted butter, rolling it in caster sugar and adding a light sprinkle of salt before microwaving.

If you have kids (or like me are immature and easily excited), microwave the cob on a plate covered with an upturned Pyrex or glass bowl. That way, you can clearly see each kernel explode as it pops. This is so dramatic the cob often leaps up into the air with every pop! Now what conventional allotment vegetable can do that?

Quinoa *Chenopodium quinoa*

The sacred grain of the Incas that'll grow like a weed in sunny Scotland

Once as sacred to the Incas as maize, this trendy South American 'superfood' grain was first planted each year by the emperor using ceremonial golden tools. Yet despite its exotic roots and vibrant technicoloured hues, quinoa's high-altitude origins mean that it positively prefers cool, wet climates, making it the perfect crop for the UK. It produces ultra high yields – an astonishing pound of grain from just ten plants so you don't need hectares of land to produce a worthwhile harvest either. No 24-carat trowel necessary.

Growing

Closely related to 'fat hen', a common garden weed, the plants are extremely easy to grow. They are impervious to droughts, pests and the unpredictable nature of the British summer. The only thing you really need to look out for is not accidentally weeding out young quinoa plants,

1.75m

30cm

assuming they are 'fat hen' seedlings, as the two really do look virtually identical when young.

Generally, quinoa is grown in pretty much the same way as callaloo (see *Leaves & Greens*, page 76). Here are my tips for growing:

• You can grow plants from seeds by simply sowing the grains from supermarket-bought packets, but going the extra mile and hunting down seeds of the highly coloured varieties like 'Brightest Brilliant Rainbow' will fill your garden with psychedelic shades and result in a quirky multicoloured grain harvest.

• Scatter the seeds over a well-raked bed of soil in a bright, sunny site in mid April and water in well.

• When the little seedlings pop up, thin them out to 30cm apart.

• In colder districts, you can always sow the seeds in modules indoors to give them and extra head start and plant them out at the end of May.

Young quinoa plants do take a little while to get started, growing slowly at first. However, once they reach 30cm in height they suddenly change gear: shooting up to 2m, in only a week or two.

Harvesting & eating

In the early months of autumn, the vibrantly colourful seed heads will be ready to harvest when the leaves start to yellow and drop off, leaving just the grain-filled clusters. Snip the whole 'ears' off with a pair of secateurs, pop them in a large paper carrier bag and leave them to dry in a cool shed or garage for a week or two. The plants are hardy enough to handle a few light frosts so don't panic about harvesting before this cold weather strikes if they aren't quite ready yet.

30cm

Just like callaloo, both the quinoa grains and young quinoa leaves are edible, giving you two crops for the price of one. The greens can be snipped off, cooked and eaten in exactly the same way as spinach.

Once fully dry, the grains will come away from the seed heads very easily if rubbed gently between two hands. Alternatively, put whole heads through the food processor on a slow setting for a minute or two to rip the grain off the stalks.

To separate the grain from the chaff, you need to embark on the rather biblical (and daunting) sounding process of 'winnowing', which I promise is far easier than it sounds. Simply:

• Get out into the garden on a breezy day and tip the quinoa from one mixing bowl to another, holding the bowl high so the wind catches the light, fluffy chaff and blows it away, leaving just the heavier quinoa grains in the bowl. It might take a few pourings to get the hang of it, but I can guarantee you'll be a winnowing expert in 30 minutes or less.

• Alternatively you can run the seed through a fine garden sieve (also called a riddle) to achieve a very similar result. A gauge of about 3mm gauge would be perfect.

• The grain is now ready to store in a cool, dry place and will stay fresh in an airtight jar for up to a year.

Now here comes the only slight catch … Quinoa grain is so untroubled by greedy birds and other potential pests because the seeds are coated in bitter soap-like chemicals called saponins. Fortunately, these are easy to wash off by giving seeds a quick soaking in a couple of changes of water just before cooking (note that shop-bought quinoa has been presoaked and rinsed).

To prepare the grain for cooking, tip the amount of quinoa you want to use into a blender, fill with water, leave it for five minutes to soak and then whizz for a minute or two. Drain off the water and repeat the process (you only need to soak it once) until the water is sud-free and runs relatively clear. This also gives you a chance to skim off any pesky remains of chaff that might have floated to the surface.

Your quinoa can then be cooked just like rice or couscous, used in all manner of salads, pilafs and risottos or added to simmering soups and stews as you would barley. You can even roll croquettes or chicken fillets in the cooked grains, after a quick dip in egg wash as a fun and super-healthy alternative to bread crumbs, before frying them until crisp and golden. I cook it by placing about 180g of the washed grain in a saucepan and pouring over 500ml of stock or water. Cover and simmer on a low heat for 10–15 minutes. Then turn off the heat and leave covered until all the liquid has been absorbed and the quinoa is tender.

Olives *Olea europaea*

Make home-cured olives from that tree on your patio

Twenty years ago, we Brits saw olive trees as hopelessly tender specimens, only suitable for greenhouse growing on our chilly little island. Today however, like wine production, olive growing is one of those once far-fetched Mediterranean ideas that is now a real possibility in the UK (for green olives at least).

Growing

Although capable of battling through winter freezes down to −10°C, olive trees thrive best in the milder southern or western regions of the UK, especially in coastal and city-centre locations. Having said this, I have seen fruiting trees as far north as Edinburgh. So as long as you get your growing conditions and varieties just right, almost anywhere in Britain could be potential olive-growing country.

Varieties to try

Most garden centres frustratingly sell you generic *Olea europaea* without specifying its variety. However, tracking down a named cultivar is well worth the effort because different olive trees behave in very different ways. Some tried-and-tested varieties well suited to UK conditions include:

• **'Veronique'**, an ultra-hardy variety reported to withstand freezes down to an arctic −20°C.

• **'Arbequina'**, forms a beautiful small tree with an attractive weeping appearance.

• **'Frantoio'**, has a rich fruity flavour and is reported to be the heaviest fruiter in our cool summers.

Although most varieties (including those mentioned above) are self-fertile, you will get the heaviest crops by planting trees in 'micro groves' of two or three plants to ensure maximum pollination. Picking the biggest plants you can afford will provide the largest,

earliest crops and come with an extra in-built frost tolerance.

To get your new tree (or trees) off to the best possible start:

• Pick the sunniest site available, preferably south-facing with protection from chilly north winds. A south-facing wall to keep them cosy is ideal.

• Unless your container is dustbin-sized, growing olives in pots makes them more at risk to plunging temperatures giving only modest amounts of fruit.

• Create a free-draining soil to plant these into by incorporating plenty of grit and organic matter – particularly if you are gardening on heavy soil. You want to avoid having the plants sit in wet, cold soil for prolonged periods because this will damage their roots. Super-fast drainage often gives them several extra degrees of frost tolerance.

• In extremely cold regions, an extra layer of warmth, such as a sheet of bubble wrap loosely shrouded around the trunk and the crown when hard frosts are predicted, will help fend off the worst of the winter weather.

• Feed your tree with regular doses of a high-potash liquid fertiliser like comfrey feed every fortnight between May and September, and leave it to get on with it.

Don't go too heavy on the pruning though as fruit appear on branches in their second year of growth. Being too scissor-happy will greatly reduce your harvest for the next year.

Harvesting & eating

British olives are produced from early autumn, starting green then slowly ripening to black. I would harvest them when green as the fruit only fully ripen in the UK in extremely long summers.

Fresh olives naturally contain a bitter-tasting substance called oleuropein, which is why they are usually cured before they are eaten. This treatment extracts the water-soluble chemical by prolonged soaking over several weeks. Despite sounding a little tricky, home-curing is a fun, surprisingly easy technique that will give you a result that's pretty much identical to that of the fanciest Italian deli. Here's how:

• Wash a cupful or two of olives and lay them out on a chopping board.

• Give each olive a quick whack with a mallet or rolling pin to lightly crush it (this opens up the olive, allowing the bitter-tasting oleuropein to escape). Alternatively, score down both sides of each with a knife. Pour the olives into a Kilner jar and fill it right to the brim with cold water, flip the lid on and pop it in the refrigerator.

• The next day, pour away the soaking water, refill the jar with a fresh supply of cold water and return to the refrigerator. Repeat each day for anywhere between two and four weeks (or as soon as the bitter flavour has disappeared – check by tasting). I promise it will only take a maximum of two minutes a day and the results are more than worth it.

• Once they have lost their bitter taste, drain the olives for a final time and replace the liquid with a brine made from 125ml water, 125ml red wine vinegar and one tablespoon of salt. Any combination of herbs and spices can be added to this mix for flavour. My favourite combination is garlic cloves, peppercorns, coriander seeds and orange peel.

• Finally, pour a thin layer of olive oil (works as a liquid seal) on top of the mix and leave to soak for a further two weeks. This will keep well in the refrigerator for over six months.

Easily as delicious as anything you can find in the shops, homecured olives are lovely served on their own with drinks, plonked into Martinis or scattered over salads, pizzas or pasta dishes.

4m

4m

Buried Treasure

Mooli *Raphanus sativus var. longipinnatus*

A dim sum favourite that's as foolproof to grow as a garden radish

Quick-growing and unbelievably easy, radishes are a perennial favourite among garden writers and seed catalogues, but sadly not with cooks! I mean, they are not exactly the most exciting or versatile veg are they? Enter its exotic oriental sister, the mooli, and all that changes. Just as easy in the garden but infinitely more fun in the kitchen, these Asian radishes are as versatile as they are stunning and come in a huge array of dazzling shades.

Growing

Although extremely closely related to the little red orbs of the European types (found in supermarkets), oriental radishes are definitely the big, badass sister in the family – growing up to ten times the size of your European radish and equipped with an intense, fiery kick.

As long as you follow these simple rules, moolis are a fantastically basic and quick-growing crop:

• Sow your seeds directly in the ground no earlier than July and no later than September. Moolis like to sprout in warm weather and sowing them outside this time period will result in instant 'bolting' (going into flower production mode), creating fibrous midgety roots. Once established, however, the crop is surprisingly hardy and will tolerate pretty arctic freezes.

• Dig plenty of sand or grit into your soil to ensure the loose, friable growing conditions they need to swell to their maximum size.

• Moolis need full sun and rigorous watering and are partial to soil on the poorer side – a perfect plant to whack in after you've lifted your summer potatoes.

• As for feeding, treat them mean and keep them keen. Too much fertiliser will encourage

twisted, forking roots, and loads of soft, sappy leaves that can be easily damaged by autumn frosts.

Varieties to try

Moolis come in a bewildering array of colours; here are a few of the very best:

• **'Mantanghong'**, a round, ball-shaped variety with a green and white skin that belies a rosy-pink flesh. Despite its exotic name it was actually bred in Britain.

• **'Bartender Red Mammoth'**, comes with a russety-red skin and icy-white flesh.

• **'Green Meat'**, funnily enough, this variety is bright emerald to its core.

• **'Mino Early'**, Hollywood-smile-white both inside and out.

Harvesting & eating

Moolis can be harvested from as little as six weeks after sowing. Pulling them up in late August (from an early-July sowing) will give you delicate baby-veg roots, with the largest specimens (often as big as your forearm) ready for yanking out by late November.

These crisp, peppery roots can be used in exactly the same way as a regular European radish, sliced into salads, served as crudités or chopped into salsas. However, as they lack wateriness and have a much stronger flavour than radishes, these oriental types are far more versatile to cook with.

Grated mooli is delicious fried with garlic and bacon and stuffed into homemade ravioli with some crumbled cheese. For a meatier texture, first sprinkle the grated mooli liberally with salt to draw out some of the excess water, and leave for 10–15 minutes, before rinsing and squeezing dry. The same salted, squeezed

15cm

shards work wonderfully in mooli cakes. To make these morsels, mix grated mooli with grated pumpkin and fresh herbs, bind with beaten egg and sculpt into rösti-like cakes. Finally, coat in panko breadcrumbs and deep-fry until crisp and golden – certainly my favourite dim sum treat.

Strangely, once simmered until soft their intense pepperiness vanishes, leaving a delicate, creamy flavour, adding an extra dimension of interest to chicken consommé or shark's fin melon soup (see *Fruiting veg & grains*, page 106).

In India, great chunks of the roots are added to all manner of curries, as their cool, watery bite provides respite from the heat of Indian curries – a trick that is also used by the Chinese in their spicy beef brisket stews. In Japan, moolis are sliced up and transformed into sweet, crunchy pickles, which are perfect with cold meat or inside any burger or sandwich.

30cm

15cm

Skirret *Sium sisarum*

Years of sugary, skinny 'parsnips' from a single five-minute planting

I love the sweet, creamy flavour of freshly dug parsnips, but I must admit I do hate growing them because they are notoriously tricky to germinate, their roots split into contorted forks and they're also pretty uninspiring to look at to say the least. But, imagine being able to double your yields, drive up their sugar content, attract bees and butterflies *and* get beautiful flowers all for half the work – that's what you'll have if you switch to skirret.

Growing

Producing tall spikes of white, lacy flowers – much like cow parsley – these plants are a great addition to a sunny flower border, where they will blend in indistinguishably with any standard border perennial.

Being a tough long-lived species, a single planting of half a dozen or so small plants will provide you with generous harvests year after year, in fact about twice that of parsnips by weight and they'll taste far sweeter. Here's how to do it:

- Track the small plants down at a specialist or herb nursery. Plant in deep, rich soil with plenty of organic matter dug in.

- Although skirret can also be grown from seeds, this is a little trickier (similar to parsnips) and the first year's crop can have a slightly woody core, so definitely opt for small plants if you can find them for sale.

- Unlike most root crops they can tolerate a little light shade, but they will be happiest in damp, rich soil.

- Using a loose, friable mix makes their roots far easier to dig up and clean. They truly are the perfect specimen for a deep (40cm minimum) trough filled with a mix of compost and sand.

- Native to muddy stream banks, skirret are thirsty plants that need loads of water, producing the sweetest, tenderest crops when spoilt with lashings of liquid fertiliser.

- Stake the tall flower spikes as needed with bamboo canes to stop them flopping over – although this is not strictly necessary it will make them look much tidier.

Harvesting & eating

To harvest this underground bounty, lift the plants after the frosts have killed off their top growth in late November. This is a great time to propagate them too by splitting the clumps into smaller offsets and replanting these about 30cm apart. Left in the ground, the roots will keep perfectly well until the following spring, so only gather them as needed.

I find that the best way to enjoy skirret is as a deliciously sweet snack. Simply wash and peel their long, pencil-thick roots and munch on them raw. Chopped into 10cm lengths like sugar-charged carrot sticks they are fantastic on a platter of assorted raw veg with paprika-sprinkled hummus. The roots can be cooked and eaten as if they were amazingly sweet parsnips, with an added tang of carrot and a

30cm

much softer, potato-like fluffiness. I love them parboiled and then deep-fried, which turns them into the most addictive chips ever.

They can also be simply roasted in olive oil, whipped up into a buttery garlic mash or blended into creamy soups. Because skirret has a wonderful affinity with other autumnal veg like sweet potato and pumpkin, the trio makes a truly spectacular vegetarian root-veg curry.

Try them steamed and tossed in a hot frying pan with caramelised shallots and crispy shards of bacon until the roots turn golden brown – lovely served with a gremolata, that zesty, herby Italian condiment made from finely chopped lemon peel, parsley and garlic. If you really want to push the calorie boat out bake them in a gratin of cream-enriched cheese sauce, topped with breadcrumbs and a grating of fresh nutmeg – my instant remedy for the impending winter blues.

Peruvian ground apple *Smallanthus sonchifolius*

Sugary, delicate 'water chestnuts' from giant underground tubers

Once used by Incan messengers to refresh themselves as they sprinted across the empire, the crisp, sweet-tasting roots of Peruvian ground apples are nevertheless one of the most productive root crops that can be grown in the UK, regularly producing between 5–10 kilos per plant! Boasting a unique flavour somewhere between a water chestnut and an Asian pear with a hint of carrot mixed in, this once-neglected Andean crop is now causing a revolution in health-food circles as a low calorie sweetner.

Growing

If you can grow a dahlia (see *Dahlia yam*, page 135), you can grow a Peruvian ground apple. In fact, the two are very closely related and have pretty much identical growing requirements. Here's how:

• In April, start the plants indoors from little tubers planted in pots of moist compost on a sunny windowsill. You can also buy small plants by post through a number of mail order companies.

• Once they reach 30cm in height, plant out in a border of rich, well-drained soil in a sunny, sheltered site after any risk of frost has passed.

• If you're looking for more bang for your buck, once they reach a height of 15cm or so you can snip the tops off the shoots to make little cuttings, giving you several free plants from a single tuber. Just dip the cut ends in a little rooting powder and grow in pots of compost on a windowsill, planting these out in the usual way.

• Give the plot a really thorough dig to incorporate plenty of compost and grit to at least 40cm deep before planting, particularly if you are gardening on heavy soil. This helps encourage maximum tuber size and makes harvesting far easier.

• Because the tubers are mainly water, it is important to keep them well irrigated and fed throughout summer to ensure the largest, juiciest harvest.

Initially, the plants can be a little slow to start but once they get going they quickly shoot up masses of large diamond-shaped leaves on stems up to 2m tall, creating a very exotic ornamental effect.

> **Tip:** In longer summers, Peruvian ground apples produce small orange flowers at the tips of their branches, like 50p-sized sunflowers. Trim these off to direct all the plant's energies to the tubers.

Harvesting & eating

After the first frosts have blackened the leaves, cut the stems down to 10cm above ground level and use a trowel to gently loosen the soil around the tubers. These have a very thin skin

50–75cm

2m

50cm

and snap easily so don't get too heavy-handed when yanking them up.

Peruvian ground apples produce clusters of two types of tubers: long, sweet potato-shaped ones around the outside, which are the best for eating, and much smaller, short, gnarly tubers towards the centre. These, although also edible, are best saved for propagation. Store these runty ones just like you would a dahlias in barely moist compost in a cool, frost-free shed or garage, ready to plant the following year. The larger ones go straight to the kitchen.

Tasty & good for you
Rich in a complex sugar known as inulin, which despite its sweet flavour is not absorbed by the body, Peruvian ground apples are touted as a source of a natural low-calorie sweetener suitable for slimmers and diabetics alike. Research has also suggested that inulin can boost levels of friendly bacteria in the gut, prevent fluctuations in blood sugar and may even prevent certain cancers. Talk about having your cake and eating it!

In the kitchen, Peruvian ground apples can be eaten (washed and peeled) straight out the ground – they will have a fresh, crisp texture but rather watery flavour. Sat on a sunny window for a week or two, much of the inulin within them starts to break down into simpler sugars, resulting in a marked increase in sweetness. If left until their skins begins to wrinkle, the sugars in them will concentrate further, producing a flavour more like an Asian pear. However you choose to eat them, it's a good idea to sprinkle Peruvian ground apples with lime or lemon juice once they are cut (similar to apples) to avoid discoloration.

Despite being a root vegetable in South America, they are traditionally eaten more like a fruit: sliced into tropical fruit salads; pressed into juice; or cut into sticks that are sprinkled with lime juice, dusted with salt and chilli powder, and served dipped into bowls of sugar. The freshly pressed juice from the tuber is also simmered down in big pans to produce a low-calorie syrup (tasting much like a fruitier version of maple syrup), which is sublime on pancakes and French toast. The syrup is surprisingly straightforward to make with a home juicer and a large frying pan, although you do need at least 10kg of tubers to make just 250ml of syrup.

Although Peruvian ground apples are traditionally eaten in desserts, I think they work just as well treated like a radish in salads or as a convincing replacement for water chestnuts in stir-fries and Asian stews. Grated and fried with bacon, sliced shiitake mushrooms and grated carrots, they can be used to stuff Asian-style wonton dumplings or Italian-style ravioli, fantastic with a drizzle of olive oil and grating of Parmesan cheese.

Salad of Peruvian ground apple, watercress & coconut

The sweet, fruity flavour of crisp, fresh Peruvian ground apple works brilliantly in this savoury fruit salad.

Serves 4 as a light starter or side

Ingredients
2 green apples
1 medium Peruvian ground apple (about 200g)
finely grated zest and juice of 1 lime
100g fresh coconut pieces, finely sliced
1 small red onion, finely sliced
1 small bunch of watercress sprigs
1 tbsp of sugar leaves, finely sliced (optional) (see page 207)
salt and pepper
2 tbsp extra virgin olive oil

For the syrup
2 tbsp cranberry jelly
1/2 tsp chilli powder
salt and pepper

Wash, peel, core and finely slice the green and Peruvian ground apples and sprinkle with the lime juice to prevent discoloration.

Arrange the green and Peruvian ground apples, coconut, red onion and watercress on your serving plates. Add the sugar leaves if you are using them.

Sprinkle with salt, pepper, lime zest and drizzle with extra virgin olive oil.

To make the syrup, simply melt the cranberry jelly in a small saucepan and whisk in the chilli powder, and a little salt and pepper with a fork until well combined. While still warm drizzle the syrup over the salad.

Serve immediately either as light starter or as a zesty side to grilled fish or (my personal favourite) barbecued chicken satay.

Dahlia yam *Dahlia spp.*

The long-lost Aztec 'sweet potato' that's sold in every garden centre

Before you dismiss the idea of eating dahlia yams as some kind of weird, hippy idea, consider this: dahlias were originally brought to our shores as a prized edible crop, while runner beans were ironically first introduced as an ornamental plant. It seems like we just got our horticultural wires crossed. Cultivated for hundreds of years by the Aztecs, and still popular in Mexico today, their sweet, starchy tubers are delicious as crisps, chips and roasties – and even in ice cream!

Growing

Available from just about any garden centre, the stunning showy flowers and starchy tubers of dahlias are a real cinch to grow:

• Start by picking up a few tubers of the largest flowered 'cactus' types, as these generally produce the biggest possible roots with the added bonus of having the most enormous flowers.

• Choose a bright sunny site and dig in plenty of organic matter such as well-rotted manure or blood, fish and bone.

• When all risk of frost has passed in May or early June, plant the tubers about 10cm deep, water in well and stake with bamboo canes because these will provide support for the plants as they get larger.

• Keep on top of the watering, spoiling your plants with regular applications of fertiliser to ensure the largest, most fibre-free roots.

In theory, to get the very best tuber harvest you really should pick off all the flowers as they emerge to direct the plant's energies into root production, although I must admit I can never bring myself to do this because they are just too pretty.

Varieties to try

Although 300 years of breeding has produced thousands of cultivars, dahlias have sadly only been selected for their pretty flowers, not for the flavour of their roots, so they vary widely in quality. The good ones have a delicious subtle Jerusalem artichoke sweetness with nuances of celeriac and carrot; others are rather watery and bland with a slight bitter edge – so it can be a little bit of a culinary Russian roulette. This does mean that you have the opportunity to give a few varieties a try, and, who knows, you might discover the best-tasting one yet! After two years of my own trials I found that the yellow-flowered cactus types are superior in size and flavour. Good examples include: 'Lemon Chiffon', 'Amhurst Regina', and 'Inland Dynasty'.

There is one variety I have yet to try but according to a few online plant geeks it is by far the best – the small pom-pom shaped 'Yellow Gem'. I can't personally vouch for this, but if you strike upon an even better one do get in touch via Twitter.

2m

50cm

50-75cm

Harvesting & eating

The tubers will be ready to harvest when the first frosts blacken the leaves, at which point the plants should be cut down to leave just 10cm of stem and carefully forked out the ground.

If you do hit on a particularly good flavoured one, please don't scoff them all, as a handful buried in a tray of just damp moss or compost will last perfectly fine all winter in a cool, dark place, ready to be planted out next spring for a repeat harvest year after year.

Safety tip: Avoid eating tubers bought straight from the garden centre because these will almost certainly have been chemically treated.

In flavour and texture, dahlia tubers possess the sweet richness of Jerusalem artichoke and the crisp, wateriness of a Peruvian ground apple, which are both closely related to dahlias.

Like aubergines, dahlia tubers benefit immensely from having their flavour concentrated

by a quick dusting of salt to draw out excess water. Simply slice or grate the peeled tubers, sprinkle a tablespoon of table salt on top evenly and leave to drain over a colander or sieve for 30 minutes or so. Give them a really thorough rinse to wash off all the salt and squeeze out any remaining moisture and they're ready to cook with.

Try the tubers roasted like parsnips with a little brown sugar or a drizzle of maple syrup as a last-minute glaze. They are mouth-wateringly good made into rösti, or better yet the Eastern European equivalent latkes, served with slices of smoked salmon and a generous dollop of sour cream. Dahlia tubers make a wonderfully warming winter soup. Just sauté in a little butter with loads of chopped onions and garlic before simmering in chicken stock and milk. Follow with a sprinkling of chopped parsley, a good glug of double cream and blitz until smooth. If this all sounds a bit too indulgent, the roots can also be eaten raw. Simply grate, drizzle with lemon juice (to stop them browning) and toss into salads – lovely with slivers of runner beans, black olives and roasted red peppers in a honey mustard dressing.

The innate, sweet creaminess of the tubers means they are a wonderful addition to desserts, grated into cakes much like you would carrot or parsnip. In fact, a roasted syrup extract from dahlia roots with a sweet, malty, chocolatey flavour was once widely sold in US health-food stores as a caffeine-free coffee substitute marketed as 'Dacopa' until as recently as a decade ago. Inspired by this curious sweet-treatment for dahlias, I've concocted a pretty impressive roast dahlia ice cream recipe. Simply roast the pre-salted, rinsed and drained tubers (see above) in plenty of butter and brown sugar. Separate the sticky golden result in two, chopping one-half into small cubes and blitzing the other half in a food processor with a little milk to form a fine paste. Fold the creamy purée into a tub of softened, good-quality vanilla ice cream along with the caramelised dahlia chunks. Refreeze the ice cream for an hour and you can enjoy this sweet either on its own or over hot apple pie or a slice of chocolate brownie straight from the oven.

a recipe idea

Dahlia rösti with smoked salmon & dill

You will never think of dahlias the same way again after one bite of these crisp and nutty fritters.

Ingredients
For the rösti
1kg dahlia tubers
1 small onion
juice of ¹⁄₂ a lemon
¹⁄₂ tsp ground nutmeg
6 tbsp plain flour
2 free-range eggs
salt and ground white pepper
1 tbsp butter
1 tbsp olive oil

For the topping
75g sour cream
¹⁄₂ a small onion, very finely diced
1 tsp chopped dill
100g smoked salmon
small handful fresh dill

Start by making the rösti by finely grating the dahlia tubers and onion. In a large bowl, mix the dahlia and onion with the lemon juice. The juice will prevent the tubers from oxidising (going brown). Place the grated dahlia and onion into a clean tea towel, twist the top and squeeze out as much moisture as you can.

In a medium-sized bowl, mix the dahlia and onion with the nutmeg, flour, eggs, salt and white pepper.

Now heat the butter and olive oil in a frying pan until bubbling and place heaped tablespoons of the mixture into the pan. Lower the heat to medium, flatten each pancake with the back of a spoon and shallow fry for about 5 minutes on each side, turning the rösti over once the edges turn golden-brown.

Remove the rösti from the pan and drain on kitchen paper.

Serve topped with soured cream, diced onion, slices of smoked salmon and a sprinkle of dill.

Mashua *Tropaeolum tuberosum*

Vanilla-flavoured tubers hidden beneath Incan nasturtium flowers

1.25m

50cm

50cm

Once fuelling the great Incan armies, these highly nutritious tubers are still prized in the Andes for their near indestructibility, as they seemingly flourish on pure neglect. With a multifaceted flavour that begins with peppery watercress, through to roast chestnut and finally a lingering vanilla, these tubers come buried beneath a stunningly exotic, flowering climber. Now, could you really ask for more?

Growing

Outside the unique habitat of its Andean home, this plant prefers similarly overcast, misty climates without extremes of heat or cold meaning it positively loves British weather, particularly in milder, wetter areas like Cornwall and western Scotland. Here's all you need to know to get started:

• Source young plants or tubers from a broad range of nurseries and online retailers, but note that they're almost always sold as an ornamental rather than an edible.

• Plant young plants outside in May after all risk of frost has passed in a sunny site in rich, friable, well-drained soil, with plenty of organic matter dug in and water in well.

• If starting with tubers, pot these up in a little good-quality compost in late March through to early April and leave to grow on a sunny windowsill, planting them out (as per above for young plants) in May.

• Once you have them growing strongly, give the plants a support to clamber up and a good, thick layer of mulch to keep the roots cool in summer. Conveniently, this layer will double up as an insulating blanket in winter.

• In milder areas, they are hardy enough to be left outdoors all year.

Mashua look great planted under tall, skinny crops like sweetcorn, where their rampant leafy growth helps smother all weeds and their insecticidal compounds deter pests. The corn stalks also act as a convenient climbing frame for their stunning flowers, showing them off to best effect.

> **Tip:** Although mashua will cope well in even the poorest growing conditions, spoiling them a little with generous applications of water and fertiliser does create a huge spike in yields.

Varieties to try

Although in the Andes the tubers come in a veritable rainbow of colourful varieties, only a few are suitable for growing as crops in Britain, the most reliable being 'Ken Aslett', which was originally developed as an ornamental for the UK climate. This is because most mashua varieties, like many Andean crops, will only start to produce flowers and tubers when the day length falls below 12 hours. In the UK, this frustratingly coincides with the arrival of the back end of the growing season, so they may not have long enough a growing season to produce a worthwhile crop, particularly in colder

Northern regions. 'Ken Aslett' however, is day-length neutral, so will flower and root up brilliantly regardless of light conditions.

Harvesting & eating

When the first hard frosts have cut down the leaves, harvest the tubers by lifting them out gently with a fork. These can be stored in a cool garage in a tray of moist compost or vermiculite in colder areas, or, if given a generous mulch they can even be left in the ground in milder regions.

Mashua tubers can be eaten both raw and cooked, and their edible leaves and flowers also make a delicious peppery addition to all kinds of salads. Straight out of the ground, the raw tubers have a powerful spiciness because of their high concentration of mustard oil. Although many people (including me) love this, in the Andes they traditionally undergo a 'sweetening' process in which the tubers are laid out to dry in the sun for 15 days so that the UV light slowly breaks down their pepperiness and simultaneously raises their sugar content. Once cooked, however, much of this pepperiness disappears anyway so it really is up to personal taste.

Kitchen tip: Putting mashua by a sunny windowsill for about two weeks will increase its sugar content, making the tuber sweet enough to be treated as a dessert ingredient. Try it grated into cakes (like you would carrots).

The tubers are simply delicious mashed, baked or fried, but possibly the best way to eat them is in a rather lovely Andean twist on a Spanish omelette. This was one of my usual breakfasts from the market stalls of Quito while conducting research in the region. There, parboiled chunks of mashua are fried with onions and garlic in lard until soft and golden, then a generous scattering of chopped parsley, yellow chillies and a couple of well-beaten eggs are poured over to create a thick omelette – perfect with a crusty bread roll first thing in the morning.

While they are entirely safe to eat, mashua tubers have a long history of medicinal use in the Andes for their perceived effect as a potent (although temporary) dampener of the male sex drive. I must say that I can't attest to the tubers' 'botanical bromide' effects though, having scoffed my way through plenty of these while living there!

Chinese artichoke *Stachys affinis*

Nutty, witchetty grub-shaped 'artichokes'

The nondescript mint-like leaves of these tough perennials belie a rather wonderful secret: a massive underground store of bizarre, witchetty grub-shaped tubers, that have a deliciously mild, nutty, artichoke flavour. Known in China as stone silk worms, these crunchy morsels have been valued for centuries throughout the Far East for not only their flavour but also for their creamy, pearlescent appearance that is virtually identical to the surface of pale white jade.

Growing

Hailing from the chilly provinces of northern China, these quick-growing plants will rapidly form a super low-maintenance carpet of green leaves and offer many years of subterranean crops from a single ten-minute planting session. To get growing:

• Start them off from either small ready-grown plants bought at specialist nurseries or save yourself a few quid and order the tubers from a seed catalogue. The plants are so quick growing that tubers will soon sprout shoots, making up for any lost time.

• Plant the tubers 10cm deep and about 20cm apart in April and water in well. If starting from young plants, simply set them out at a similar spacing and let them get on with it.

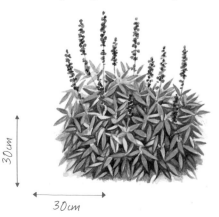

• Chinese artichokes are generally pretty indestructible, being unfussy about site, soil, water or fertiliser, however, I would strongly recommend growing them in tubs or troughs of compost (a minimum of 40cm deep) unless you have particularly sandy soil. This is because it can be exceptionally difficult to get rid of the dirt on these knobbly tubers once harvested, especially if grown on a heavy clay soil.

• Ideally choose a site in full sun to generate the largest crops, although they will also produce quite respectable yields in even considerable shade.

Apart from watering in the driest weather you can forget all about them.

Harvesting & eating

The tubers are ready to harvest in late autumn when the first frosts cut down the leaves. Simply plunge your hand into the soil and gather up great fistfuls of creamy white roots. Only do this as and when you need them as they keep far better just left in the soil than they do in the fridge or freezer.

Freshly pulled out of the ground, the little tubers are crisp, watery and sweet – a bit like

a green cobnut crossed with a water chestnut. Given a good wash, they are great chopped into salads, mixed with slivers of crisp, raw veg in crudités or even as part of a fruit platter – their flavour is just sugary enough to get away with as a sweet ingredient.

Once cooked, Chinese artichokes take on a completely different character, becoming starchy and potato-like with a nutty, artichoke flavour. Try them as an elegant substitute to spuds in a creamy leek and 'potato' soup, or serve cold in the fancy French vichysoisse. In fact, the one place outside Asia where they are now popular is France, where they are known as *crosnes* and prepared braised in herbs and butter to create a curiously familiar-tasting comfort food – lovely with a few lardons tumbled in for good measure.

In Japan, Chinese artichokes are made into fantastically crisp, sweet pickles known as *chorogi*, which are dyed a deep vermillion using the leaves of the Japanese beefsteak plant (see *Experimental herbs, spices & flavours*, page 183). Combine a mix of dyed and undyed pickled tubers in a little dish as an accompaniment to a cheese platter or fondue next time you have guests around and watch the expressions of delight or horror ...

Jerusalem artichoke *Helianthus tuberosus*

The 'potato' with a roasted artichoke flavour

Neither from Jerusalem nor an artichoke, this plant apparently gets its name from a corruption of the Italian word *girasole*, meaning 'sunflower', which is an extremely close relative. Yet being up to four times as productive as potatoes, super-low main-tenance and with a far more sophisticated artichoke-like nuttiness, I think this deli-cious Native American crop can be forgiven for having a confusing name.

Growing

Jerusalem artichokes really are foolproof to grow. In fact, once established, you can largely ignore the clumps for years, pulling them up as and when you fancy scoffing them. All you need to do to start growing them is:

• Get hold of a few tubers, either from a seed catalogue or even the fruit and veg section of fancier supermarkets.

• Plant out in April into deep, well-drained soil in a sunny site. Bury each tuber about 10cm deep and 50cm apart, water in well and watch them grow. Be mindful where you site them though because these sunflower relatives will grow into towering plants 2.5m high.

• Once they reach about 45cm in height, earth them up (lightly burying their bases by 15cm) to help keep them stable during high winds.

Apart from the above, you won't really have an awful lot else to do until harvest time.

50cm

2.4m

50cm

Harvesting & eating

Generally speaking, plants betray when their tubers are at their very plumpest by the change in colour of their leaves in autumn. At this point, wade in there and tidy them up by hacking down their foliage to leave about 30cm of stem to mark the location of each clump of tubers. Yank on these stems and a whole bundle of tubers should come up easily, unless you are on particularly heavy soil. Have a quick root around with a hand fork to dig up any stray ones, but because these will keep far fresher in the ground over winter than in the fridge, you should only harvest what you are planning to use that day.

The plants are so enormously productive that I generally leave between a quarter and half of them in the ground for the rest of the winter (with yields of up to 3kg of tubers per plant being common, this won't be a problem), where they will pop back up the next spring to produce years of crops from a single planting.

The fat thumb-shaped tubers are as amazingly versatile as a waxy new potato and can be served in exactly the same ways: be it baked, mashed, boiled, roasted or sautéed. However, because Jerusalem artichokes have a far more grown-up autumnal flavour that's almost like a mix of globe artichoke and roast mushroom, they are really far more special than the standard potato. They can even be eaten raw, grated into salads or sliced into wafer-thin slivers. However, their effect on the bowels is infamous even when cooked, so I wouldn't indulge too heavily on them in their raw state for your family's sake – they aren't called 'fartichokes' without good reason!

> **Kitchen tip:** Cut or peeled tubers can be popped into a bowl of water with a squeeze of lemon or splash of vinegar to stop them browning.

I particularly love them steamed and whizzed up in a food processor with cream, butter, salt and pepper for a truly indulgent mash that is out of this world when eaten with seared scallops and lightly blanched runner beans. They work well in creamy dishes, so try them diced into cubes, parboiled and stirred into the filling of a chicken pot pie with a glug of white wine and loads of freshly chopped tarragon or in place of potatoes in classic leek and potato soup. However, my absolute favourite way to serve Jerusalem artichokes has to be roasted with homegrown oyster mushrooms (see *Fruiting veg & grains*, page 117), chestnuts and bacon. True autumnal bliss on a plate.

Queensland arrowroot *Canna indica*

The Amazonian root veg that grows in every council bedding scheme

Before you double check the Latin name, yes gardeners I am talking about the canna lily, the exact same species that decorates the centre of seemingly every council bedding scheme each summer. These plants have been cultivated for thousands of years in the Amazon for their deliciously starchy rhizomes and are now a major crop from Mexico to Vietnam to Australia (hence the name Queensland arrowroot).

Growing

Queensland arrowroot is of huge sentimental value to me, as it is one of the very few crops in my London garden that I also grew 7,000 miles away in the steamy heat of Singapore as a child. As adaptable as it is resilient and despite hailing from the Amazonian jungle, Queensland arrowroot is an extremely unfussy crop. Given the right treatment it will produce very respectable harvests even in the most average UK back garden.

To get started:

• Buy small plants from a garden centre in spring and plant them out in May after any risk of frost has passed.

• Alternatively, start them off from a packet of bare roots that appear in nurseries from late autumn onwards. Just pop them in large, 30cm containers of compost between March and April, barely covering the surface of the roots. Plonk the pots in a light place indoors, water well and leave them to grow on until planting them out in May.

• The keys to runaway success are full sun, a sheltered site, loads of water and lashings of organic fertiliser throughout summer.

• Dig in as much organic matter as you can bear into a sheltered planting bed, sprinkling in a good couple of handfuls of chicken manure and your plants will thank you with a basket of swollen roots come autumn.

Varieties to try

Choosing your variety is rather important as there are hundreds to choose from and they can have extremely variable root yields. Three of the most productive ones recommended by my buddy Keith, a freakishly knowledgeable Queensland arrowroot expert and fellow exotic crop geek, are:

• **'Russian Red'**

• **'Musifolia'**

• **'Robert Kemp'**

All of the above varieties produce the most stunning to look at, tropical-effect plants not to mention their enormous leaves that can be used to wrap all manner of foods – but more on that later.

Word sense: Do bear in mind that in horticulture those plants are known not as Queensland arrowroot, but by their Latin name *Canna*.

2m

50cm

Harvesting & eating

The rhizomes will be ready to harvest in late autumn, once the first frosts have blackened the leaves. Cut their foliage down to 15cm and carefully lift the roots with a fork, shaking off all the soil. Unless you fancy splashing out on new plants every spring, avoid the temptation of eating all these roots so you still have some left to plant come spring. The roots can be easily stored for growing by placing them in trays of barely damp compost, moss or vermiculite in a cool, dark, frost-free place like a garage or shed.

> **Safety note:** Don't be tempted to eat rhizomes bought straight from the garden centre as these will almost certainly have been chemically treated. After a season in your garden though, they will be fully detoxed and ready to eat.

Queensland arrowroot can be cooked in the same way as Jerusalem artichokes, having a similar sweet starchiness and deliciously smooth, silky texture. They are lovely in soups (just take a classic Jerusalem artichoke soup recipe and swap the artichokes for arrowroot), roasted like regular potatoes, whipped into a creamy mash or even in a spud-free gnocchi. Try slicing into wedges to make crispy oven chips – just scatter on a tray, sprinkle with salt, spray with olive oil and bake in a 200°C oven until golden. Serve with aioli and a light dusting of paprika.

In the Andes, they are processed into a flour used to make cakes, biscuits and bread and sold in spectacular wicker baskets at local markets. I have found that by simply swapping potato for Queensland arrowroot in any Irish potato bread or cake recipe you get a surprisingly similar result. In their native Ecuador and Peru, it is not only the roots that are used, but the large, banana-like leaves too. The leaves can be used to wrap whatever tasty concoctions you like and add a subtle lemony fragrance to all manner of steamed, baked or grilled foods.

a recipe idea

Ecuadorean humitas with chicken, black beans & cheese

Queensland arrowroot leaves make a great flavour-imparting botanical foil. This recipe uses the leaves to lend a sweet, grassy freshness to delcious Andean corn cakes.

Serves 4

For the cornbread
85g corn kernels, fresh or frozen
120g softened salted butter, plus
  extra for frying
250g quick-cook polenta
1 tsp baking powder
2 tsp salt
350ml cold water

For the filling
½ a medium-sized onion,
  finely chopped
2 garlic cloves, finely chopped
2 tbsp olive oil
4 chicken thighs, finely sliced
2 tsp smoked paprika
1 tsp brown sugar
sea salt and pepper
12 Queensland arrowroot leaves
25g mozzarella cheese, grated
200g tinned black beans, rinsed
  and drained
non-plastic string (for tying
  each parcel)

Start by making the cornbread by frying the corn kernels in a knob of butter until they look golden and crisp, then pop them into a large mixing bowl and set aside to cool. In a food processor, blitz the polenta, baking powder, salt and butter until thoroughly combined and crumbly in texture. This should take about 2 minutes. Pour the water in a little at a time pulsing between additions for about 2 minutes or until you have a light, fluffy mix. Tip the polenta mix into the bowl with the corn and stir. Cover with a damp tea towel and leave to rest while you make the filling.

Gently fry the onions and garlic in the oil until soft and translucent. Tumble in the chicken pieces, sprinkle over the smoked paprika and sugar, season well and continue to fry until the chicken becomes thoroughly cooked and browned.

Place each Queensland arrowroot leaf flat on a chopping board and spread a 1cm-thick layer of the corn dough evenly over the centre, leaving a clear border all around the edge of the leaf. Spread a spoonful of the chicken mix in a line over the surface of the corn dough (just as you would fill a tortilla or fajita) and sprinkle over a little mozzarella and some black beans.

Roll the leaf to create a Mexican burrito-like parcel. Tie each little parcel up with a length of string. Place in a hot steamer and steam on a high heat for 15 minutes. Once done, untie the parcel and serve immediately.

Sweet potato *Ipomoea batatas*

The 'new kid on the block' providing two crops for the price of one

Exciting breakthroughs in sweet-potato breeding have resulted in a new range of varieties that will yield a decent crop of sweet, tender little tubers when grown in the UK. Producing attractive trailing vines with delicious edible leaves, the plants rarely reach over 20cm in height, making them the perfect underplanting for taller, shallow-rooted crops like corn, fennel or quinoa.

Growing

In the UK, sweet potatoes are conventionally grown from 'slips' – little cuttings available from most seed catalogues that are posted out in the spring. Recently, a few companies have improved on this method, selling far more established little plants instead. In my trials, these young plants are vastly superior to slips, which often prove annoyingly fragile and are comparatively expensive considering the potted plants are usually the same price.

If using slips:

• Pop these in a glass of water as soon as you can and soak for 12 hours to revive them.

• Dip the cut ends into a hormone-rooting powder and then plant them up in pots of gritty compost. For best results place them in a heated propagator to encourage quick rooting.

For both slips and young plants:

• When you see white roots emerging from the bottom of the pots, transplant into tall plastic pots of compost and place on a sunny windowsill ('long tom' pots are perfect for this use).

• If your young plants come in fibre pots, gently tear the pots before planting in tall plastic pots to allow for rooting and improved final yields.

• In June plant these established plants out into the border in rich, well-drained soil in the most sheltered and sunny site you have, about 20cm apart. Bury the plants deeply, with at least half of the stems covered to encourage tuber formation.

• UK-adapted varieties will grow happily out-doors but if you happen to have a cold frame or cloche to give them that extra bit of warmth they crave they will reward you with far larger crops.

> **Tip:** Sweet potatoes will thrive in pots too, although these will need to be as large as possible because the bigger the pot the better the crop.

20cm

20cm

Varieties to try
These are my recommended varieties – give them a go and you won't regret it.

- **'Beauregard Improved'**, as close as it comes to a sweet potato on a supermarket shelf, boasting vibrant orange flesh and a rich, sweet flavour.

- **'Georgia Jet'**, particularly well flavoured, this early maturing, high-yielding type will produce good yields of orange-fleshed tubers throughout the UK.

- **'T65'**, despite their unconventional cream-coloured flesh and bright red skin, these for me, have proven to be the most reliable variety for UK growing, producing good yields even in the most miserable of summers.

- **'Okinawa'**, this exciting variety with bright purple or pink flesh is the only one not stocked by the seed catalogues. It has an incredibly sweet, fruity flavour and is often available in Asian supermarkets. Its small tubers mean that it is often able to mature fast enough to provide a decent crop in our short summers.

> **Tip:** With the exception of 'Okinawa', it is not a good idea to plant supermarket-bought tubers as these varieties will almost certainly not be adapted to the UK climate.

Harvesting & eating

With regular feeding and watering the plants will start to produce tubers in August, triggered by the short days, but as sweet potatoes can take a while to develop in our cool summers, I would leave them in the ground as long as possible to ensure maximum yields. Covering them with a cloche from September onwards will improve your chances in colder regions. Once the leaves are blackened by the first frosts, the tubers will be ready to lift. Grown in our cool summers the sweet potatoes will be far smaller but sweeter than the giant supermarket types.

Reserving a couple of these little tubers from your harvest in pots of moist compost in a frost-free shed or garage will mean you can create your own slips the next spring, saving you a fortune. In March, simply plant the tubers up in pots and place them on a sunny windowsill. Once these send up little sprouts about 20cm long, snip these off and treat them just as you would slips.

Sweet potatoes can be eaten in exactly the same way as regular potatoes but are even more versatile. They can be eaten raw simply sliced up as part of a crudité platter or grated into coleslaws. Their leaves can also be cooked and eaten, having a spinach-like flavour. Just snip the leaves off the stems (the stems can be rather fibrous) and throw them into stir-fries and soups. As for the tubers, try them baked, roasted, mashed or boiled, or fried as chips, crisps or battered in tempura.

Used in a huge range of desserts throughout Asia and Latin America, sweet potatoes are delicious in pies (think pumpkin pie without the pumpkin), grated into cakes, simmered in coconut cream and brown sugar to make the most warming, comforting dessert.

Maple & sweet potato muffins

This savoury-sweet muffin combines sticky, sweet maple syrup with crisp bacon to bring out the best in the humble sweet potato.

Serves 6

Ingredients
120g purple sweet potatoes
1 egg, beaten
100g caster sugar
50g lightly salted butter, melted
40ml milk
100g plain flour
½ tsp ground cinnamon (or Carolina allspice)
½ tsp bicarbonate of soda
¼ tsp baking powder
¼ tsp salt
50g pecan nuts, coarsely chopped
5 rashers smoked bacon, crisp-fried and crumbled

For the frosting
2 tbsp maple syrup
2 rashers smoked bacon, crisp-fried and broken up
50g purple sweet potato, peeled and cubed into 1cm chunks
50g unsalted butter, softened
200g icing sugar, sifted
¼ tsp mixed spiced

Preheat the oven to 180°C. Prepare a muffin tray by greasing it lightly with butter or lining with paper muffin cases. Peel and chop the sweet potatoes into 1cm chunks. Place the sweet potato in a steamer or microwave and cook thoroughly for 2–3 minutes. Mash it into a fine purée and leave aside to cool.

In a large bowl mix together the egg, sugar, mashed sweet potato, melted butter and milk. In a separate bowl, combine the flour, cinnamon (or Carolina allspice), bicarbonate of soda, baking powder, salt and pecans.

Add the wet ingredients into the dry ingredients with the crumbled bacon and fold gently. Fill the muffin cups three-quarters of the way full and bake for 20–25 minutes (or until a skewer inserted into one of the muffins comes out clean). Cool on a wire rack.

For the frosting, heat the maple syrup in a small saucepan until just simmering. Break up the bacon rashers into rough shards and tip them into the maple syrup. Simmer gently for 1–2 minutes, take off the heat and remove the bacon and set aside. Cook the sweet potato as per above and mash until you have a very smooth purée. Beat together the butter, sugar, cooled sweet potato and mixed spice. Once the muffins have completely cooled, smooth the frosting on top and sprinkle the crispy bacon shards.

New Zealand yam *Oxalis tuberosa*

The shamrock-leaved 'designer potato' with the flavour of green apples

Second only in importance to potatoes in their Andean home, these delicious, lemony-flavoured 'spuds' are also a much-loved vegetable in New Zealand. Producing masses of edible shamrock-like leaves with the flavour of Bramley apples followed by knobbly little 'potatoes' that come in every colour of the rainbow, this generous plant provides two gourmet-veg harvests in one.

Growing

Forming billowing 30cm-high mounds, these plants are excellent weed-suppressing ground cover under tall skinny annuals like sweetcorn or outdoor vine tomatoes, helping trap moisture around their roots and doubling the number of species you can grow on the same plot. There are a multitude of vividly coloured varieties to choose from in shades of orange, yellow, red, green and purple, each with subtly different flavours and textures.

New Zealand yams are essentially grown just like a regular spud, with the only exception that they are immune to almost every ailment that so often trashes a spud grower's hopes (including the dreaded potato blight). Here's how to get growing:

- Plants can be started off from the little seed tubers, which are increasingly available from many specialist mail-order nurseries. Begin by planting them in small pots of compost on a sunny windowsill in late April.

- Kept warm and well watered these little guys will soon spring up several little shoots and will be ready to plant out about 30cm apart in May after the risk of frost has passed.

- Like most veg crops, they grow best in full sun and in rich, fertile soil packed with organic matter.

- Until late July the stems will form neat little mounds. However, these will then soon flop over to create long trailing runners, which should be lightly buried with about 10cm of soil to stimulate the biggest harvests.

The tubers won't form until quite late in the year, as the plants are sensitive to day length and only initiate their production when they are exposed to less than 12 hours of daylight. In colder northern districts, it might well be an idea to cover the plants with a cloche if frosts are predicted in October and early November to help extend the boundaries of their growing season.

Harvesting & eating

Your multicoloured stash will be ready to harvest when the first frosts blacken their leaves in late November and early December. Lift the tubers carefully out of the ground with a fork, holding a few back for planting next spring. Reserved tubers will keep astonishingly well in barely damp vermiculite inside a paper bag and stuffed in your chiller cabinet. They

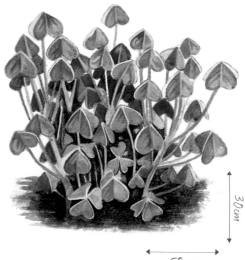

30cm

50cm

30cm

will even survive outside down to −5°C if protected with a good thick layer of mulch.

Fresh New Zealand yam leaves add a zingy lift to all kinds of summer salads and are particularly lovely tossed with homegrown rocket and watercress, some grated Parmesan cheese and a drizzle of olive oil – there is no need for vinegar or lemon as the leaves are perfectly acidic enough.

Tip: Avoid picking off too many leaves at once as being too greedy will dent your tuber harvest later in the year.

The tubers have an intense, tangy lemoniness when pulled straight out of the ground caused by oxalic acid – the same stuff that gives rhubarb and sorrel their characteristic taste.

Their sourness can be greatly reduced by placing them on a sunny windowsill for a few days. This traditional Andean practice uses UV light to set off a chain reaction within the tubers, which breaks down the acid content and simultaneously causes a rise in sugar levels causing them to taste markedly sweeter. They are delicious steamed whole (no need to peel them) before slicing in half lengthways then serving with a drizzle of olive oil, a sprinkling of sea salt and smoked paprika. Alternatively, try adding New Zealand yams to rich, coconut-based curries as their fresh acidity cuts through the heaviness of the spices and coconut milk. For a truly marvellous treat, you can even try them in fruit crumble or sweet pies, where their lemoniness works wonderfully with fruit like Bramley apples or gooseberries.

a recipe idea

Honey-roasted New Zealand yams with ginger & lime

Sticky, rich with a light lemony tang, these roasted New Zealand yams are true autumn bliss.

Serves 4

Ingredients
1 kg New Zealand yams, cleaned and scrubbed
4 tbsp olive oil
2 tbsp mild honey (orange blossom or eucalyptus)
2 garlic cloves, crushed
zest of ½ a lime
1 tsp ground chilli
½ tsp ground ginger
½ tsp of salt
1 tsp chopped fresh lemon thyme
1 tsp chopped fresh basil

Preheat the oven to 200°C. Halve the yams lengthways and arrange them in a baking tray.

In a small bowl, mix the olive oil, honey and crushed garlic until well combined and brush this glaze lightly over the yams.

Combine the lime zest with the chilli, ginger, salt, thyme and basil. Sprinkle this seasoning over the yams and bake for 30–45 minutes, or until the yams are cooked and appear caramelised around the edges.

Experimental Herbs, Spices & Flavours

Curry leaves *Murraya koenigii*

Ready-made 'curry powder' that grows on living room-sized trees

Super easy to grow in the UK, curry leaves are packed with all the flavour of premixed curry powder so you can cook up a stonking homegrown korma or jalfrezi to rival anything your local takeaway can produce.

Growing

Not to be confused with the silvery-leaved 'curry plant' *Helichrysum italicum*, which smells like curry but has virtually no flavour, these little trees from India are fantastically easy houseplants that anyone with a sunny windowsill can grow.

The only catch is that the plants can be tricky to track down in the UK. A couple of independent mail-order herb nurseries stock these as small plants, as do some of the more specialist seed catalogues, but the good news is they are easily grown from cuttings of the fresh stems. Pop to your local Asian grocer, choose the greenest leaves and, most importantly, a few firm, healthy little branches poking out between the foliage. Then all you need to do to get your plant growing is:

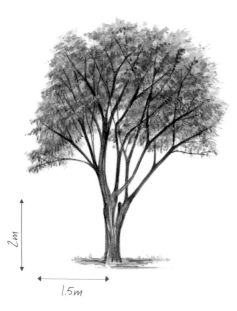

2m

1.5m

• Strip all the leaves off and quickly plunge the stems into a bowl of water for two hours.

• Snip the branches into 10–15cm lengths and dip the lower ends in a rooting hormone powder (available at all garden centres), then simply plant them, burying half their length in moist, gritty compost and water in well. These will root best in the warmth of a heated propagator, but failing that an upturned clear ziplock bag placed over the whole pot will retain moisture and heat. Whether you choose cuttings or a mail-order plant, here are my growing tips:

• Curry leaves love humidity, so they are best grown indoors all year round in a sunny, draught-free room. For best results, pot them up in a rich ericaceous compost with a good handful of vermiculite or grit mixed in to ensure fast drainage.

• Water liberally, but make sure they do not get waterlogged, and keep well fed on a diet of a dilute ericaceous feed once a fortnight in the summer.

Harvesting & eating

When the urge for curry hits you, carefully snip off the lower leaves at the stem with a pair of secateurs. Generally with curry leaves, the larger and more mature the leaf the more intense its flavour.

The leaves can be added to any dish in which curry powder would work and fried up with a little garlic, chilli, salt and a bit of ground turmeric (just for colour) they make a surprisingly convincing substitute. Throw in some prawns, coconut milk and a ladleful of stock and simmer for 15 minutes and no one will be the wiser. Don't believe me? Test it out on some unsuspecting house guests and see for yourself.

30cm

Kaffir lime leaves *Citrus hystrix*

A taste of Bangkok in a pot on your patio

Zesty and uplifting with an incredibly fresh citrus fragrance, Kaffir lime leaves are indispensable to a whole host of authentic Thai dishes. More aromatic than any Kaffir lime leaves you can buy in the shops, a single plant on your kitchen windowsill will earn its keep providing an endless supply of leaves all year round.

Growing

Grown in exactly the same way as calamondin limes (see *Dessert fruit*, page 240), Kaffir lime plants are the perfect small, slow-growing bushes for a sunny patio in summer and bright porch or windowsill over winter. Give them a regular splash with an organic citrus fertiliser every month or so and you will be rewarded with a regular supply of more leaves than you could ever eat.

2m

1.5m

Harvesting & eating

To get cooking with Kaffir lime leaves, all you need to do is snip off the largest (mature) leaves where they meet the stem with a pair of scissors or secateurs. Used in a similar way to bay leaves, Kaffir lime leaves can be popped into all sorts of broths, curries, soups and stews to impart a fresh zestfulness. Alternatively, slice extremely fine to create a lemony confetti and mix into marinades for chicken or fish or toss into stir-fries. Try them scattered in a salad of shredded green mango, sliced chillies, coconut flakes and roasted peanuts for a mouth-watering treat.

One of my all-time favourite guilty pleasures is a sort of citrusy Singaporean take on the common Bombay mix, which is simply amazing with a bucket of cold beers on ice at a summer party. Just flash-fry half a dozen leaves with four large, dried red chillies (broken in half) in a pan of hot oil until the leaves are crisp. Fish the leaves and chilli out of the oil and toss with a handful each of roast peanuts and wasabi peas, and crack open a bottle or three. Cooked this way the fibrous leaves are transformed into crispy, citrusy morsels, which combine amazingly well with the salty crunch of peanuts and the fiery chilli.

n/a

Cardamom leaves *Elettaria cardamomum*

The perfect edible houseplant with the gingery warmth of cardamom

Cardamom *pods* might be cheap to buy and it's almost impossible to coax a plant into producing them in the UK. However, the plants' warm, gingery *leaves* – prized in Asian cooking – are just the opposite, being foolproof to grow in the UK, yet nearly impossible to track down in shops. Keep one of these beautiful, architectural houseplants on your kitchen windowsill for a ready supply of fresh, rich spiciness.

Growing

Native to the dense understorey of the Indian rainforest, these low growing, leafy plants will form cascades of lush green foliage whether it be in the Bengal jungle or in your living room. All you need to do to create the perfect conditions for these little guys is:

- Give them a bright position in a warm room (ideally a south-facing windowsill), a rich compost, and keep well watered.

- Occasionally mist with water to ensure humidity levels are high and stand them on a tray of pebbles filled with water.

If you live in a very mild part of the country, larger plants can be planted outside in a warm, sunny part of your garden (I know this goes against all the conventional advice). They can withstand temperatures down to −2°C (when fully mature), so in theory, even if they get totally cut down by winter frost, they should be able to pop back up in spring if planted in a sheltered position and covered in a thick layer of bark mulch.

To get harvesting, snip off the long strappy leaves near the base of the stem with a pair of scissors. When the plant is in active growth you can remove up to a third of the leaves every couple of months without damaging the health of the plant.

50cm

1m

50cm

Although cardamom leaves have a more complex taste than their pods, their underlying similarities in flavour means that they have the same uses in the kitchen. Popped into a pot of freshly brewed coffee or tea, cardamom leaves exude spicy, exotic warmth. Concoct your own homegrown chai tea by steeping them with builders' tea, chilli and a few pieces of Carolina allspice. Try adding a couple whole to rice dishes like pilafs and biryanis or very finely chopped to stir-fries or Asian-style salads. They are spectacular in rice puddings too with sprinkling of nutmeg, scattering of chopped pistachios and a large dollop of clotted cream.

Vietnamese fish mint *Houttuynia cordata*

The exotic Mekong herb you can grow in your patio pond

Creating a vivid multicoloured tapestry of reds, oranges, yellows and greens, these lush, carpet-forming plants have an intense flavour of coriander (now officially the UK's favourite herb) with the added tangy whiff of orange peel, making it much more complex and interesting. It's tastier, far easier to grow and infinitely more ornamental, so why bother with the shop-bought version? Also known as: chameleon plant, fish leaves, fish mint, lizard's tail, *dokudami*.

Growing

Hailing from the banks of the Mekong River, where it is grown in paddy fields and catfish ponds Vietnamese fish mint is one of the most esteemed herbs in South-East Asia. Surprisingly, it also lives a double life as an extremely common garden plant in the UK, able to withstand temperatures down to −15°C. Yet despite the fact that packets of the herb sell for a fortune in Chinatown, no one seems to have twigged that the two are one and the same.

Here's how to get growing:

- Pick plants up in the aquatic section of any garden centre – normally labelled as chameleon plant.

- These plants thrive best in very damp, rich soil, either in the garden border or in the boggy margins of a pond, being perfectly happy with their roots entirely submerged in water.

- In full sun, they will have a stronger taste and the most intense colour. But if you are keen on a milder flavour, site them in partial shade which will give you larger, less pungent leaves.

- These plants are extremely vigorous and will spread out in all directions through ad-venturous underground roots, creating ever-expanding colonies of edible colour year after year. However, if they stray too far they are very easy to uproot and get rid of so they won't ever become a noxious weed.

Varieties to try

Although the most common form in the UK is *Houttuynia cordata* 'Chameleon' for its mottled technicolour splodges, the variety used in Asia is plain leaved, much more similar to the pure green *H. cordata* 'Flore Pleno' with its double white flowers. However, in Chameleon's defence, they do all seem to have a virtually identical scent, so I imagine are pretty interchangeable culinarily speaking.

Harvesting & eating

Getting Vietnamese fish mint from garden to kitchen could not be easier. Just pick off the young tender shoots with a quick whip of the secateurs.

However, I must make a confession before I go any further: I have never actually cooked with Vietnamese fish mint, despite having grown it for years as an ornamental. The problem is, I can't stand coriander leaves, and a tiny sprig of this plant is like a fistful of the supermarket stuff. Having said that, if you, like so many people it seems, love coriander this really is the plant for you.

Vietnamese fish mint can be eaten in all the same ways as regular coriander – sprinkled in salads, stir-fries and added to soups and stews. It makes a pretty garnish and is traditionally used in Cambodia chopped up and tumbled over a salad of sliced hard-boiled duck eggs with fried ground chillies, mint, chopped raw shallots and roasted peanuts. In Malaysia, the leaves are added to spicy coconut laksas, in Thailand into endless salads, in Vietnam to fresh summer rolls and in Laos simmered in fish soup.

30cm

30cm

no standard width

Herbal remedy

Apart from being a popular culinary herb and stunning garden plant, Vietnamese fish mint also moonlights as one of the most important herbs in traditional Chinese medicine. Used for nearly 5,000 years to treat coughs, fevers and even cobra bites, the herb became the Chinese government's key weapon in the war against the SARS outbreak in 2003 to 2004 when conventional antiviral drugs proved of limited value. The herb is often cited as one of the pillars behind the disease's effective control.

a recipe idea

Vietnamese summer rolls

Crisp, fragrant and deceptively simple to make, these fresh summer rolls are far removed from the greasy takeaway spring rolls.

Serves 4 (makes 12 rolls)

Ingredients
For the dipping sauce
2 tbsp crunchy peanut butter
1 tbsp fish sauce
juice of ½ a lime
2 tbsp light brown sugar
1 tbsp hot chilli sauce
60ml water

For the rolls
12 x 22cm extra-thin dried Vietnamese rice papers
  (available in Asian supermarkets)
18 cooked king prawns, sliced in half lengthways
2 large handfuls of fresh Thai basil leaves, mint,
  Vietnamese mint leaves
16 Chinese chive leaves
½ a cucumber, cut into matchstick-sized pieces
2 carrots, grated
150g crisp lettuce leaves, washed and dried

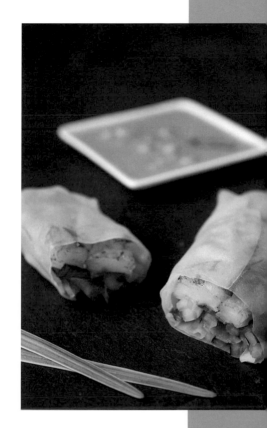

Make the dipping sauce by mixing the peanut butter, fish sauce, lime juice, brown sugar, hot chilli sauce and water together in a small bowl.

Working with one rice-paper round at a time, dip it into a shallow bowl of cold water and leave to soften for 1 minute. Then remove and lie on a damp paper towel and cover it with another damp paper towel. Continue to build layers of paper towels and rice-paper rounds until you've done six.

To assemble the rolls, take the first round that was moistened and place it on a clean work surface. Arrange a few prawn halves across the centre of the round. Top with Thai basil, mint, Vietnamese fish mint, cucumber, carrot, chives and lettuce leaf (torn or folded to fit).

Fold the edge of the paper closest to you over the filling, then fold in the sides and roll the whole thing up like a burrito into a tight cylinder. Set the assembled roll aside and cover with a damp tea towel to prevent it from drying out. Repeat the process with the remaining papers, making sure to distribute the ingredients evenly between them.

When they are all assembled, arrange on a serving platter, seam side down, to and serve with the dipping sauce.

Carolina allspice *Calycanthus floridus*

Cinnamon bark on shrubs with strawberry-scented magnolia blossom

With a rich, aromatic bark that combines the flavours of nutmeg, cinnamon and cloves into a single easy-to-grow spice, this pretty garden shrub will even reward you with a summer-long flourish of scarlet mini-magnolia flowers. Also known as: strawberry shrub, common sweetshrub.

Growing

Native to the woodlands of the southern United States, these small trees are as beautiful as they are low maintenance, making it puzzling why these aren't planted in every front garden. Here are some planting tips:

• Carolina allspice bushes are happy in full sun or partial shade, but will have stronger flavour and more flowers if situated in the hottest, sunniest sites.

• Dig the planting hole deep and incorporate plenty of compost and a good scattering of chicken manure or blood, fish and bone to get your little spice bush off to its best start.

• Keep well watered while it is establishing, and then leave it to its own devices.

Harvesting & eating

Carolina allspice bark can be harvested any time of year, but because it keeps extremely well, I usually do this once a year in November, taking advantage of this time to prune out any dead, congested or crossing branches. Then all you need to do is snip the leaves and small twigs off these pruned branches, and let them dry for a couple of days in a cool, dark place. Once dry, the bark is easily scrapped off with a serrated knife, with the flakes keeping their fragrance for up to a year if stored in an airtight container (again, in a cool, dark place).

A versatile store cupboard ingredient, Carolina allspice can be used in all the same ways as

3m
3m

cinnamon, nutmeg, cloves or indeed regular allspice. To prepare it for use in the kitchen, grind the dry strips of bark with a pestle and mortar into a fine powder and sprinkle over rice pudding, pancakes, hot chocolate or layers of brioche to make a delicious bread-and-butter pudding. Try mixing Carolina allspice with some sugar – spectacular sprinkled on top of buttery hot toast. Of course, it works just as well in savoury dishes too, adding sweet-spicy notes to curries and meat marinades, and even a rich warmth to Bolognese sauce.

Sweet galingale *Cyperus longus*

The exotic medieval spice you can grow in a bucket of water

Once as central to British cuisine as pepper or mustard, this vital medieval spice combines the warmth of ginger with the fragrant, floral notes of galangal (the Thai ginger relative from which it gets its name). Super hardy and low maintenance, it'll even grow in an old bucket on your patio. Also known as galyngale

Growing

Being a British native, the plant can handle anything our northern winters throw at it. Here are my essential planting tips:

• Sweet galingale needs full sun and permanently moist soil to thrive. This makes it a perfect candidate for that patch of boggy soil at the bottom of the garden, the edging of your pond, in a water-filled half barrel on the patio or even in a large bucket or pot with no holes in the bottom.

• The plants can be propagated by dividing the clumps in spring: simply uproot established plants and split them into smaller clumps. Replant each of these into a large 5-litre pot filled with a 50:50 mix of aquatic compost and sharp gravel. Then plunge them into a pond or water feature or just plant these little clumps directly into moist garden soil where they will grow quickly.

Apart from remembering to keep water levels topped up, you won't have much else to do.

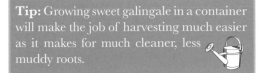

Tip: Growing sweet galingale in a container will make the job of harvesting much easier as it makes for much cleaner, less muddy roots.

Harvesting & eating

Harvest sweet galingale when it is at least 1m tall in early autumn to allow the underground stems

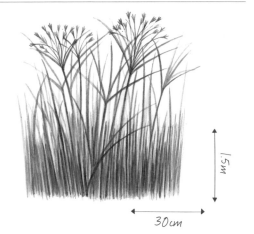

15m

30cm

(rhizomes) to reach their maximum size – the taller the plant, the larger the buried stems. Here are some tips on getting them kitchen friendly:

• Lift them out their pots and wash off as much soil as possible from the roots. Trim off the leaves and fibrous roots and give the rhizomes another thorough rinse under the tap.

• Finally, drop the rhizomes in freshly boiled water with a splash of vinegar added and leave to soak for ten minutes to remove the last traces of dirt and eliminate bacteria.

The rhizomes have a similar flavour to fresh ginger or galangal albeit with a floral fragrance and can be used in exactly the same way. Note that they can be quite woody, so bruising them slightly will release their aroma (make sure to remove the bruised rhizomes before serving).

Sweet galingale works wonders in all sorts of dishes from eastern-inspired curries, soups or flavouring the milk in old-fashioned comforting sweets like steamed ginger sponge, custards and rice puddings. Perhaps the most creative way to cook with it is to dig out recipes from old-school cookbooks and adapt to modern tastes. On page 167 is one of my most successful recent experiments, adapted from the *Forme of Cury* – an infamous medieval cookbook – just without eels and a team of kitchen lackeys.

a recipe idea

Tea-smoked haddock
with galingale

This medieval recipe was originally made with freshwater eels. I've adapted it so anyone can now make it at home – no cauldron necessary!

Serves 4

Ingredients
60ml vermouth or sherry
finely grated zest of ½ a lemon
60ml water
2 tsp sugar
1 tsp salt
5cm section of sweet galingale rhizome, sliced into
 fine matchsticks
4 medium haddock fillets
2 tbsp olive oil
a small handful of rocket leaves
2 calamondin (or regular) limes, sliced into wedges

For the smoking mixture
100g rice
110g brown sugar
3 tbsp of chamomile or jasmine tea (just rip open 3 tea bags)

Mix the vermouth, lemon zest, water, sugar, salt and sweet galingale in a shallow bowl. Add the haddock and spoon the marinade over the fish. Cover and leave to marinate in the refrigerator for at least an hour, but preferably overnight.

Cut off a length of extra-wide kitchen foil (about twice as long as it is wide) and use this to line the base of a large wok. Mix the smoking ingredients together and scatter them over the base of the wok.

Place a bamboo steamer (or small wire rack) on top of the smoking mix, arrange the haddock on top of the steamer and spoon over the marinade. The fish and the smoking mix should not be touching. Gather up the ends of the foil to form a tightly sealed parcel, folding over the edges and crimping them closed with your fingers to stop the smoke you are about to generate from escaping and place the lid on the wok. You have created a miniature oven and smokehouse.

Now set the wok on a high heat for 5 minutes. This will cause the smoking mix to char a little. Lower the heat and leave to cook for a further 5 minutes or until the fish is cooked right through. Serve scattered with the olive oil, rocket and lime wedges.

Sumac *Rhus typhina, R. glabra*

The Moroccan spice that grows on a common British garden tree

Known to foodies as 'sumac', the deep red Arabic spice with a tart, lemony richness, and to gardeners as 'sumach', the small common garden tree with spectacular crimson autumn colour, it seems that despite their virtually identical names no one in the UK knows these are really one and the same thing. Also known as: Stag's horn sumach, smooth sumach, sumaq.

Growing

These small trees need full sun and a rich well-drained soil in a sheltered location to thrive. Water them in well when newly planted, but once these ultra low-maintenance specimens are established they should be able to fend for themselves.

Varieties to try

Although the authentic sumac used in the Middle East is the southern European *Rhus coriaria*, the far more commonly available North American species *R. glabra* and *R. typhina* look and taste virtually identical and can be picked up in any garden centre.

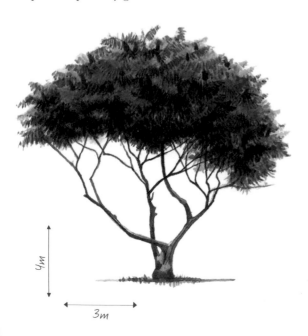

Harvesting & eating

The berries appear on fuzzy 'cones' in late August and can be harvested by simply snipping them off as soon as they are fully red. Autumn rains can wash out the water-soluble compounds that give them their characteristic flavour and colour, however, so don't be tempted to leave them on all winter. Try to avoid getting the milky sap on your skin when harvesting as this can cause irritation for those of you with sensitive skin.

Hung up in a cool, airy place to dry for a few days, the cones will keep fresh for up to a year. You can either strip off all the tasty fuzz in one go and store it in a glass jar or simply pick it off the dried cones as and when you need it.

In Middle Eastern cooking, sumac is treated rather like lemon juice, vinegar or tamarind to add a bright, fresh zing to all sorts of pilafs, tagines, salads and grilled meats. Its tartness is largely provided by ascorbic acid, a powerful antioxidant otherwise known as vitamin C. Sumac also adds a tangy bite to herb blends like the oh-so-trendy za'atar which is made from grinding dried sumac with equal quantities of oregano, ground cumin, toasted sesame seeds and a little sea salt. Extremely good sprinkled over a couscous salad.

Try sumac mixed with some sea salt and rubbed over a whole chicken just before roasting, sprinkled over hummus with a drizzle of olive oil or as seasoning for pretty much anything that needs a fresh zingy lift. I find it works best used raw and added at the end of cooking (roast chicken being my one exception) as I think this spice can lose a lot of its edge or fragrance when cooked. You can even use sumac to make a pink 'lemonless lemonade' by soaking two cones in a litre of cold water overnight and sweetening to taste.

Eucalyptus *Eucalyptus spp.*

Outback flavour from your backyard.

Anyone who has tried cooking with whole eucalyptus leaves will know just how rich, complex and unrecognisably different these are to the super-concentrated essential oil that is added to menthol-laced flu remedies. Combining the foresty herbal scent of the Australian bush with warm, toffee-like notes to create a sweet, woodsy flavour, the aroma will work its magic on anything from crisp roast pork to cocktails with a twist. Also known as gum tree.

Growing

Here's how to get your gum tree off to a good start:

• Go for young plants less than 1m tall as larger ones hate being transplanted and can result in stunted, unstable trees.

• Eucalyptus thrives in fast-draining soil in a sunny location that is sheltered from cold, drying winds. As with all larger trees, don't plant them within 5m of your house because their roots can damage building foundations.

• Keep young plants well watered while establishing, but don't worry about staking as eucalyptus develops far stronger root systems if grown unaided.

Growing rapidly to form enormous trees when left to their own devices – a 1m sapling planted out in spring can turn into a 2.5m mini tree by that very same autumn, and a towering specimen within just five years – eucalyptus has the interesting habit of popping back up from the base when hacked right down to the ground. This evolutionary adaptation to survive rampant bush fires means that these jungle giants can be grown in even small urban gardens if chopped back down to ground level each spring to control their size.

Varieties to try

There is a broad range of varieties that are perfectly hardy in the UK. My favourites are: *Eucalyptus dalrympleana*, with its bronze new foliage; *E. gunnii*, for its peeling brown and white bark; *E. pauciflora* subsp. *niphophila*, a dwarf variety with red tips and a stature perfect for small gardens; and *E. citriodora*, a fantastically lemon-scented species, which has a zingy, sherbet flavour that almost fizzes on your tongue and will, however, need to be grown in a pot and brought under cover in winter.

Harvesting & eating

To harvest, it is as simple as pulling or snipping off a couple of the mature, sickle-shaped leaves from each branch. Eucalyptus can be persuaded to impart its unique flavour in a number of ways, from infusing the leaves into cooking liquid to smoking food in the charred foliage (just stick a few handfuls of twigs over the coals at your next barbecue). You can even rub the leaves directly onto hot slices of toast as you would with garlic on bruschetta – amazing with a rich, spiced pâté.

Perhaps the most versatile way to extract the tree's woodsy sweetness is by adding the leaves whole (just as you would bay leaves) to hot milk, stock, syrup or oil. Leaves simmered in double cream with a generous pinch of homegrown saffron make a fantastic base for a rich, exotic ice cream, even better studded with handfuls of chopped pistachios. Like saffron, eucalyptus also works surprisingly well in cocktails – just whizz a few leaves up with sugar syrup in a blender, strain and shake with gin, lemon juice (to taste) and plenty of crushed ice. Bubbling away in an otherwise rather boring fruit jam, they add an instant hint of wild outback fragrance, transforming plain blueberry, grape or blackcurrant into a thing altogether more faraway and exciting.

3m

25m

8m

Saffron *Crocus sativus*

Turn the walk onto your patio into your very own spice route

Far and away the world's most expensive spice, saffron is literally worth its weight in gold – yet it's as easy to grow as a regular 'park lawn' crocus to which it is closely related. Saffron also has the added benefit of flowering in the dark days of October when little else dare raise its head, and if you need further convincing, a patch the size of your average dining table will provide you with more saffron than the average family could ever eat.

Growing

Despite conjuring up exotic images of Iran and North Africa, saffron is deceptively hardy and will shrug off the coldest winter in somewhere as unexotic as Saffron Walden in Essex, where the plant was grown for over 500 years for its fragrant stigmas (hence the town's name).

The corms are available from a range of good garden centres and online catalogues in late summer and are best planted straight away. Make sure to choose the largest bulbs you can. To start your own mini plantation:

• Plant the corms (pointy end up) in July and August, spaced about 10cm apart in free-draining soil in a bright, sunny site and water in well. For a natural look, plant them in loose groupings of three, as part of a large drift.

• Digging in extra sand or grit and a good few handfuls of compost into the planting area will really pay dividends, particularly if your plot has a heavy soil.

• A quick dusting of black pepper or chilli powder sprinkled in and around the planting area should deter raiding grey squirrels – the only real pest you might encounter. They love nothing better than snacking on the corms.

• You should see blooms in as little as eight weeks, with the number of flowers – and of course therefore your harvest – increasing year on year for at least the next five to ten years. Simple as that!

Harvesting & eating

To harvest saffron all you need to do is pick the long floppy stigmas (bright red saffron threads) out of the centre of each flower with a pair of tweezers, being careful to avoid the shorter, orange, upright stamens and purple petals. This way you won't ruin your display by ripping off the whole flower head as done in commercial harvesting. Sandwich the fresh threads between two pieces of kitchen roll and place on a hot radiator for a day or two to dry them out. Then transfer to an airtight jar, where they will keep for a good few years.

Saffron contains a hefty dose of antioxidant chemicals, including crocins and safranal, which apart from being of great nutritional value also have demonstrated antidepressant and mood-enhancing effects. At the right dosage, these can give you a mild (and entirely legal) psychoactive buzz. Okay, so you won't exactly be seeing pink elephants dancing across your ceiling – but you should notice a genuine mild giggly 'lift' for up to 30 minutes.

To get the most out of its 'side effects', forget the paella and try a saffron Martini – alcohol being the most potent solvent to extract these constituents most efficiently. To make this concoction, simply add a couple teaspoons of saffron threads along with five cardamom pods to a 350ml bottle of vodka. Leave it for a week. In a cocktail mixer, shake together a shot of vermouth, two shots of your flavoured vodka, a squeeze of lime and a splash of maple syrup and voila, you have the most giggle-inducing Martini known to man.

10cm

A deadly doppelgänger!

It's important to be 100 per cent sure that the corms you are buying are those of saffron crocus (*Crocus sativus*) as there are many lookalikes (including a plant confusingly named 'Meadow Saffron') that are toxic. Look for the Latin name *Crocus sativus* on the packet, which should also specify clearly that this is the edible saffron species. If in any doubt, do not buy. However, all reputable suppliers will make it very clear which are safe to eat and which are not.

***Deadly: Colchicum* spp**. (i.e. meadow saffron) Notice the lack of leaves, multiple flowers per plant, and no bright red saffron threads in the flowers or leaves.

Delicious: Crocus sativus Three distinct red saffron threads present in each flower, one flower per plant and many grass-like leaves.

Colchicum spp.

Crocus sativus

15 cm

15 cm

Sichuan peppercorns

Zanthoxylum simulans

Delicious tongue-numbing pods that grow on blizzard-proof trees

The flowery pink pods of these Himalayan 'peppercorns' are possibly the most exotic spice that can be grown in the UK. Closely related to citrus with a flavour that blends orange peel, chilli and eucalyptus, its minty orange flavoured leaves in my view, taste even better than the berries themselves. Also known as: flower pepper, Chinese prickly ash, *sansho, hua jiao*.

Growing

Despite their exotic flavour Sichuan peppercorns are very easy to grow in the UK and their high-mountain origins make them hardy enough to fend off even the most bitter, northerly winter. Simply plant them in full sun or partial shade in rich well-drained soil and water in well while establishing. They are happy grown in a large pot or in rather deep shade. For a neater, more statuesque tree, trim the lower branches – reducing the risk of anyone being snagged by the occasional thorn. Apart from avoiding these rather vicious thorns, you really will have to do very little else.

In saying that, there is one catch. Although these shrubs are relatively easy to find, they are rather pricey. But, on the other hand, their stunning scent, bewitching flavour and beautiful flowers and fruit make the £20–£30 investment more than worth your while.

Varieties to try

There are quite a few species to choose from, each with its own unique flavour. For me, the best option is *Zanthoxylum simulans*. This self-fertile species is quite happy to pollinate itself so you only need one plant to generate a huge harvest of peppercorns, unlike *Z. piperitum* and *Z. schnifolium*, which need to be planted in groups to achieve the same result.

Harvesting & eating

Once the shrubs get to about 2m high, they will produce a huge, annual crop of bright red berries in late summer and early autumn.

Once the berries start to split, revealing their little black (rather tasteless) seeds and giving the opened aromatic fruit a flower-like appearance, they are ready to pick. All you need to do is simply snip off the berries and dry them off on a sunny windowsill for a few days. Store the berries in an airtight jar, where they will keep for well over a year.

Even the tiniest shrub will offer up handfuls of tangy leaves ready for being chucked straight in your frying pan. The leaves are at their tenderest and least fibrous in spring and early summer – just be careful to trim off any thorns! The leaves can be used just like bay or curry leaves.

In the kitchen, Sichuan peppercorns differ from regular peppercorns because generally they are added only towards the very end of cooking. This is because prolonged heat can diminish their complex flavour. I love rubbing crushed Sichuan peppercorns into a steak just before searing it or adding them to a honey-sweet sticky marinade for barbecued pork ribs or chicken wings (see *A recipe idea*, page 176). Try throwing the leaves and peppercorns into any stir-fry or stew for an instant flavour uplift or simply add the dried peppercorns to your peppermill as a homegrown pepper alternative.

Tip: The edible leaves and young shoots are known in Japan as *kinome* and are scattered whole or finely minced over all manner of seafood dishes, but most famously over hot bamboo-shoot dishes.

2-4m

2.5m

Honey Sichuan chicken wings

Combining the piquant kick of both Sichuan peppercorn leaves and pods, these sticky sweet wings were my favourite childhood treat.

Serves 6

Ingredients
4 tbsp Chinese rice wine
2 tbsp light soy sauce
½ tsp salt
1kg chicken wings
2 egg whites
6 tbsp cornflour
500ml vegetable oil (for deep-frying)
1 tbsp Sichuan peppercorns
7 cloves of garlic, finely sliced
2cm piece of ginger, grated
6 spring onions, finely sliced
8 whole dried chillies
8 tbsp light soy sauce
4 tbsp runny honey
10 Sichuan pepper leaves
4 tbsp toasted sesame seeds

Make the marinade by combining the rice wine, soy sauce, salt and chicken wings in a small bowl. Leave to chill in the refrigerator for at least 30 minutes or preferably overnight.

Whisk the egg whites and cornflour together in a separate bowl until smooth and pour this mix over the chicken. Stir to create a roughly even and thick coating on the chicken.

Heat the oil in a wok or large pan until smoking. Deep-fry the chicken for about 10 minutes or so until crisp and golden brown. Remove the chicken with a slotted spoon, drain well on a paper towel and set aside.

Lightly bruise the Sichuan peppercorns by crunching them with a pestle or rolling pin and dry-fry in a pan for a couple of minutes so that they just begin to release their aroma.

Pour 2 tablespoons of the leftover deep-frying oil into a wok along with the garlic, ginger, spring onions and dried chillies, and stir-fry over a medium heat for about 5–10 minutes until the spring onions start to wilt.

Add the chicken to the pan and give it a good stir for 1 minute. Finally add the soy sauce, honey, Sichuan pepper leaves and sesame seeds, and stir until thoroughly combined and heated through. Serve with steaming hot white rice.

Tasmanian mountain pepper

Tasmannia lanceolata (aka Drimys lanceolata)

Two exotic spices that grow on a single super-hardy plant

With berries that taste like a strange fusion of black pepper and blueberries and leaves that somehow blend wasabi and bay leaf, this plant has some serious 'Willy Wonka' appeal. Used for centuries by the Australian Aborigines, Tasmanian mountain pepper is now a seriously trendy new bush food down under. Lush evergreen leaves, fluorescent pink stems and frothy white blossom make this exotic spice a true horticultural multitasker that looks just as good as it tastes. Also known as: bush pepper, pepperberry, mountain pepper.

Growing

Hailing from the cool, damp forests of Tasmania, the plant is surprisingly hardy in the UK, withstanding temperatures as low as −15°C. Mine have certainly pulled through several subarctic winters without so much as a discoloured leaf.

It strikes very easily from both cuttings and seeds (as long as they are planted quite fresh), but for instant impacts mature plants are also available relatively cheaply from the ornamental section in most good garden centres. Here are my tips:

• Plant in a sunny site in rich, well-drained soil. Tasmanian mountain pepper will also tolerate a fair amount of shade and even remain happy in a pot on the patio for years – great news for city gardeners.

• If you want berries, you need to plant several bushes together as the species needs both a male and female to bear fruit. However, if your space is at a premium, don't worry as one plant will produce more than enough leaves to keep even the most insatiable pepper-fiend happy.

Harvesting & eating

The evergreen leaves can be harvested all year round, with the pepper berries dotting female plants in early autumn. Both can be dried (place them on a piece of kitchen towel on a radiator for a few days) and used as an exotic, fruity substitute for black pepper.

Strangely, the flavours do not arrive all at once, but in successive waves – with the fruit tasting at first sweet and blueberry-like, only to then hit you with a wave of pungent spice. I love using the leaves exactly as you would with bay leaves, having all of bay's fragrance but with an extra spicy dimension.

Trendy Aussies use it in everything from brewing fancy-flavoured beers to chocolates, curries, scented liqueurs, fish, cheese and fiery fruit salads. The adventurous Japanese have even started using the deep purple, antioxidant-rich fruit to make a beetroot-red wasabi. After a list like that anything is possible, so go on, give it a go!

2m

2m

2m

Tasmanian mountain pepper & macadamia-crusted beef

Blending both the fruity spice of Tasmanian mountain pepper berries with the herbal fragrance of the leaves from the same plant, here is quite possibly the best steak recipe ever – if I do say so myself.

Serves 4

Ingredients
½ tsp Tasmanian mountain pepper berries, dried
1 tbsp Tasmanian mountain pepper leaves, dried
20g roasted macadamias, finely chopped
sea salt
600g beef fillet or sirloin steaks
2 tbsp olive oil or coconut oil
a small handful of rocket leaves

For the peach salsa
1–2 peaches, plums or nectarines, stoned and sliced
½ a red onion, finely sliced
2 tbsp balsamic vinegar
1 tbsp lemon juice
100ml extra virgin olive oil

Start by grinding the dried Tasmanian pepper berries and leaves in a pestle and mortar until you have a fine powder. Mix in the chopped macadamias and sea salt to form coarse crumbs. Firmly press the mix over each steak, coating them evenly.

Heat a large grill pan and pour in the oil. Once the oil begins to smoke, pop your steak in the grill pan, frying for 2–3 minutes on each side. Take off the heat and allow the steak to stand for a couple of minutes before slicing into strips.

To make the salsa, toss the peaches, red onion, balsamic vinegar, lemon juice and extra virgin olive oil together and serve alongside the steak with some rocket leaves.

Wasabi *Wasabia japonica*

Japanese green horseradish worth more than £125 per kilo

Wasabi fans, I want to let you in on a little secret: probably as much as 95 per cent of 'wasabi' products in the West actually contain little or no wasabi at all – just a counterfeit blend of horseradish, mustard, artificial sweeteners and food colouring. In fact, genuine wasabi (the root of which sell for over £125 per kilo) loses nearly all its flavour within 24 hours of being grated. So, sushi fans, if you want to get your hands on the real thing you'll have to grow it yourself! Also known as Japanese horseradish.

Growing

Wasabi plants can't stand the sunshine, preferring cool, wet, overcast climates – making them perfectly at home in old Blighty, particularly in our mild, moist western regions.

Here are my tips for success:

• Plant out small plants (half a dozen is plenty) in a shady spot at anytime between early spring and early autumn, covering the area in a thick mulch of organic matter. Spread a layer of sharp sand or gravel around the base of the plants to help deter their only real pests, slugs and snails.

• Wasabi needs a moist, humid position to thrive. You're basically after a boggy patch of ground rich in organic matter, though a few pots of aquatic compost sitting in a large tray of water, regularly topped up, will do just fine.

• They need loads of shade throughout the summer, as too much sun will result in their leaves wilting and quickly· turning yellow. Soggy, overshadowed plots are ideal. Check your garden for patches where moss or little ferns have sprung up and you will have found a perfect spot.

• Although hardy, wasabi grows most rapidly in spring and autumn when temperatures are between 7–18°C, so to prolong their growing season cover the plants in a thin layer of horticultural fleece through winter. I like to plant them under a canopy of evergreen trees, which will shade out the hot summer sun, and trap warm air around them in winter.

Harvesting & eating

Although frequently called the 'root', the edible part of wasabi is its partially buried stem, which take about 18–24 months to reach full size and flavour. This may be a bit of a wait at first, but the plants will soon start to develop small offshoots from their bases, meaning that an established clump will provide you with a succession of 'roots' for years to come. Harvest these when they reach about 10–15cm long and 1–2cm wide, remembering that a good 5cm of this may well be below ground. While you wait, the plants will offer up masses of beautiful lily-pad-shaped edible leaves with a wasabi tang that make the perfect wrapping for sushi – simply folded over a piece of raw (or smoked) salmon, slice of pickled ginger and an optional smear of cream cheese.

Wasabi is traditionally grated fresh at the table, as its rich, complex flavour components are highly volatile, degrading within just a few hours of being grated. The intact root however, will keep in the fridge for up to 30 days, and the dried root will last for several months.

The key difference between genuine wasabi and its many imitations is a far more complex, rounded flavour and a fresh, sweet aftertaste. It works surprisingly well in salad dressings, marinades for grilled chicken or fish, whisked into homemade mayonnaise or stirred into herby mashed potatoes. If you fancy getting a little more adventurous tip a tablespoon of grated root into a bottle of vodka for a really spectacular Bloody Mary, stir it into a mango or gooseberry jam or even fold it into vanilla ice cream (a surprisingly popular flavour in Japan).

20cm

30cm

30cm

Thai basil *Ocimum basilicum var. thyrsiflora*

Succumb to the sweet, liquorice bootlace-scented basil

Perhaps it is purely due to geography, but I really can't understand how every corner supermarket is stacked with pots of fresh Italian basil while its exotic Siamese cousin languishes in foodie obscurity. It's just as easy to grow, much prettier, with burgundy stems and pink flowers, and has a far more interesting anise-like flavour. Give this a go in your next pesto and you will never look back! Also known as Thai sweet basil.

Growing

Thai basil is an extremely close cousin of the regular kind and can really be grown in pretty much the same way:

• Sow the seeds indoors in early May on a sunny windowsill and grow them on until they get to about 15cm high in mid-June before planting outside. Although most mainstream advice says to start them off far earlier in the year, I find that sowing in these warmer, sunnier months means that plants establish far better, soon catching up on any missed time to produce larger, lusher plants.

• Choose the brightest, sunniest outdoor spot, as their flavour will be infinitely more intense the higher the UV index.

• Dig plenty of grit into the soil to allow a sharp drainage, keep well watered and get cooking!

Harvesting & eating

Thai basil is so widely used in South-East Asian cooking meaning you can scatter it over any Thai, Vietnamese, Burmese or Malaysian dish and it will work perfectly. Stuff the leaves into summer rolls, toss them into fresh coconut and peanut salads or steep them in a spicy noodle broth or tamarind laksa (fellow Malaysians, I know this isn't exactly traditional, but boy is it good).

The only rule here is to enjoy the leaves raw or add them right at the end of cooking time, as they lose their unique aromatic properties with prolonged cooking – anything over a five-minute blanching is sacrilege. Of course, there is no reason why you should let their origins be a culinary barrier, as Thai basil works in any dish that its plainer Italian cousin does, adding sweet, aniseed notes to homemade pesto, cannelloni or spaghetti Bolognese.

20cm

30cm

30cm

Japanese beefsteak plant *Perilla frutescens*

Giant multicoloured 'nettle' with a flavour that lives up to its name

Already a hugely popular bedding plant for its frilly, colourful foliage, it's a surprise that so few people in the UK know that the leaves are also edible, especially considering how much a tiny packet sells for in fancy Japanese grocers. Scatter a few of these plants through your flower border for a savoury, spicy ingredient that will happily sit incognito amongst the herbaceous perennials. Also known as *shiso*, perilla, Chinese basil, purple mint.

Growing

If you can grow basil (those designed-to-fail supermarket pots don't count) you can grow Japanese beefsteak plant – they are after all in the same family. To get started, simply:

• Buy small pots from the herb (or bedding plant) section of your local garden centre in spring or sow a pack of seeds on your windowsill between late March and May.

• Plant them out after all risk of frost has passed. Being annuals, these plants will only last until the first frosts, but if you let them self-seed, a new generation of young plants will often pop up in the footprints of last year's crop.

• Choose a site with full sun and rich, well-drained soil.

• Situate towards the back of your border so the plants don't shade out its more diminutive residents (these plants will grow tall).

• Pick off any flower buds that appear throughout the summer, to divert the plant's energy into producing the maximum amount of leaves. However, from September onwards you can give these poor things a little respite, and allow them to set seed, sowing themselves freely in the soil.

1–1.5m

40cm

30cm

Harvesting & eating

To harvest, simply snip the leaves off with your secateurs. Culinarily, there are three key types of Japanese beefsteak plant, neatly grouped by colour: green, purple and a two-tone variety whose leaves have a mossy green topside, flushed with burgundy undersides.

The green variety is the most favoured in Japan and is used to flavour all manner of sushi, soups and rice dishes. In Korea, the whole leaves of the green variety are pickled in sweetened rice wine vinegar with sliced chillies and served with all manner of grilled beef and seafood dishes, and being more laissez-faire than the Japanese, the Koreans prize the two-toned and purple versions just as much.

The darkest, deepest burgundy variety has a colour so intense that it is also used to make a fluorescent pink, cumin-flavoured food dye (see 'Nature's E-numbers', page 209). In Japan, the seeds are sprouted to produce a maroon-coloured cress called *hojisu*, which is used to garnish an array of noodle, seafood and egg dishes, adding a rich and almost meaty savoury flavour.

a recipe idea

Mixed vegetable tempura with cinnamon salt

Encased in crisp tempura batter, this is a satisfying treat. I use sweet potatoes and figs but peppers, mushrooms and aubergines will work brilliantly too.

Serves 4

Ingredients

For the dipping sauce
2 tbsp Japanese soy sauce
1cm piece of fresh ginger, finely grated
finely grated zest of ½ an orange
½ tsp Sichuan peppercorns
small pinch of ground chilli
15ml mirin

For the tempura
¼ tsp ground cinnamon
¼ tsp salt vegetable oil, for deep-frying
125ml sesame oil, for deep-frying
1 egg
300ml ice cold soda water
75g plain white flour
75g cornflour
½ tsp bicarbonate of soda
a selection of vegetables, sliced
10 Japanese beefsteak plant leaves

Make the dipping sauce in a small saucepan by heating the soy sauce, ginger, orange zest, Sichuan peppercorns, chilli and mirin over a low heat and gently simmering for 5 minutes. Set aside to cool.

In a small bowl mix together the ground cinnamon and sea salt (this is your cinnamon salt). Set aside. Half-fill a large saucepan or wok with vegetable oil and sesame oil and heat to 180°C or until the oil begins to smoke.

Once the oil is ready, prepare the batter as this needs to be done just before frying to ensure you end up with crispy rather than soggy tempura. Whisk the egg and soda water in a bowl (the cold water ensures the batter does not absorb too much oil, while the bubbles in the soda gives it lightness). Now add both the flours and the bicarbonate of soda and mix quickly to create a lumpy batter – if your mixture looks like air bubbles with small pockets of flour you are on the right track.

Dip your vegetables one by one (saving the Japanese beefsteak plant leaves aside to fry last) into the batter and fry in the hot oil. Only fry a few pieces at a time so they don't overcrowd. Fry for 1–2 minutes or until crisp and golden. Serve with a sprinkling of cinnamon salt and the dipping sauce.

Peruvian mint marigold *Tagetes minuta*

A marijuana lookalike with a minty, tropical fruit flavour

Guaranteed to raise a few horticultural eye-brows, these tall, leafy plants look, at least from a distance, very similar to a prize clump of marijuana. However, if you can keep ma-rauding teenagers away, these fantastically easy-to-grow South American plants will not only provide you with a limitless supply of powerfully scented, tropical fruit flavoured leaves, but will even act as a natural pes-ticide. All these aspects combined make Peruvian mint marigold far more exciting than its illicit lookalikes. Also known as: *huacatay*, black mint, stinking Roger.

Growing

These plants are actually just a regular garden marigold that has swapped its blousy golden flowers for a towering leafy stature, and are just as easy to grow. Here's all you need to know to get started:

• Sow the seeds in April indoors on a sunny windowsill in a tray (or pot) of gritty compost, spacing them about 2cm apart.

• When the little seedlings have between four to five true leaves, they can be transplanted into their own little pots, ready to be planted out in their final position at the end of May.

• These half-hardy annuals are unfussy as long as they are given plenty of sunshine but will be happiest in well-drained soil to mimic the dry Meditteranean-style climate of their Latin American home.

The aromatic chemicals responsible for the plant's flavour evolved as a natural pesticide and helps to deter everything from eelworms to whitefly. As this fragrant protection is also conferred to neighbouring crops, Peruvian mint marigolds are perfect bedfellows for susceptible plants like tomatoes.

Varieties to try

If you really can't do without the big, blousy blooms, I would go for the following species:

• *Tagetes tenuifolia* – ubiquitous and more manageable in size, it erupts in a stream of tangerine blooms on 30cm-high plants from early summer to the first frosts. The leaves have a flavour similar to those of *T. minuta*.

• *T. lucida* – a Mexican species, which has a rich tarragon-like flavour and golden flowers that are highly esteemed in many 'south of the border' dishes.

Harvesting & eating

To harvest Peruvian mint marigold, simply snip off the soft, ferny leaves about 10cm from the growing tips. You want fully opened leaves that are still quite young and not yet fibrous.

> **Tip:** When harvesting the leaves on hot days, be careful to wash off any sap that gets on your skin as this can cause photodermatitis in people with sensitive skin.

Widely used in Ecuadorian, Peruvian and Bolivian dishes, the knockout fragrance of this plant mixes tropical fruit with a zesty grapefruit and vibrant peppermint. Used in higher quantities this evolves into a distinct coriander-basil aroma, creating a totally bewildering fruit salad of flavour in just one leaf. I love chopping small quantities of Peruvian mint marigold extremely finely – a little goes a long way – and sprinkling over a tropical fruit salad with a twist of lime and sugar. They add an exotic touch to a simple red onion and peach salsa served with grilled fish or chicken. For a modern take on a retro favourite, mix the finely chopped leaves with orange zest and powdered ginger to make a delicious citrusy herb butter. Alternatively, add a couple of bruised leaves to a boozy fruit punch for a flavour one of my mates described as 'Rio carnival on a leaf'.

2cm

30cm

2m

Manuka *Leptospermum scoparium*

All the flavour of the New Zealand Bush in a pretty garden shrub

Mainly known in the UK for its delicious (albeit scandalously expensive) honey, the eucalyptus, mint and honey-flavoured leaves of these New Zealand Bush natives add a lingering foresty note to all manner of dishes. It's also pretty easy on the eye, with blossom in shades of white, pink or red that's like catnip to butterflies and bees – hence the honey. Also known as New Zealand tea tree.

Growing

If you want to fill the air in your garden with manuka's honey-like fragrance, all you need to do is:

• Spoil these fast-growing, subtropical plants by giving them the warmest, sunniest spot you have available, preferably against a south-facing wall.

• Although these shrubs are reputedly hardy in all but the coldest areas in Britain, it might be worth draping them in a couple of layers of horticultural fleece if a particularly cold snap is predicted.

• Provide very well-drained soil, adding plenty of horticultural sand or grit to the mix and keep well watered while establishing.

If you follow the above rules, they will form fantastically low maintenance, drought -tolerant

shrubs that will last up to 20 years with very little intervention from you.

Varieties to try

If you don't have much space to play with, there is a stunning dwarf variety with dark-purplish-green leaves and dark-eyed, crimson flowers that won't grow more than knee high called 'Nichollsii Nanum'.

Harvesting & eating

Throughout the summer, you can snip off the long leafy twigs found at the end of each branch. If you hang them up to dry in a cool, dark place they will keep their fragrance for well over a year.

Prized for its anti-bacterial and anti-fungal properties, manuka honey sells for a fortune in health-food stores all over the world. However, even if you don't have the luxury of your own beehive, you can still create a convincing counterfeit version with much of the same medicinal properties. Simply tip a plain jar of honey into a saucepan and heat it gently until it is about the temperature of hot bathwater (test with your finger). Pour this warmed honey back into its original jar with a few large sprigs of manuka, leave for a week or so in a cool, dry place and few people will be able to tell the difference between your version and the shop-bought alternative.

Manuka leaves also make a warming tea with a comforting camphor-like lift. Simply wash and then bruise the leaves slightly by scrunching them in the palm of your hand. Drop them into a mug of hot water and you have a cold-busting hot drink. Try manuka leaves infused in syrup over desserts. Just add great handfuls of the leaves to simmering sugar syrup, strain and spoon this over a fresh fruit salad, fold into a peach or orange sorbet, or add to blueberry or blackcurrant jam for a fragrant tang.

1.2m

50cm

2m

Meadowsweet *Filipendula ulmaria*

Plumes of almond-flavoured flowers with the power to relieve pain

A native wild flower that's foolproof to grow, beautiful to look at, tastes exquisite and even has the power to relieve pain – what more could you ask for? As the original source of aspirin, the frothy white plumes of meadowsweet combine the marzipan-like flavour of almonds with a fragrant hint of elderflower, backed up with a hefty dose of pain-relieving chemicals.

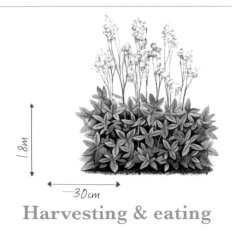

1.8m

30cm

Growing

One of the best things about growing native edibles is that they are guaranteed to be perfectly adapted to our climate and, given the right conditions, will happily take care of themselves – even spreading out naturally to colonise your beds and borders. All these plants need is:

• Full sun, a fertile soil rich in organic matter and lashings of regular watering.

• They're perfect for damp ditches and even the boggy margins of your pond – just make sure you don't fall in amid a harvesting frenzy.

Harvesting & eating

The frothy flowers emerge from early summer and will continue for far longer if you keep on top of watering and pick them regularly – a great excuse to knock up a good couple of batches of sweet treats. Almost anything that works with a dash of almond essence or swirl of elderflower cordial will make an ideal culinary bedfellow for meadowsweet. Simmer a dozen of the blossoms in half a litre of hot cream for an absolutely blinding panna cotta.

Stewed in a simple fruit compote or homemade jam, like gooseberry or cherry, meadowsweet adds a fleeting floral uplift – making it equally incredible soaked in white wine with sliced strawberries for a lazy patio drink on a warm summer's night. One of my all-time favourite ways to use meadowsweet is in a granita. Simply simmer the flowers with peaches and plenty of sugar and press the mixture through a sieve. Pop this fragrant purée into the freezer, scraping the icy crystals with a fork after three hours or so to create a fluffy pain-relieving granita so fresh and delicious you will almost wish for a headache to come on!

Allergy note: Because the substances found in meadowsweet are chemically very similar to aspirin, lay off them if you are pregnant, breastfeeding or allergic to aspirin or related painkillers. It is also not a good idea to feed it to kids under 12, meaning all the more for you …

30cm

Vanilla grass *Pandanus amaryllifolius*

Emerald-green 'vanilla' extract you can grow in your living room

Unless you have access to a giant Kew Gardens-style glasshouse, growing real vanilla orchids for their pods is nearly impossible in this country. Good news then that the strappy green leaves of vanilla grass are easy house guests and will provide you with a fresh supply of custardy, vanilla-scented extract to transform even the most plain sponge cake into a cloud of heavenly deliciousness. Also known as: pandan, pandanus, screwpine leaves.

Growing

Native to the steamy rainforests of South-East Asia, there is only one golden rule for growing vanilla grass – keep it indoors. Unlike many houseplants, this jungle species needs constant chill-free conditions to be happy, so won't even enjoy a brief holiday on your patio over summer. Don't let this scare you though – the temperature of your average living room (18–20°C) is absolutely fine.

To get vanilla grass off to a good start:

- Give these little guys a bright, warm home on a sunny windowsill (a steamy bathroom would be perfect).

- Keep them well watered with a dilute ericaceous fertiliser throughout the summer and a roomy pot of rich compost, and you're all set.

- An occasional mist of water from a spray gun a couple of times a week will ensure a healthy rosette of leaves all year round.

As the plants get larger, they will produce little suckers at the base, each one a tiny botanical 'mini-me'. Once these get to about 10cm high, they can be gently prized away from the parent and potted up in new containers of fresh compost to increase your stock for free. These incidentally make great gifts for any other like-minded plant geeks with an incorrigible sweet tooth.

Harvesting & eating

All you need to do to get harvesting is snip off the largest, longest leaves at the base of the plant (the older the leaf, the more intense the flavour). The easiest way to extract vanilla grass's flavour is to make a food-mile free 'vanilla essence', as in the recipe on page 193. Although still largely unknown in the UK, vanilla grass is a standard dessert flavour in South-East Asia and is found in everything from ice cream to coconut rice pudding, and it's far more popular and delicious than the dried-up, black-podded form. Vanilla grass will colour any food it's stirred into a pale, jade green and infuse it with a faint fragrance of freshly mown grass. A trick often used in Asia to give regular rice a more refined fragrance (like posh jasmine varieties) is to pop whole leaves of vanilla grass into rice during cooking.

Vanilla grass's sweet, creamy flavour is caused by an aromatic compound known as 2-Acetyl-1-pyrroline, which, despite a rather unfortunate name, is also responsible for the biscuity, almost-floral aroma of white bread, jasmine rice and butter cookies.

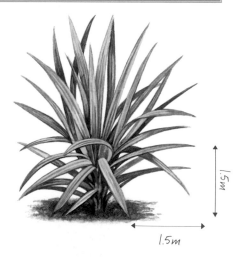

30cm

1.5m

1.5m

a recipe idea

Pistachio & coconut Swiss roll

Homemade vanilla grass essence works brilliantly in mousses, crème caramels and cakes such as this delicious treat.

Serves 6–8

Ingredients

For the vanilla grass essence
7 large vanilla grass leaves,
 washed and torn into small pieces
2 tbsp sugar
45ml vodka

For the sponge
1 tbs melted butter
4 large eggs, at room temperature
125g caster sugar, plus 2 tbsp
125g plain flour
2 tsp vanilla grass essence

For the filling
200ml double cream, whipped
100g white chocolate, chopped
 into small pieces
50g desiccated coconut
50g roasted pistachios, chopped

Preheat the oven to 190°C and line a 25 x 38cm Swiss roll tin with baking parchment. Brush the base and the sides of the tin with melted butter and dust with a little flour.

To make the vanilla grass essence, pulse the vanilla grass leaves, sugar and vodka in a food processor until the vanilla grass leaves look very finely chopped. Strain the chopped leaves through a sieve, retaining the liquid. This is your vanilla grass essence.

In a large mixing bowl, beat the eggs and sugar together until the mix is extremely light and fluffy. This may take a few minutes but the more air you can work in the lighter the resulting cake. Carefully fold in the flour and the vanilla grass essence, making sure you don't over-stir.

Pour the mixture into the prepared tin and bake for 12–15 minutes or until the centre is slightly springy to the touch and has shrunk away from the sides. While the cake is still warm, place a clean sheet of baking parchment over your work surface and sprinkle evenly with the remaining caster sugar. Flip the sponge out of the tin, on to the baking parchment, and with the shortest side facing you, lift one end of the baking parchment and carefully roll the cake. Leave to cool for 30 minutes. This step will minimise any chance of the sponge cracking once the cake has cooled.

Once the cake has cooled completely, carefully unroll and evenly spread the whipped cream on top. Sprinkle over the white chocolate, desiccated coconut and roasted pistachios. Carefully roll the whole thing up again and you're ready to slice up and serve.

Lemon verbena *Aloysia triphylla*

Semi-hardy bushes of exotic lemongrassiness

It is a huge shame for us curry-obsessed Brits that fragrant, zesty and oh-so-trendy, lemongrass is so frost-phobic. But swap it for the sherbet-scented foliage of lemon verbena and you will be rewarded with the same burst of citrus flavour *and* a beautiful bonsai-style shrub. As an added bonus, it can often stay outdoors all year round. Also known as verbene, *cedron*.

Growing

Native to areas with a dry, Mediterranean-like climate in southern Latin America, these shrubs do best if in a hot, sunny position that is sheltered from strong winds on all sides. Although lemon verbena is almost always described as tender in gardening textbooks, I have found that given a sheltered site and some winter protection, larger plants will fair perfectly well in all but the coldest regions. Here are my tips for growing:

• Pick a shrub that is at least 1m high as the more mature the plant, the stronger its cold resistance will be. Plant them against a sunny south-facing wall and dig in plenty of grit into the ground to create fast drainage. Give them a regular douse with water throughout the summer.

• Keep them well irrigated but don't let their roots sit in cold, stagnant water, particularly over winter because this will cause them to rot.

• If you don't live in a milder southern area, as winter looms drape them in a light cocoon of horticultural fleece to keep the worst of the frosts off. Alternatively, as the plants are very easy to grow in pots, just protect them from severe frosts by bringing them indoors.

• Keep pinching out the young tips to promote a dense, bushy growth and spoil them with a dilute liquid feed every fortnight throughout the summer.

• Plants take very easily from cuttings about 10–15cm long, poked into pots of gritty compost and kept well watered and shaded in summer.

Harvesting & eating

I find that the oldest leaves found at the base of the plant are the richest in scent. To harvest, simply pull them off gently with your fingers. For most of the other leaves, simply snip off the young stems at the ends of the branches. Either way, you are just seconds away from a fizzy-sherbet bounty.

Unless you've crushed one of these fresh lemon verbena leaves, it is almost impossible to explain just how zingy and intoxicating they smell, with a captivating, effervescent character. This means they can be used to replace lemongrass or lemon zest in a whole range of recipes, both sweet and savoury.

A few large sprigs of lemon verbena added whole to curries or Asian-style broths like tom yum, pho or laksa work wonderfully. Their clean, vibrant tang can also cut through rich meats like pork or duck. Try stuffing a few lemon verbena leaves into the cavity of a whole chicken and roast, or over fish prior to steaming, grilling or roasting.

The leaves can, however, be rather fibrous to eat, so whip these out prior to serving. You can even tie up the bundle of leaves with a piece of string to keep them all in one place, so they are easier to remove. Steeped in hot sugar syrup, the leaves make a delicious cordial, which can be diluted to make summer coolers, drizzled over fruit salads or even stirred into palate-cleansing sorbets.

50cm

2m

1m

Japanese hardy ginger *Zingiber mioga*

Yes, you can grow an edible ginger outdoors in the UK

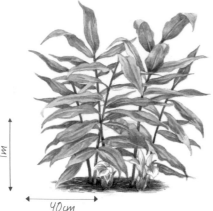

1m

40cm

In medieval Britain, ginger carried for thousands of miles atop caravans from the Far East was an expensive commodity – a sort of 13th-century equivalent of a silicon chip or jewel-encrusted watch. If only they knew about this über-hardy Japanese species that provides all the flavour with none of the fuss – offering up bumper harvests of spicy shoots and delicious, gingery pink flower buds. Also known as myoga ginger.

Growing

These Japanese forest natives originate in a habitat that's not all too dissimilar to our own British woodland, growing on the edge of the canopy in dappled sunlight, making them one of the most northerly members of the ginger family. To get growing, simply:

- Give the plants a rich, moist soil filled with as much organic matter as you can bear digging in, on a site in full sun or partial shade (they really aren't too picky either way). Spoil them with regular dousings of liquid feed throughout summer.

- To get more plants from just the one planting, uproot established clumps in early spring, divide them into smaller clusters and plant them back out into the bed, spacing them 30cm apart.

Japanese hardy ginger will grow quickly to produce large thickets in only a year or two, offering up generous harvests of young shoots and flower buds, so you only need to start with a patch of three or so young plants to provide you with more than the average family could ever eat.

Harvesting & eating

One trump card Japanese hardy ginger holds over the supermarket variety is that it produces not one but two crops a year, starting with fresh green spears in spring, giving way to a fleet of bright pink buds that emerge from beneath the ground in late summer. Both are delicious sliced and used just like regular ginger – in salads, stir-fries or simmered in curries and spicy broths.

Electric daisies *Acmella oleracea*

Edible daisies that taste like a jolt of electricity

Pop one of these unassuming little yellow flowers in your mouth and you will soon find out how it got its range of colourful common names. An initial burst of citrus tang is quickly followed by a curious, tingly sensation – like a jolt of electricity – that fills your whole mouth, ending in a mild local anesthesia that can last for up to 15 minutes. Also known as buzz buttons, toothache plant.

Growing

Native to the tropical forests of South America the plant is nevertheless incredibly easy to grow as a summer bedding plant in the UK where it is already a popular ornamental plant.

Here's how to get growing:

• Sow the plants from seeds on a bright windowsill in March or April and plant them out in a warm, sunny location in rich, well-drained soil after all risk of frost has passed (usually late May).

• Perfect for pots and tubs, the plants will grow quickly, producing 30–40cm of rich bronze, green foliage and yellow button-like flowers right through summer. Regularly keep the growing tips pinched back to promote bushy growth and treat them to a high-potash feed fortnighty to encourage flowering.

• Avoid damage from slugs and snails (the only real pests they will suffer from) by mulching the surface of the pots with sharp gravel.

Although unlikely to survive a UK winter outdoors, the plant is extremely easy to start each year from seed. Alternatively, lift it in late autumn, pot it up and treat it as a houseplant, or take several cuttings and put in pots of compost on a warm windowsill and plant these back out the following spring.

Harvesting & eating

Simply snip the button-like flowers off when they reach their full colour and remember as with almost all flower crops, the more you pick the more they will produce.

The fizzy 'space dust'-like effect of electric daisies – which some have likened to licking a 9-volt battery – is produced by the plant's high levels of a pain-relieving agent called spilanthol. This unique factor explains its traditional use in treating toothache and sore throats for centuries, as well as the current facination it attracts from experimental chefs.

For a truly quirky twist on a simple watercress and grapefruit salad, slice up a flower or two with a little red onion and sprinkle over for an effervescent tang. In Brazil, both the leaves and flowers are mixed with sliced chillies and garlic as a condiment for all sorts of dishes, from grilled fish to fried chicken to give a fizzy kick. Be careful though as a little does go a long way.

Try electric daisies in place of tabasco sauce with oysters, or instead of wasabi on sushi. Or better yet, grind up a few flowers, mix with salt and coat the rim of a margarita glass. Their fresh, sparkly flavour makes them perfect in a palate-cleansing sorbet, combined with fresh mangos and ripe red chillies.

Electric daisies' medicinal effect

Electric daisies can be used to make a pain-relieving mouthwash. Just blitz a few flowers in a blender with a shot or two of vodka, strain and add the mix to an equal quantity of water and bottle up. The electric daisies' pain-relieving agent spilanthol, also acts as a muscle relaxant, and an extract of the plant has managed to find its way into high-end face creams that claim to have a natural 'botox' effect. Ladies, form an orderly queue …

30cm

30cm

30cm

a recipe idea

Mango & electric daisy sorbet

Whether it's a tongue tingling dessert or the ultimate between-course palate cleanser, this curious 'fizzy' sorbet is guaranteed to bring a smile to your mates' faces.

Serves 4

Ingredients
3 fresh mangoes, peeled, stoned and sliced
  finely grated zest and juice of 2 limes
250g icing sugar, sifted
1 small red chilli, finely chopped, plus a little
  extra for garnishing
9 small electric daisies, finely chopped, plus
  a little extra for garnishing
flaky sea salt

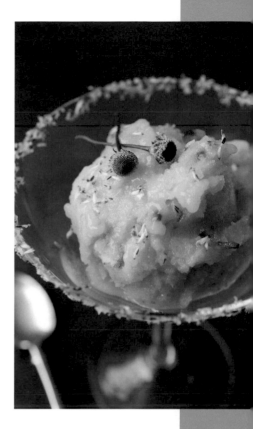

Blitz the mangoes, lime zest and juice and icing sugar in a food processor to produce a smooth purée. Pour into a Tupperware container, stir through the chillies and the electric daisies and pop in the freezer for 1 hour.

Give the mixture a quick stir with a fork once every hour until fully frozen (this will take about 4 hours). The aim is to create a fluffy slush of ice crystals rather than a solid block.

Wipe the rim of a Martini glass with a slice of lime to coat it in a thin layer of lime juice, flip it over and dip the rim into a mixture of sea salt and chopped electric daisies.

Serve the sorbet in the salt-rimmed glass and garnish with electric daisies and freshly sliced chillies.

Wintergreen _Gaultheria procumbens_

Scarlet root beer-flavoured berries on creeping evergreen plants

Prized by the Mohawks and Objiwe tribes for their delicious, effervescent flavour and pain-relieving properties, the fragrant leaves and red berries of wintergreen are the key ingredient in old-fashioned American-style root beer – originally brewed (like Coca-Cola) as a medicinal drink. Wintergreen even has the added benefit of being one of the few fruit crops that positively loves growing in shade, livening up dark corners as well as your palate.

Growing

Spreading out to form an evergreen mat of shiny green leaves, white bell-shaped flowers and aromatic scarlet berries, these easy-to-get-hold-of ornamental plants are awash in garden centres around Christmas time. Here's what you need to know:

• Native to the moist forests of eastern North America, these plants require consistently damp soil in dappled, filtered sunlight.

• Wintergreen needs an acidic growing medium to thrive, so if you have rhododendrons and camellias growing away happily in your soil you won't have to do anything but dig in a couple of spadefuls of rich organic matter.

20cm
20cm

• For those who live in an area with alkaline soil, wintergreen is best housed in a trough or raised bed, filled with ericaceous (acidic) compost.

• Water well right through the summer, preferably using rainwater if you live in a hard water area.

• Spoil your plants with a liberal scattering of chicken manure each spring to keep them romping away to create a living, root beer-scented carpet.

Harvesting & eating

Gathering wintergreen leaves could not be more straightforward, just snip off the tips of the branches with your secateurs or alternatively if it's the berries you are after just use those nifty fingers. Wintergreen's characteristic flavour and medicinal value is provided by the chemical methyl salicylate, otherwise known as oil of wintergreen. This is an antiseptic pain reliever and when applied topically, stimulates circulation to skin and muscles. Wintergreen's properties causes it to wind up in all sorts of well-known household products like toothpastes, mouthwashes, antiseptic creams and warming mentholated muscle rubs; many of which (like Germolene and Deep Heat) smell pretty much identical to how the leaves taste.

I like to add the mild-flavoured berries to fruit salads and jams or simply slice them in half, macerate in a little elderflower cordial and scatter over Greek-style yoghurt, muesli and an assortment of autumnal puddings. In the US and throughout Asia, wintergreen is immensely popular in sweets, chewing gum, cakes and of course brewed up into root beer.

Fresh leaves are very subtle in flavour but can be intensified by soaking them for a few days in water (this is caused by naturally occurring yeasts, which break the leaves down, releasing

their aromatic compounds). To do this, stuff a glass jar loosely with fresh, washed leaves and fill it up to the brim with boiled water that has first been cooled to room temperature. Cover with a loose-fitting lid and leave it in a warm place for three to five days. Simmer the liquid (leaves and all) for a few minutes and, once strained, the 'tea' can be used to flavour cakes and sweet treats. To transform this into a root beer simply add a stick of cinnamon, a teaspoon of anise seeds, a couple of cloves and the zest and juice of a lemon to 1 litre of the simmering liquid. Chill and sweeten to taste. Enterprising American chefs often reduce this down to syrup to add to everything from a glaze for a slow roasted Christmas ham

to packaged cake mixes to make 'root beer float' cupcakes. Try using red autumn and winter leaves, which will result in a lovely pink-blushed hue for your wintergreen syrup.

Allergy advice

Being chemically similar to aspirin, wintergreen's methyl-salicylate content means that I would avoid taking this if you are allergic to aspirin or any similar painkiller. Although perfectly safe to eat in the quantities suggested here, excessive consumption of the leaves is not advised because wintergreen contains compounds that can be toxic if eaten in vast amounts on a frequent basis.

Green tea *Camellia sinensis*

Bring a whole new meaning to 'English tea'

Despite the romantic images of sari-clad women gathering tea from tropical hillsides, you don't need a vast colonial estate to grow your very own morning cuppa. In fact, tea plants positively dislike high temperatures, growing best in cool, wet and slightly miserable climates – hence the reason why farms in the tropics are always high up on mountain tops with their heads buried in mists.

Growing

Native to regions of China with climates that are surprisingly similar to Cornwall or western Scotland, there were once actually wartime plans to create vast tea plantations in the UK as Churchill believed that if our supplies were ever cut off we simply couldn't have won the Second World War. Half a century later, there is now a commercial plantation in Cornwall growing the world's only truly English tea. If they and I can do it so can you!

Closely related to the common garden camellia and hardy down to about −5°C, the tea plants are definitely a viable option for outdoor growing throughout much of southern Britain and milder areas of western Scotland. Still, in colder areas, plants can be grown outdoors in pots for most of the year and then moved (only if a strong freeze is forecasted) to an unheated porch or greenhouse. To get growing, simply:

• Choose either a sunny or partially shaded site on rich, well-drained soil.

• Tea plants hate alkaline, chalk-rich soil, which causes their leaves to slowly turn yellow and drop. If you live in an area with such soil or are unsure about your soil type, plant them directly into large pots of ericaceous compost (pH4.5–7), designed for acid-loving plants. This can be boosted with the application of ericaceous liquid feeds that should quickly green up any pallid or yellowing leaves.

• To help protect your plants against the cold weather, plant against a sheltered west-facing wall and give them a quick drape in horticultural fleece during cold snaps, especially during those late spring frosts. A little hedge of these planted up against a sunny wall will work brilliantly.

• Water regularly throughout the summer.

• Propagate by cuttings – either from firm-heeled shoots in June or near-ripe shoots with a heel (a small section of woody growth) taken in September. The resulting saplings should be taken into a cold greenhouse or sat on a bright windowsill for their first winter or two before planting outside the next spring.

Harvesting & eating

The bit you are interested in here are the fresh, young growing tips; because adult leaves quickly develop a much stronger, bitter flavour. These can be harvested any time during the season – as often as once a month on healthy adult plants. It is important, however, that you harvest regularly as tea plants can grow to enormous trees over a few years if left to their own devices. In one part of China, local people have even trained monkeys to harvest the young shoots off the canopies of some particularly ancient, revered wild trees, the tea from which sells for a premium price in Beijing.

All types of tea – be it black tea (aka builders' tea), the newly trendy green tea or the highly prized white tea – come from the same plant. The only difference between them is in their processing.

White tea
For white tea, only the two smallest, youngest leaves are harvested from the very tips of new

1.25m

1.25m

growth. These are then dried to form the most expensive and antioxidant rich form of tea.

Green tea

For green tea, a more generous portion of the fresh young growth is picked off and left to wilt slightly. A similar procedure can easily be done at home by spreading the freshly picked leaves out on a baking sheet and leaving them on a windowsill for 20 minutes or so.

The wilted leaves should then be lightly bruised, causing them to oxidise (just like when a cut apple goes brown). It is this process that creates tea's characteristic flavour. At home this bruising can be done by rolling the wilted leaves gently in the palms of your hands for a

minute or two, before scattering them over the baking tray and leaving them in a warm place to oxidise for about an hour.

Then all you need to do is dry out the tea leaves to preserve them. To do this, simply bung the tray in a very low oven (100°C or lower) for an hour or two, until the leaves are just crisp to touch. Alternatively, leave it in a warm airing cupboard for a day or so.

Black tea

The preparation of black tea is a little more complicated and the process destroys many of the delicate, fresh flavours and antioxidants found in the leaves, so I would stick to the tastier and far easier green tea.

Floral-scented tea

By far the most popular type of tea in China is jasmine tea, which uses fresh jasmine flowers to scent the tea leaves, imparting a delicate floral fragrance. Industrially, these are usually blended with the tea leaves during the drying process, but at home simply popping a couple of fresh blossoms straight into the pot along with the tea leaves will give you a virtually identical result.

Here is just a small range of flowers that are traditionally used in the great Chinese tea houses.

Gardenia *Gardenia jasminoides*

There are now two exciting new hardy varieties of this delicate, tropical flower, which not only imparts a glorious scent but also has stunning visual appeal while floating in your teapot. Gardenia 'Kleim's Hardy' and gardenia 'Ice Diamonds' will tolerate temperatures down to −10°C and, as long as they are given acidic soil and a warm, sunny spot, will reward you with flushes of flowers in spring and autumn every year.

I would normally pop in about four flowers per pot of tea.

Honeysuckle *Lonicera japonica*

Added to tea for both for its lingering fragrance and medicinal qualities, honeysuckle blossom has been prized throughout Asia for centuries. Containing antiviral chemicals that can help reduce inflammation, packets of the sweetly scented flowers used for tea sold out nationwide during the bird flu outbreak in China. Who said medicine was supposed to taste horrible?

Add six to eight flower clusters per pot. The addition of sugar markedly brings out its flavour.

Jasmine *Jasminum sambac or Jasminum officinale*

Although the stronger-scented tropical species *Jasminum sambac* is traditionally used, the more common UK garden plant *Jasminum officinale* makes a fine substitute.

I would use four flower clusters per pot.

Bergamot *Monarda spp.*

Oil of bergamot, extracted from the peel of a Mediterranean citrus fruit, is what gives Earl Grey tea its refreshing fragrance. Fortunately for those living in less idyllic climes there are a group of entirely unrelated, but resolutely hardy, plants that possesses a nearly identical scent: *Monarda* spp. In fact, they are so similar they are sometimes confusingly called bergamots. Used medicinally by the native people of North America, they have demonstrated mild antiseptic and digestive properties too.

Simply pop four large leaves into the pot with the tea leaves.

Tea flowers *Camellia sinensis*

In the late summer and early autumn, tea plants reveal their extremely close relation to garden camellias, when buds burst into pretty white flowers. Although smaller than regular camellias, these are sweetly scented with a refreshing aroma akin to orange blossom.

Try adding four or five of these to a pot for a 'double tea'-scented brew.

Making matcha

In Japan, matcha is made by grinding dried green tea leaves to create a pale green powder. Traditionally, this is whisked into hot water to produce a truly verdant green, green tea. In recent years, matcha has found its way into some pretty cool fusion cooking, used to add a fragrant, grown-up flavour to a whole range of trendy Japanese ice creams, cheesecakes, puddings, and even cookies and cakes.

Because green tea is ground up so finely the entire leaf is consumed, including the insoluble bits that are normally tossed away as spent leaves, despite being by far the part highest in antioxidants. The best thing is, this fancy powder is extremely easy to make at home by simply grinding broken-up dried green tea leaves using a pestle and mortar. Stir a teaspoon or two of the resultant powder into a tub of softened vanilla ice cream or vanilla cheesecake mix and you instantly have a legitimate way to proclaim it as health food.

Natural 'artificial' sweeteners

Sugar companies beware. There is, surprisingly, a range of naturally occurring, calorie-free sweeteners found in plants that can provide an astonishingly sugary flavour that won't ruin a diet or make your teeth rot. Don't believe me? Here are a few examples to try …

Sweet cicely *Myrrhis odorata*

The ferny leaves of this relative of dill and fennel have long been used as a flavouring herb in continental Europe for their delicious sweet tang and rather strong aniseed flavour. Enormously popular in Germany and Scandinavia, they are added to all sorts of jams, jellies and pies, especially with tart fruit like gooseberries, to impart a pleasant, herbal sweetness – significantly reducing the amount of sugar you need to add. Three fat sprigs tucked in among ten sticks of chopped rhubarb, for example, is enough to slash the amount of sugar needed to sweeten your summer crumble from 100g to just a mere tablespoon. An amazing 75 per cent reduction that instantly cuts out nearly 300 calories!

The frothy white sprays of flowers and dried seeds also possess the same haunting sugar-free sweetness, and are both used in Scandinavia to flavour the perilously strong liqueur known as akvavit. You can easily make a counterfeit of this at home by stuffing two to three teaspoons of the seeds in a bottle of vodka with a teaspoon each of fennel and dill seeds and a few strips of lemon peel. Leave this to steep for at least a week, strain and get sozzled. Try ripped-up lacy spring flowers of sweet cicely scattered over fruit salads and puddings for a decoration that is equally as beautiful as it is delicious.

Growing
• Plants can be bought in small pots in the herb section of most good garden centres, sown from seeds directly into your beds in autumn (they need a touch of frost to trigger germination) or propagate by lifting and dividing established clumps.

• With a preference for rich, well-drained soil in light shade they will happily self-seed all over your garden.

• If you want to keep sweet cicely's spreading tendencies in check and get a second fresh flush of leaves as a convenient side effect, simply cut right down the ground directly after flowering.

Sugar leaf *Stevia rebaudiana*

Containing a chemical 300 times sweeter than sugar but with none of the calories, this pretty green herb from the Bolivian Andes is already widely used as a natural high-intensity sweetener in Japan, Australia, Brazil and the US. A single teaspoon of the dried, powdered leaves can be used to replace up to a cup of sugar in all sorts of drinks, desserts and even in baking – with its fluoride content and antibacterial compounds meaning it is actually good for you teeth!

In Japan, where most artificial sweeteners have been outlawed on the grounds of safety, sugar leaf extract has been used for the last 40 years as a standard sugar-free sweetener, including in huge household brands like Diet Coke, Wrigley's chewing gum and Sunkist.

The leaves can be chopped and mixed into fruit cups, minced up and blended into mousses, smoothies and cream cheese frostings. You do need to add quite a few leaves to get intense sweetness, but the bushy plants are so productive this shouldn't be a problem.

A sugar syrup with a difference
You can make a simple, concentrated sugar leaf 'syrup' by chucking three cups of chopped fresh sugar leaves into a blender with 250ml vodka (don't worry this will all be evaporated off in the next stage) and 500ml water and blitz for a minute or two. Pour into a jar and leave to sit in the fridge for any time between 24 and 48 hours for the sugary flavour to leach out of the leaves and into the liquid. Line a sieve with a piece of muslin and strain out the leaves. Simmer the whole mix over a medium-low heat for about 30 minutes in order to concentrate the liquid and evaporate the alcohol.

Stored in the fridge in a sterile bottle (to do this just run it through the hottest cycle in the dishwasher) it can be added to pretty much anything in the place of sugar. The only exceptions perhaps are when the sugar crystals are chemically necessary for the recipe to work, for example in feeding yeast in bread baking or when making caramel.

Growing
• The plant can now be bought as small plug plants, as well as grown very easily from summer cuttings or seeds in spring. Seed germination can be a little slow and erratic but be patient as the little shoots will pop up when you least expect it.

• Choose a sunny site on well-drained soil and sugar leaf will kick out great handfuls of leaves throughout the summer.

• Its only fussy point is that it needs a very well-drained soil to mimic its scrubby habitat, as it will simply hate having its roots sitting in cold, soggy compost.

• Treat it as you would other tender herbs (such as basil), bringing it inside before the risk of frost and standing it on a bright windowsill over winter before planting it back outdoors the next summer.

Aztec sweet herb *Lippia dulcis*

In the 1570s, the Spanish physician Francisco Hernandez wrote of a magically sweet plant known to the Aztecs as *Tzonpelic xihuitl*, translating literally as 'sweet herb'. Over 400 years later, his description and sketching of the plant led a group of scientists to track it down in Central America – leading to the discovery of the previously unknown natural sweetener that they named hernandulcin in homage to him.

An astonishing 1,000 times sweeter than sugar, the plant has what I can only describe as a radioactive sweetness, like biting into a pack full of pure Canderel. Used in small amounts, a little goes a very, very long way, the pretty white flowers and little green leaves add a sweet, minty sugariness as a garnish on any dessert from mango sorbet and summer fruit salads to rhubarb and gooseberry pies and elderflower jelly.

Growing
• The plants strike very easily from cuttings, but can be rather tricky to cultivate from seeds, so opt for small plants or pinch a tip from a friend who has one.

• They grow quickly to create long, trailing stems adorned (even on newly rooted cuttings) with tiny white button-shaped flowers.

• They look great in hanging baskets or bedded out for the summer in gravelly, Mediterranean-style gardens, where they can bask in full sunlight on sharply drained soil.

• Although large adult plants can take a degree of frost or two, they are so pretty and easy indoors, I would bring them undercover for a year-round supply.

Too much of a good thing
I would not recommend eating Aztec sweet herb, however, in excessive quantities or very regularly as the leaves are rich in camphor (but because they are so intensely sweet this probably won't be too much of an issue). Although camphor is commonly found in rosemary, lavender and certain types of basil, and has an extremely long history of medicinal and culinary use, it has recently been found to be toxic to the nervous system in large quantities. For this reason, I would stay well away from this herb if you are pregnant or breastfeeding, and do not give it to young children. However, when used in the occasional treat it is generally recognised as safe for most people.

Natural colours

Create a living paint box of botanical food dyes in every colour of the rainbow – from deep red and vibrant green to rich purple and even shocking blue. These pigments are not only all natural, but in many cases powerful antioxidants capable of turning cake into 'superfood'. Well, almost!

Ruby red

For a rich ruby colour, peel and slice a couple of scarlet beetroots (not the purple supermarket kind) and run them through a juicer. Good varieties to go for include:

• 'Detroit 2'

• 'Pablo'

Alternatively, beetroot can also be grated and popped in a pan with two thirds of its volume of water, simmered for 20 minutes and strained to extract their scarlet colour (or fresh juice). A tablespoon of the simmered liquid can be added to any recipe to create a deep ruby hue; with just a drop or two enough to give a pale pastel pink. This quantity is so small and the earthy beetroot flavour so mild that it will be completely imperceptible in cakes, pastas and even dyed eggs at Easter.

Hot pink

In Japan, purple leaves of Japanese beefsteak plant (see page 183) have been used for hundreds of years to create a brilliant fuchsia tint in all sorts of savoury dishes. All you need to do is:

• Take 20 large purple leaves, chop them finely and pop them into a saucepan with a squeeze of lemon juice to bring out the colour.

• Add about 125ml water. Bring to the boil and then remove from the heat and leave to cool.

• Press the leaves through a sieve to extract the bright pink liquid. You can now use it in everything from a savoury pancake batter to making pink homemade pasta dough.

For sweet dishes and desserts, try using the juice of a few raspberries, pressed through a sieve with the back of a spoon to remove the seeds or a drop or two of beetroot juice (scarlet varieties will give you a powder pink, while regular supermarket ones will give you an altogether more disco hue).

Yellow & orange

Although turmeric is the cheaper alternative when adding a golden shade to a broad range of dishes, it is both inferior in flavour and far harder to grow in the UK than the rich, luxuriousness of homegrown saffron threads (see page 172).

To get the most out of homegrown saffron threads:

• Toast a generous pinch of threads (about ten) over a medium heat in a dry frying pan for a minute or two until they lightly crisp up.

• Transfer to a pestle and mortar and grind to a fine powder.

A pinch or two of this golden dust will not only infuse a sunny yellow and orange hue to dishes but will even transform any pallid dish into a deliciously warm golden hue.

Electric blue

If you fancy taking shocking food colours to the next level there is no better candidate than the electric-blue hue provided by the butterfly pea (*Clitorea ternatea*), a pretty garden climber with an unfortunately anatomical Latin name (take one look at the flowers and you will know why). In South-East Asia the dried flowers are used to dye all manner of cakes, rice dishes and cookies by simmering the flowers in the cooking liquid or brewing them up into a strong tea that is added to any recipe.

To have a go at growing butterfly pea:

• Lightly knick the coat of each seed with a nail file and sow them on the surface of a tray of free-draining seed compost, covering them with a layer of vermiculite.

• To kick start germination place the tray in a plastic bag or heated propagator. Site plants in the warmest, sunniest location available outdoors after all risk of frost has passed, but for the very best results grow in a conservatory and spoil with weekly lashings of a dilute high-potash fertiliser.

Jade green

The chlorophyll in many types of leaves can be extracted and used as a bright green food pigment. One of the best candidates I have found for this is New Zealand spinach (see *Leaves & greens*, page 84) for its intensity of colour and ease to extract. Either run a cupful of leaves and tender stalks through a juicer or whizz them in a food processor and press the resultant mulch through a sieve to extract a rich, dark green juice. Alternatively for a lighter green tint coupled with a sweet buttery flavour, try using vanilla grass leaves (see page 191) or matcha powder made from homegrown green tea (see page 202).

Chocolate-wrapper purple

The shiny, jet-black fruit of huckleberries (see *Dessert fruit*, page 238) produce the deepest, darkest purple I have ever seen, which becomes even more intensified on cooking. Just half a teaspoon of the cooked berries or jam made from huckleberries is enough to turn the colour of any icing, cake, jelly or mousse a rich burgundy.

Oregon grapes were once used by Native Americans as clothing dye. A simple spoonful or two of their jelly will give you the most potent E-number free purple colouring.

Natural flavours

You might think that you need a fancy lab and a couple of white coat-clad boffins to brew up homemade and natural 'artificial' flavours, but follow my tips and you too can play Willy Wonka with the best of 'em.

Lemon sherbet

Lemon verbena sugar is wonderful instead of plain old caster in everything from lemon drizzle cake, to sweet and scented butters. Pop a dozen fresh lemon verbena leaves (see page 194) into a ziplock bag with a cupful of sugar and give the whole thing a good few bashes using a rolling pin until the leaves are thoroughly bruised. This scented sugar can be used immediately or left in the refrigerator for a week to intensify the flavour. Remember to discard the leaves from the sugar before adding it to cakes, scones, mousses or pancakes.

Vanilla

The lush green leaves of vanilla grass can be blitzed up into a homegrown version of vanilla extract in mere minutes (full instructions on page 193). Use the vanilla grass extract as you would the shop-bought vanilla version but bear in mind you will need about double the amount.

Rose

Rose petals straight from the garden can be convinced to give up their floral fragrance if layered between sprinklings of sugar in a glass jar, a cupful of each at a time. Left overnight in the fridge, the sugar draws the fragrance out of the petals leaving you with rose-scented crystalline slush. Used to infuse its sweet fragrance in sophisticated jams it can perk up plain old sponge cake or enliven a simple vanilla ice cream. Pop a jar in your fridge and crack it open in the depths of winter for the instant flavour flashback of an English garden in mid summer.

Coca-Cola, Old Spice and more

Scented geraniums *Pelargonium* spp. come in every imaginable flavour from peppermint to rose, pine and orange peel. There is even one called 'Old Spice', which really does live up to its name. But my favourite has to be 'Cola Bottles', for the weirdly identical aroma to those gummy, pick-and-mix sweets. Any of these varieties of geraniums can be used to impart flavour to syrups, teas, chicken or fish dishes, either simmered gently for a minute or two at the end of cooking time or chopped and scattered straight over. Perhaps the easiest way though is to add them to the base of a greased cake tin, prior to pouring the cake mix in, with the perfumed flavour infusing through the batter as it bakes. Yum.

Root beer

Presoaked wintergreen leaves (see page 200) add the unmistakable flavour of root beer to fruit salads, fizzy drinks and even roast hams. Follow my instructions on page 201 to brew up your own 1950s soda fountain.

Almond

The foamy white blossom of meadowsweet (see page 190) adds an almond flavour to really anything that takes your fancy, ending in a faint fragrance of elderflower cordial. Because meadowsweet also has the benefit of pain relief due to the aspirin-related compounds it contains, it gives the perfect excuse to eat cake in the name of its 'medicinal value'.

Sour apple

The flowers of the tuberous begonia have an acidic green apple flavour and come in every colour of the rainbow – making an unexpected garnish to apple crumble, or better yet an apple crumble ice cream. The leaves of New Zealand yams (see *Buried treasure*, page 151) and wood sorrel (see *Leaves & greens*, page 82) also offer a virtually identical 'bramliness' to salads, soups and sandwiches.

Fruit salad

For a zesty tropical fruit flavour blend up the leaves of the Peruvian mint marigold (see page 186) in a little sugar or hot syrup and stir into drinks and desserts to create the culinary equivalent of a cocktail umbrella.

Maple syrup

Douse pancakes and waffles in homemade Peruvian ground apple syrup (page 132) for a caramelised sugariness that'll make you wonder what all the fuss over maple syrup was about in the first place. Add to that the fact that it contains far less calories and is packed with probiotics, simply pour away to your heart's content.

Space dust

Nothing describes the sparkly sensation caused by an electric daisy (see page 197) inside your mouth better than licking a 9-volt battery! Chop up a couple of the small flower heads and shower over cocktails or even chocolate truffles, for a curiously fizzy tingle that will have your guests shocked out of their seats.

Dessert Fruit

Asian pear *Pyrus pyrifolia*

Crisp, sugary, apple-shaped pears, wrapped in a golden skin

These curious golden orbs, with their crisp juicy texture and refreshing sugariness, were once an esteemed fruit of the royal households of Japan and China. Unlike the buttery, silkiness of their European sister, these pears are far more crunchy and fragrant, looking and tasting like an intriguing fusion of tart Bramley and juicy Comice, but with an altogether more refined flavour. Also known as: Chinese pear, crystal pear, apple pear, sand pear.

Growing

An extremely close relative of its European sister (although actually a distinct species), Asian pears are just as easy to grow as your regular Comice or Conference varieties. All you need to do is:

• Choose a good sunny site with a rich soil, preferably on the light and loamy side. Like European pears, they will grow perfectly well out in the open in southern regions, but may require the protection of an adjacent wall when grown further north. Although capable of withstanding freezes down to −25°C when fully dormant, the delicate newly grown blossoms are vulnerable to damage from late spring frosts.

• As with most fruit trees, plant out in early spring or autumn, with the scion (a little scar on the lower part of the trunk, where the graft has occurred) well above the soil surface and apply a liberal sprinkling of mycorrhizal fungal powder in the planting hole.

• Keep well watered throughout summer while they are establishing, with a fortnightly dose of high-potash feed.

• Plant a minimum of two Asian pears in your garden, each of a different variety, as this will greatly improve the pollination of the trees (i.e. the number of flowers that turn into fruit) not to mention giving you two different-flavoured crops.

• Asian pears don't demand slavish devotion to pruning and will produce a very respectable crop simply by trimming their new non-fruiting tips back to five to six leaves each summer. This will encourage the formation of fruiting spurs, which in turn will boost the amount of fruit produced.

• Finally, as with pretty much all fruit trees, the occasional late-winter prune to remove any congested, dead or crossed branches as well as thinning out the newly formed clusters of fruitlets in late spring to just two per bunch, will ensure you get the juiciest harvest.

Varieties to try
I find the variety 'Nijisseiki' (aka '20th Century') has the best flavour and is the most common popular commercial cultivar, though there is an increasing range of options available.

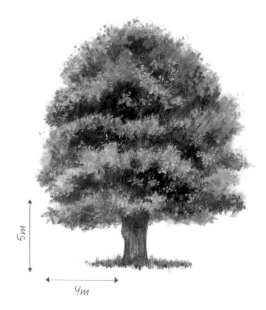

3–4m

5m

4m

Harvesting & eating

The fruit will be ready to harvest when they reach a fully golden hue in September and October. Simply pick from the tree with a gentle tug.

In their native northern east Asia they are prized for their fragrance and golden hue, not to mention the premium prices they sell for. Here Asian pears are part of tradition at feasts, celebratory family banquets, served to visiting guests or given as auspicious gifts – far more special than our equivalent – a box of Milk Tray chocolates.

In Japan their sugary freshness has seen them being ground and mixed into vinegar or soy sauce to create a sweet dipping sauce or as part of a marinade for meat dishes like beef.

Asian pears' crisp, rather grainy texture and fresh wateriness make them wonderful in salads, with walnuts, blue cheese and watercress, finely sliced in roast beef and horseradish sandwiches or shredded in fresh, mayonnaise-free coleslaw. Unlike European pears though, their high water content and lack of acidity make them rather unsuitable baked or roasted, although they are lovely blitzed with fresh green chillies in a watercress soup.

You can even make a modern, grown-up (and let's face it, rather pretentious) take on a toffee apple, by spearing a fresh pear on a stick, rolling it in a pot of hot liquid caramel and sprinkling with a dusting of flaky sea salt and chilli powder.

5m

4m

Medlar *Mespilus germanica*

A medieval fruit that tastes of ready-made spiced apple compote

Once a much-loved fruit in medieval Britain, the last 100 years has seen medlars inexplicably fall out of foodie fashion. But with their rich, mellow sweetness akin to apple butter laced with cinnamon and chopped dates, it is high time we succumb to this ancient fruit's delicious autumnal charms.

Growing

Medlar fruit may have a quirky appearance, like a small Russet apple with a gaping star-shaped scar on the base – resulting in the French name *Cul de Chien* (literally 'dog's arse'). However, I implore you to put any culinary squeamishness aside and plant one of these stunning ornamental trees with their character-filled canopies and large pink 'apple blossom'. They are wonderfully unfussy about both site and soil, as long as the ground is relatively well drained. Being self-fertile and extremely productive, a single tree should produce enough fruit to keep even the most resolute medlar fiend content. To get them off to a flying start:

• Treat them to a sheltered sunny patch with a good few spadefuls of organic matter and a scattering of chicken manure pellets in the planting hole. This will ensure that you get the largest crops.

• Keep well watered while the plants establish and give them a boost each spring by applying an extra scattering of organic all-purpose fertiliser around their bases.

• As for pruning, all they need is the standard annual thinning out of dead wood, congested growth and cross-eyed branches to create an open, airy structure.

Harvesting & eating

Although borne on the trees from as early as August and September, the fruit fully matures in late October and early November. At this point it loses its rock-hard firmness and yields easily to the pressure of a finger, taking on a caramel colour. This maturing process is traditionally known as 'bletting' and is basically an advanced stage of ripeness where the starches in the fruit begin to break down, reducing the astringent tannins and causing a pronounced spike in sugariness. This is *not* a sign of decay or fermentation as many claim, but a part of the normal ripening process, just like when a banana develops freckles on its outer skin and gets softer and sweeter.

For me, medlars are best enjoyed simply cut in half, the flesh scooped out and eaten with a teaspoon, with an optional (although frankly marvellous) sprinkling of brown sugar and drizzle of double cream.

Traditionally the fruit were also simmered up with sugar and a squeeze of lemon to create all manner of jams, jellies and relishes – particularly lovely at Christmas with a good old cheeseboard.

In my kitchen trials, I have found that medlars have a distinctly similar taste to tamarind paste making a surprisingly convincing food mile-free substitute. To do this, scoop out the flesh from five medlars and simmer it with the juice of half a lemon, a teaspoon of sugar and half a cup of water for ten minutes or so. Strain the pulp through a sieve to remove the seeds and hey presto, homegrown tamarind paste! This is wonderful mixed up with water, sweetened with a good few teaspoons of sugar and poured over a tall glass of ice to make a Mexican-style 'Tamarindo Fresco'. Alternatively, simply spoon it into Asian salad dressings, soups, curries and stir-fries to add an instant tart richness, just as you would shop-bought tamarind. Then sit back and feel deservedly smug about your homegrown creation.

4–5m

Quince *Cydonia oblonga*

The super-fragrant, Middle Eastern fruit your great grandpa grew

With a rich and spicy aroma powerful enough to fill a room and stunning spring blossom – not to mention the extortionate prices they sell for at farmers' markets – quince come pretty close to the top of my long list of 'must grow' fruit for UK gardeners.

Growing

Once as common as the humble pear in Victorian markets, this exotic Middle Eastern fruit was grown all over the UK as an indispensable ingredient in British cuisine for almost a millennium. Yet for some unknown reason, the last 100 years has seen them become relegated to a mere anecdote in historical cookbooks, elbowed out of our orchards (and diets) by boring old apples and pears. Closely related to both of these, quinces are just as easy to grow as their more common cousins, but offer up an altogether more delicious reward.

To get them off to a good start simply:

• Pick a sheltered site in full sun on moist, slightly acidic soil for best results and plant them out in autumn or winter, setting trees about 4m apart.

• If you have particularly chalky alkaline soil, it's worth digging in a good bucketful of pine needles or trimmings from conifer trees into the planting hole to help lower the pH of the soil a little.

• Keep them well watered while establishing and feed with a high-potash fertiliser throughout the summer.

• A nice thick layer of mulch around their roots will help seal in moisture and quash any potential competition from weeds.

Apart from the occasionally watering, once you have planted your little sapling all you'll have left to do is stand back and admire its pink spring blossom, golden fruit and gorgeous autumnal tones when the leaves flush a bright butter yellow.

In their early years young quince trees benefit from a little light pruning to help establish an open canopy of well-spaced branches. Simply remove any dead, diseased or crossing branches to create a rough 'wine glass' shaped tree, with an open centre that allows light and air right into the middle of the canopy, and snip off any suckers (vigorous, sappy branches) that arise from the base. Once you have a decent structure going though, you can pretty much leave them to their own devices.

Varieties to try

Popular tried and tested varieties include:

• **'Sibley's Patio'** – if you don't have a huge garden, there's a fantastic British-bred dwarf variety that will not grow much over 2m tall in a pot, bearing up to 50 tennis ball-sized fruit just a couple of years after planting.

• **'Meech's Prolific'** – an early-bearing American variety.

• **'Vranja'** – a large-fruited variety from Serbia.

Harvesting & eating

Quinces are ready to be picked when they begin to emit their powerful fragrance and turn a golden yellow in hue. Simply twist and gently tug the fruit off the branch. Let your nose be your guide as, generally, fragrance is a better indication of full ripeness than colour. In fact, bowlfuls of the fruit were even once used as a room fragrance, far prettier and more seductive than any chemically laden air freshener. After a 100-year break from our diets, however, most of us Brits will need a little guidance on how to prepare and eat quinces as in their raw state they are extremely dry and astringent. However, prepared the correct way

– baked, boiled, grilled or poached – they are possibly the single most delicious fruit that can be grown on our chilly isles.

One of the simplest and most traditional ways to eat quince is cooked down into a jam made thick enough to slice by the sky-high pectin content, and served with cheese. This quince paste (otherwise known as membrillo) is lovely sliced into thin slivers and scattered between flour tortillas for the ultimate cheesy quesadilla or melted down as a gooey topping for cheesecakes. You can even incorporate the cooked, puréed fruit into marinades and cooking sauces for all manner of meats.

Membrillo is also wonderful stirred into a honey-mustard rub for barbecue chicken or as the base for a spectacular homemade sweet and sour sauce, lovely drizzled over crisp roast pork.

Sliced into chunks, parboiled and tossed in butter and brown sugar, quinces are particularly good roasted until golden and served with chicken, pork or game. Of course the fruit can be used in sweet dishes too, chopped up into regular apple pies, strudels and crumbles, for example. Remember to parboil or poach the fruit for a good 20–30 minutes before adding these to the raw apples as they do take far longer to cook.

4m

4m

Membrillo with lime, chilli & ginger

Perhaps the easiest way to use quince is to extract its perfumed spiciness and transform it into membrillo (a candied fruit paste). Extremely versatile, this can be eaten with cheese or on top of steamed puddings, tarts or cheesecake (pictured).

Makes enough for a 20cm x 30cm square tin

Ingredients
500g quince (about 2 large quinces), washed and
   coarsely grated
500ml water
finely grated zest and juice of 1 lime
5cm piece of fresh ginger
2 large dried red chillies
a pinch of salt
500g sugar

Place the grated quince into a medium-sized saucepan. Slice up any remaining cores into little slivers and chuck these into the pan too, as they will help with the setting.

Pour the water into the saucepan and bring to the boil. Simmer partially covered, over a medium heat for 30 minutes.

Once the grated fruit has become translucent, add the remaining ingredients, return to the heat, then simmer again, partially covered, for 1 hour.

Remove the pan from the hob and blitz the cooked fruit up using a stick blender to give you fine, smooth paste. Return to the heat for a further 10–15 minutes stirring it slowly to prevent the mix from sticking to the bottom of the pan. Test the thickness of the mix by drawing a line with your wooden spoon along the bottom of the pan. If the mix separates and leaves a clear trail of metal visible for a couple of seconds, it is ready.

Line a 20cm x 30cm square tin or a shallow tray with tin foil. Pour your mix into the tin and leave to set. If you find it doesn't quite set as firmly as you like, you can always return the mix to the heat, melting it down and reducing it further until it reaches your desired consistency. Once set, store in the refrigerator where it will keep for up to a year.

Black mulberries *Morus nigra*

The Haribo-sweet, tree-blackberries that money simply can't buy

'Money can't buy' might be a bit of an overused expression, but in the case of the succulent black berries of this Middle Eastern fruit, it literally is the case. Despite being vastly superior in every way to blackberries and raspberries, these delicate-skinned fruits are virtually impossible to transport or store for more than 24 hours without them turning into a juicy pulp. So if you want to revel in their delicious wine-like flavour you will just have to grow them yourself.

Growing

Mulberries are wonderfully easy to grow and will form extremely long-lived trees, offering up knockout harvests for well over 300 years in return for the 15 minutes it takes to plant one – not a bad investment in the current climate really. Here are my growing tips:

• Pick the largest specimen you can afford, as they can take a little time to come into fruit, with 90–120cm high saplings, for example, producing their first harvest after two to three years.

• These unfussy trees are happy on all kinds of soil, as long it is relatively well drained and the site enjoys full sun for most of the day.

• In smaller gardens the size of trees can be radically contained by training them against a wall or by planting them through a root-trainer bag, which will restrict the spread of their roots and thereby keep their canopy a far more manageable size.

• They will even be happy in a large pot of soil-based planting mix for the first 10–15 years of their lives, as long as they are kept well watered using a high-potash liquid feed like comfrey tea, with the top 10cm of planting mix refreshed each spring.

• Mulch around plants with a thick layer of bark or compost once a year to help both suppress weeds and retain moisture, with a liberal scattering of fertiliser around their roots at the same time.

Pruning is largely unnecessary for mulberries, apart from the occasional removal of overcrowded, dead or broken branches, which is best done before trees come into growth in the spring as actively growing plants do have a tendency to bleed sap.

Varieties to try

Planting one of these stately trees is really like growing a living piece of history, with most of the cultivars available coming directly from cuttings of the original trees planted by King Charles I, such as 'Charlton House' or in the Chelsea Physic Garden like 'Chelsea' (also rather confusingly known as 'King James I').

Whatever the variety, always make sure that the plant you are picking is indeed black mulberry *Morus nigra* and not of its white cousin *Morus alba*, whose small, dry berries are sadly nowhere near as much of a treat.

8m

6m

4m

Harvesting & eating

Mulberries are at their most delicious straight off the tree in the August sunshine – no need for any sugar or cooking – with the ripe purple berries having an intense syrupiness that is made all the more addictive by their curious gumdrop-like bite.

Don't wear white when you set off to pick them though, as their vivid, antioxidant-laden juice will stain anything it comes into contact with an indelible shade of burgundy. Frankly, don't be surprised if you end up with enormous splodges all over yourself!

If you can get any mulberries back to the kitchen without scoffing them all first, they are spectacular in jams, pies, crumbles and jellies, blitzed into cocktails and smoothies or just scattered over Greek-style yoghurt with a generous drizzle of honey.

Although the whole berries don't keep or even freeze well, once simmered for five minutes or so the resultant compote (with or without sugar) should last at least until the next harvest if cooled and frozen in ziplock bags or poured into sterilised jars while still bubbling hot and sealed. Simmered with diced Bramley apples, a couple of chillies, a dash of soy sauce, a generous scoop of sugar and a sprinkling of Tasmanian mountain pepper, they make an unbeatable sticky glaze for pork ribs.

Cocktail kiwi *Actinidia arguta*

Grape-sized mini kiwis from the wilds of Siberia

If the board of Haribo were to sit down and reinvent the kiwi fruit, it would no doubt look a bit like these. Bunches of miniature grape-sized kiwis with fuzz-free edible skins and flesh that's twice as sweet as a regular kiwi hang on these vines each autumn, offering up to 400 fruit per plant. If you grow one berry crop this year, make this it! Also known as: baby kiwi, kiwi berry, Arctic kiwi.

Growing

In the wild the cocktail kiwi is a rampant bramble-like vine native to northern Asia and Siberia meaning that despite its tropical appearance, it is hardy enough to withstand arctic blasts down to −35°C. Here's all you need to know to get started:

• Plants like a rich, well-drained soil, and although they will grow happily in both full sun and part shade, the plants will produce much bigger yields and sweeter fruit on sites in full sun.

• Generally they suffer from few pests and diseases but the most common complaints are fungal infections, which can be avoided by ensuring the soil is well drained prior to planting by digging in plenty of grit.

• A sturdy, weight-bearing support to train them over is a must — the plants can grow up to 2m in a single season and produce over 20kg of fruit when fully mature. They look great growing over trellises, pergolas and even well-spaced wires along a south or west-facing wall.

• Keep plants well watered during the growing season — as often as two or three times a week in hot, dry weather — in order to replicate their moist woodland habitat. They are not heavy feeders and only require an annual sprinkle of all-purpose feed (like chicken manure) around the base of each plant in spring.

In the wild, plants will only produce berries on the very tips of their branches, which scramble up above the forest canopy, enjoying the full rays of the sun. Clever pruning, however, can cheat the plant into producing berries on vines on at least a far more manageable scale (i.e. not 30m overhead) and with a major increase in yield to boot.

Most textbooks advise pruning in the espalier fashion – almost exactly as you would prune a grapevine – however this can be rather daunting or overcomplicated for most homegrowers not to mention leaving you with a cat's cradle of branches. I prefer a more laid-back American technique called 'spur pruning', which is just as effective but so much simpler. All you need to do is keep snipping back the vigorous new growth about every four weeks during the summer, reducing these lanky, snaking shoots by half – from about 20cm to 10cm long. This encourages the plant to produce many side shoots, creating a compact, branching bush rather than a lanky tangled mess. It is on these side shoots that the flowering 'spurs' are produced, which later turn into fruit.

3m

4.5m

6m

Varieties to try

Most conventional varieties of cocktail kiwi need both male and female plants to produce a crop, leaving gardeners with small city spaces in danger of having their garden swallowed up whole by the thuggish couple. Fortunately, there is a new self-fertile variety out there called 'Issai', which is capable of bearing fruit all on its own. If you have space there is a ruby red-fruited variety called 'Ken's Red', which kicks out berries by the bucketload if planted with a male pollinator variety such as 'Weika'.

Harvesting & eating

Cocktail kiwis come into season in autumn, from September through to November, depending on your region. Harvest them when they are firm yet soft enough to have a little give (just like a plum) as this is the point when their sugar content is the highest.

The fruit are delicious on their own and work fantastically in pies and jams with a dash of elderflower cordial. My favourite thing to do with cocktail kiwis is to slice them in half and dry them out in a low oven. They will form sticky, wine-gum-like sweets without a single E-number in them.

In addition to a whole load of vitamins and minerals, kiwis contain a unique protein-digesting enzyme called actinidin, which is used traditionally in China as a highly effective meat tenderiser. It's what's responsible for that sharp, tingly sensation unripe kiwis sometimes give you on the tip of your tongue. The enzyme is literally digesting the proteins on the surface of your tongue! If you want proof, squeeze the fruit on raw chicken or squid and marinate with your favourite seasonings (say, garlic, ginger, soy and chilli) in the fridge for an hour or so. You'll notice a real difference and of course an unusual additional flavour at your next barbecue.

Pineapple guava *Acca sellowiana (aka Feijoa sellowiana)*

An exotic Brazilian guava tree, hardy enough to grow outdoors in the UK

Fusing the flavours of ripe pineapple and pink guava, the powerfully aromatic fruit are the most exotic-tasting crop that can be grown in the UK. But poolside cocktail-flavoured fruit isn't all pineapple guavas have to offer, they also come with powdery silver foliage and scarlet pom-pom blossoms, whose edible petals taste, rather unbelievably, of sweet, minty marshmallows. Also known as: feijoa, guavasteen, New Zealand banana.

Growing

Hailing from the cool mountains of southern Brazil, pineapple guavas are one of the hardiest members of the largely tropical guava family. Despite enjoying warm, sunny summers, this region is frequently characterised by some pretty harsh winter temperatures, meaning plants can shrug off chills as low as −10°C without any visible damage. Mature specimens can even hang on for brief periods down to a chilling −15°C, when severely frost-damaged plants will often regrow from the base in spring.

This inbuilt cold tolerance (roughly similar to that of an olive tree) makes them a viable crop throughout most of southern Britain and practical in pots overwintered in a porch or conservatory right across the country.

To start your own pineapple guava orchard:

• Plant them out in full sun in the warmest spot you can give them and ideally against a sunny south or west-facing wall whose blockwork will act like a heat trap.

• Enrich the soil prior to planting by digging in plenty of grit and organic matter especially if you have heavy clay as the plants need a light, fast-draining soil to perform their best.

• Apply a high-potash feed to encourage maximum fruit production once a month during summer – something like a comfrey feed would be perfect – along with a good thick mulch to retain moisture.

Once established, plants are remarkably trouble free, being resistant to almost all pests and diseases, extremely drought tolerant and even very frugal feeders. However, almost all UK growers will report a single common problem: poor fruit set. The good news is that there are three simple reasons why we Brits tend to have this seemingly universal problem, all of which are easily remedied.

• **Error 1) Single specimen planting:** The plants should be planted with a friend – in groups of twos or even threes – as they are not self-fertile. Without pollen from a genetically distinct parent, the plants will fail to fruit well. So for the heaviest crops match-make couples from different varieties.

• **Error 2) Leaving a dense canopy:** The plants flower well only on young branches that enjoy bright, direct light. This means that branches in the middle of the dense,

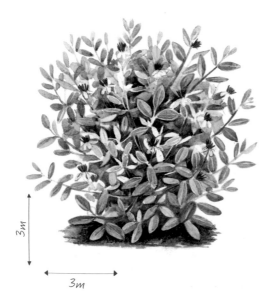

3m

3m

2m

tightly clipped canopies of traditionally grown pineapple guavas stand little chance of producing fruit. Instead, when autumn comes around, thin out old and congested branches in the centre to create a light, open shape. Don't get too trigger happy with the secateurs though as heavy pruning will ironically reduce flower production.

• **Error 3) Lack of pollinators:** In the UK, for a variety of reasons, birds and bees seem to be less effective pollinators for the plant than they are in their native habitat. Simply tickling the centre of each flower with a paintbrush (like a surrogate bee) transferring pollen from plant to plant can improve fertilisation rates by almost threefold for only a few minutes work.

Harvesting & eating

Fruit signal their ripeness by falling from the tree and becoming intensely aromatic. A bowl of these on your kitchen table is capable of filling the room with a fresh pineapple and strawberry scent, laced with hints of winter-green and spearmint. This bizarre flavour amalgamation has made them a major crop in New Zealand, where 500 commercial plantations mean it almost rivals the kiwi fruit as the national fruit.

Please do not be tempted to harvest these straight from the tree, because until they fall and release their smell they are hard and astringent. Commercial growers often cover the ground under the trees with hay or tarpaulins to prevent bruising of the ripe fruit.

The Kiwis love to eat pineapple guava simply sliced in half, scooping out the flesh with a spoon. However, I feel to do this is to miss out on the best bit of the fruit – its fresh perfumed skin. I like to slice the fruit and eat it raw in salads, salsas or sprinkled with sugar and served in desserts or over cereal.

Lightly cooked they are delicious in jams, pavlovas, ice creams and fancy liqueurs, where their high pectin content (up to 20 per cent) guarantees a smooth, firm set each time.

The thick, fleshy petals are sweet and minty and can even be picked without sacrificing the fruit, as long as the central pom-pom bit is left intact after pollination. Try them scattered in a tropical fruit salad or crystallised as an unusual garnish to cakes and trifles.

a recipe idea

Pineapple guava salsa with seared tuna

As well as in desserts, the fragrant resinous tang of pineapple guavas also works brilliantly in savoury sweet relishes, chutneys and simple salsas. Delicious with a really fresh slice of seared tuna.

Serves 4

Ingredients
For the salsa
3 ripe pineapple guavas, peeled and cubed
2.5cm section of cucumber, peeled and cubed
1 red chilli, sliced
1 spring onion, finely sliced
1 tsp chopped Peruvian mint marigold leaves (or mint)
½ a small red onion, finely diced
finely grated zest and juice of 1 lime
¼ tsp salt
½ tsp sugar

For the tuna
2 tbsp olive oil
4 tuna steaks
1 tsp light brown sugar
sea salt and pepper

To make the salsa, put the pineapple guavas, cucumber, chilli, spring onion, Peruvian mint marigold (or mint) leaves and red onion in a mixing bowl. Sprinkle over the lime zest, juice, salt and sugar and stir well to combine. Cover with cling film and place in the fridge for an hour to let all the ingredients macerate (soften).

When the hour's up, it's time to get started on the tuna. Heat the olive oil in a large non-stick frying pan over a high heat. Rub the tuna steaks with the sugar and a little salt and pepper until well seasoned. Add the tuna to the hot pan and sear until lightly browned on the outside but the inside still slightly pink. This normally takes as little as 30 seconds on each side, slightly longer if the steaks are thickly sliced.

Divide the tuna between serving plates, top with a generous dollop of salsa and serve immediately with a crisp side salad.

Blue sausage fruit *Decaisnea fargesii*

Bizarre, cobalt-blue pods, stuffed with cloudy watermelon-flavoured jelly

Now, I have eaten my fair share of weird and wonderful fruit, but this one easily takes the biscuit for being far and away the most wildly exotic looking. Split one of these fleshy electric blue pods open to reveal a row of cloudy jelly-like segments, wrapped around a shiny black seed. Not just style over substance, they have a delicate watermelon-like flavour ending with a touch of fragrant fig, making them taste almost as curious as they look. Also known as deadman's fingers.

Growing

These handsome trees of branching silver-backed leaves and smooth grey bark are surprisingly, already relatively common garden ornamentals in the UK, but despite the fruit being enormously popular with the people (and monkeys) of its native south-western China, few of us Brits have ever tasted them.

Blue sausage fruit are a woodland species, so although they will produce the largest crops on sunny sites, they are one of the very few fruit trees that will grow happily even in dappled shade. Incorporate large amounts of organic matter in the soil before planting to mimic that of their forest home, with a couple of handfuls of chicken manure pellets dug in for good measure. Also, unlike almost all conventional fruiting trees, they do not need any pruning to produce bumper crops of blue pods.

Apart from regular soakings with a high-potash fertiliser to eke out every last bit of their enormous potential productivity they will need very little intervention from you. In fact, it is not unusual to see specimens so loaded with fruit in the early autumn that half of the tree has been literally doubled over under their weight.

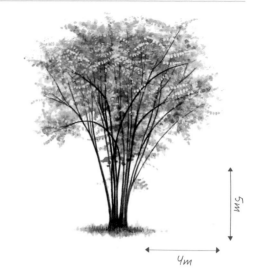

5m

4m

4m

Harvesting & eating

The bunches of bizarre blue fruit come into season in September and early October. When they are just soft to touch simply snip them off with your secateurs.

Most gardening texts describe blue sausage fruit as being rather insipid, which I think is wholly unfair. Delicate yes, but in much the same way as fresh watermelon is – clean, light, refreshing but with a irresistible gelatinous gumminess that reminds me of those pick-and-mix sweets at the cinema. Paired wonderfully with a whole range of other ingredients, I like to squeeze a twist of lime over a bowl of separated segments and toss them into a fruit salad with papaya, homegrown cocktail kiwis and chopped Peruvian mint marigolds to enhance their tropical fruit flavour. They are particularly nice mixed with finely cubed pineapple, mint, sliced chillies and red onions as an exotic salsa to spoon over grilled chicken thighs or a nice cut of seared fish. Alternatively, they are delcious simply stirred into a homemade lychee jelly (made from dissolving leaf gelatine in the syrup from a can of lychees) so they appear to float in the jelly.

Figs *Ficus carica*

The ancient biblical fruit that thrives on near total neglect

One of the oldest fruits in the history of cultivation, figs were first domesticated in ancient Mesopotamia right at the dawn of agriculture. Yet despite their origins in the searing heat of the Middle East, many varieties will fruit perfectly well in the average British back garden with little or no coaxing. Sitting underneath one of these on a hot sunny day, admiring the stunning tropical leaves and heady scent, you could almost be in your own Mediterranean villa.

Growing

Fig trees thrive on punishment and if spoilt with lashings of water or fertiliser they will kick out long, lush branches at the expense of fruit. To ensure they produce figs by the basket-load simply:

• Seek out the hottest, sunniest site available, ideally a south-facing wall where your little tree can bask in the retained warmth of its blockwork.

• Dig plenty of grit into the planting hole, even if you are gardening on a sandy plot as figs need a poor, sharply drained soil to fruit well.

Many gardeners will often line the sides of a 60cm deep planting hole with paving slabs, lowering the plant into the centre and backfilling it with a gravel-based compost to restrict the roots. The effect of this 'buried container' is both to control growth – if spoilt for root-space they can produce enormous trees – and to keep the plant under a certain degree of stress, as this is what shocks the plant into diverting its energies into producing fruit instead of leaves.

With this in mind, only water or fertilise newly planted trees to aid their establishment in their first summer and then leave them to fend for themselves. Remember, it's all about tough love with figs.

Give your little tree a quick once-over with the secateurs in the early spring to remove any frost-damaged or crossed branches as well as any suckers that are shooting up from the base. Then, in summer, pinch out the tips of the new branches to five or six leaves long to encourage the formation of embryo fruit for next year.

It is also a good idea to snip off any large partially ripened fruit left sitting on the tree in late autumn as these are unlikely to fully ripen before winter frosts set in and can put a drain on the plant's energies. Do not bin them though as these too are a delicious ingredient, cooked and eaten all over the Mediterranean in a totally different way from ripe figs. Leave any tiny green fruitlets (i.e. hazelnut-sized or smaller) as fruit of this size will often make it through the winter, carrying over their swelling and ripening phase until the next summer.

Varieties to try

If you live in a cool, Northern region your best bet would be the ubiquitous variety 'Brown

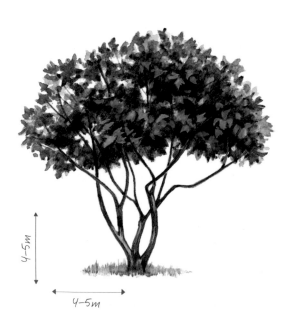

4–5m

4–5m

4m

Turkey' which is the hardiest of them all. Further south or in more sheltered areas there are a wealth of varieties to pick from like the strawberry-scented 'Panachee', super early 'Brunswick' and creamy-fleshed 'White Marseilles'.

Harvesting & eating

The fully ripened figs are ready to pick from August to early October depending on the variety, but watch the sticky white latex that exudes from the broken stems and leaves. This is corrosive on the skin – so much so that it is traditionally used to burn off warts!

To me the succulent flavour of a tree-ripened fig is best enjoyed bitten into while still warm from the sun or prepared very simply to not disguise their rich, fruity jamminess. I like to slice into the centre of each one and stuff it with a walnut and a knob of Dolcelatte (a cheese). Wrapped in a sliver of Serrano ham and drizzled in a little honey – my highlight of the summer.

As the season draws to a close in the late autumn, any large unripe figs that remain can be cooked up in all manner of treats. In some parts of the Med these are even considered superior in eating to the fully ripe ones. To do this just snip off their tough stems and plonk them whole into a pan of rapidly boiling water for ten minutes. Drain off all the water and repeat the process in a fresh change of water to leach out the last of the slightly latex 'green' flavour that raw unripe figs have, and you are ready to prepare them however you like.

I adore bubbling these cooked green fruit up with an equal weight of sugar, a splash of water and a little lemon juice to make a murderously addictive jam, as they do in Greece and Turkey. Alternatively, try simmering them up with a couple of crushed cardamom pods in the leftover syrup of stem ginger for a treat as delicious with cheese and biscuits as it is spooned over Greek-style yoghurt.

Muskmelon *Cucumis melo*

Exotic, fragrant gourds without the need for a greenhouse

Once thought of as a resolutely heat-loving species, recent breakroughs in melon breeding have transformed these natives of the African desert into something that can reliably fruit outdoors even on our blustery North Atlantic island chain. Treat a couple of these trailing vines to your sunniest site and you'll be rewarded with six fragrant gourds per vine, whose sugary sweetness is almost unrecognisable to the pre-sliced packing-foam version at your local supermarket.

Growing

There are two keys to success when it comes to growing melons outdoors in the UK, even in rather disappointing summers. First and foremost is getting your variety right. Look for the 'personal sized' small-fruited types that have a more modest stature allowing them to fully ripen even in our short growing season. Secondly, give the melons the sunniest, most sheltered position in your garden. You can further enhance this by:

• Providing a covering of thin black plastic laid over the soil, through which the vines are planted, will help absorb and retain the sun's heat around the plants' roots and stems. Even bin bags will do for this purpose, pinned down with a few hooks of wire, as long as you ensure enough water gets to the roots.

• For best results (although I have admittedly never bothered with this is in my sheltered southern garden) cover the young plants with open-ended plastic cloches to get them off to the best start until they start to come into flower. These should then be removed to allow the bees to pollinate them, ensuring a really good crop.

• If you are lucky enough to have a greenhouse or cold frame available, these plants will be even more productive in this cosy, humid environment, especially the further north you are and the higher the elevation you are gardening on.

Now you know the key to muskmelon success, here's how to get started:

• In late April, sow the seeds in little individual pots of compost on a warm, sunny windowsill, inserting a couple of seeds per pot about 1cm below the compost level. Using a heated propagator (or failing that an upturned plastic bag over the pots) will markedly improve both the rate of germination and the quality of the seedlings that pop up.

• Thin out the weaker of the two seedlings when they develop their first true leaf and transfer the remaining ones to larger pots, planting them out as described above when all risk of frost has passed in May.

• Keep well watered with a high-potash liquid feed, such as diluted comfrey tea, throughout the growing season and come September, you can expect to harvest up to half a dozen little 500g melons from each vine. Magic!

30cm

1.5m

Tip: Placing a small paving tile under each melon as it develops will help keep them off the soil, making for cleaner fruit that will also ripen evenly.

Varieties to try

All of the below have been tried and tested for the UK climate:

• **'Emir'** – with its orange flesh and netted skin and the hugely productive.

• **'Alvaro'** – with its stripy green skin and golden flesh.

• **'Magenta'** and **'Small Shining Light'**.

Recent years have also seen the introduction of some of these as small grafted plants in the spring. In my experience these modified plants, whose fruit-bearing top growth has been spliced onto the turbo-charged roots of another variety, will produce infinitely more productive vines that come into fruit much earlier in the year.

Harvesting & eating

Come September when they are at their most fragrant, the melons can be snipped off with the secateurs.

Melons have such a delicate, fresh fragrance so I generally don't like to mess around with them too much. Fresh chunks only need to be enveloped in a sliver of Parma ham, with a glass of chilled white wine in hand, to be enjoyed at their very best. Sliced into wedges and soaked in a sprinkling of sugar, chopped mint, a squeeze of lime and a dash of white rum overnight, they can be frozen stiff to make iced 'mojito' melon slices – a hopelessly easy summer treat you will be reminiscing about well into the depths of winter.

Inca berries *Physalis peruviana*

The Incan delicacy that thrives on neglect

Prized by the Incas as one of their most esteemed crops and with tiny packets flown in direct from Colombia, costing a small fortune in fancy supermarkets, you might think that these exotic berries were impossibly difficult to grow, but nothing could be further from the truth. Each wrapped in its own paper Chinese lantern, these sticky amber balls have a rich flavour of ripe gooseberries with a hint of tropical fruit, followed by a delicious bitter-sweet aftertaste. Also known as: golden berries, cape gooseberries, tipparees, physalis.

Growing

The plants can be grown just like tomatoes, to which they are related, with the one exception being that they are much less demanding. To get growing:

• Sow the seeds in shallow trays of compost in a propagator or on a sunny window in March or April. When the little seedlings are large enough to handle, plant each in its own little pot and leave to grow in a warm, bright place indoors.

• Choose a sunny site with well-drained soil and plant outdoors in late May after all risk of frost has passed. They will thrive in grow-bags or a collection of pots on the patio.

Unlike tomatoes, all varieties do perfectly well outdoors. You might even be able to get these to pull through the winter in the mildest parts of the country, meaning that if you're lucky they might just spring back year after year. To maximise your chances, plant them against a sunny, south-facing wall, and cover their roots with a thick layer of mulch, such as bark chippings or straw. Unlike tomatoes, there is no need to prune or train them and they won't need slavish devotion to lavish fertilising and irrigation. They don't even suffer from as many pests and diseases, so as long as you keep on top

of the watering they are happy to get on with the job – producing berries by the punnet-load.

Varieties to try

I recommend the following varieties:

• **'Pineapple'** – known for its huge yields on stout, branching plants and intense pineapple flavour.

• **'Little Lanterns'** – which grows no more than 20cm high and has a rich butterscotch flavour – ideal for small containers on the balcony or even in your studio flat's window box.

Harvesting & eating

Come late summer and early autumn the plants will come into a heavy crop of brown papery lanterns, which have the convenient habit of falling off when they are ripe. This means there is none of the agony about when is exactly the right time to harvest – the plant does it for you.

The shiny golden berries taste great as they are, or as an interesting ingredient in smoothies, salads and salsas. Their flesh also has a sky-high pectin content so for any would-be WI-ers out there, they make great textured jams, chutneys and preserves. In fact, these berries were once widely grown by the Victorians as a popular fruit, 'Tipparees'. Even Mrs Beeton had a recipe for a sticky, sweet jam made out of them (for more on jam making see *My ten commandments*, page 35).

Enclosed in their own little package, the fruit has an impressive shelf life – the longest of any berry I know, staying fresh for up to 3 months in the fridge. I've once eaten a September harvest on Christmas Day, and trust me, there is no kitschier Christmas cake decoration than half a dozen of these sticky sweet baubles rolled in edible glitter.

45cm–1m

variety 'Pineapple'

variety 'Little Lanterns'

1m

40cm

Huckleberries *Solanum x burbankii*

The blackberry-flavoured 'superfood' descended from a garden weed

Apart from as a prefix to words like 'Finn' and 'Hound', most of us Brits have never heard of these shiny, antioxidant-packed orbs. Yet with their delicious blackberry and plum flavour, enormous yields and indestructible ease of cultivation, take one bite of homegrown huckleberry pie and you will be as evangelical about them as I am. Also known as: sunberry, wonderberry.

Growing

Huckleberries are grown in pretty much an identical way to outdoor tomatoes, with the one exception that they are far, far easier, requiring no staking, training, fertiliser or slavish devotion to near-daily waterings.

Thriving on neglect, these tough, survivalists were originally bred in the States from two common garden weed species, so like many other plants in this book, it really is a case of 'treat them mean, keep them keen'. In fact, all that lavish watering or fertiliser applications will do is distract them from their fruit-bearing duties, causing them instead to kick out loads of lush leaf growth at the expense of berries. To put things in perspective, the most productive examples I have seen were growing in builders' rubble at the bottom of a sunny wall in a Croydon industrial estate. To get growing, simply:

• Start plants off by sowing them indoors in March or April in a small tray of damp seed compost, cover over with a sprinkling of ver-miculite and pop this on a sunny windowsill.

• Once the little emerging seedlings develop three to four leaves, carefully ease them out and transfer to little individual pots and leave them to grown in a bright, warm place.

• Plant them out after all risk of frost has passed in May. Pick a sunny place on sharp, well-drained soil (you can fake this by digging in loads of grit if you are gardening on heavy clay soil), water in well and leave them to fend for themselves.

You probably won't need to do this for more than half a dozen of the little guys though as each plant bears enough berries for an enormous pie. These should be more than enough to keep even the most huckleberry-philic family happy.

Although garden huckleberries are a delicious, much-loved fruit crop, they are very closely related (both genetically and in appearance) to a common British native the 'Black Nightshade' *Solanum nigrum*, which, as its name suggests, is *not* edible. Because of this potential mistaken identity, even I as a trained botanist will only eat fruit from plants that I have grown from seeds, and from a reputable source that clearly sells them as an edible crop. Look for the Latin name *Solanum x burbankii* and a mention of its edibility clearly written on the packet. I also dig up and remove any apparently self-seeded plants each year, just to make doubly sure there is no room for confusion about their identity.

Harvesting & eating

The berries are borne in little bunches all over the plant, ripening to an intense, shiny black from late summer to autumn. It is important to harvest these only when they are fully ripe as, like many plants in the potato and tomato family to which the huckleberry belongs, the green parts are not safe to eat. As the mature, black berries stay fresh for ages on the plants, I find the easiest way to harvest them is to wait until the late autumn and pick them off all in one go.

Simmered up into all manner of pies, jams and jellies (both the wobbly and serve-with-cheese-and-crackers kind), huckleberries are truly delicious, adding a rich plum-blackberry

50cm

flavour and intense purple hue to anything they are stirred into. The stunning colour of these berries make them a fantastically effective food dye, and as this is produced by antioxidant chemicals (like those in red wine and blueberries) they are of great nutritional value – one less reason to feel guilty about eating pie.

There is a bit of a debate about whether the fruit can be eaten raw as well. Some claim they are perfectly safe to eat straight off the plant; others that they are mildly toxic unless well cooked. What I can say is that having gingerly tried a couple of fresh berries (please don't do this at home!) they have quite an unspectacular flavour when raw. However, given a good simmer with a little sugar, they transform into rich, sticky deliciousness so I would steer well clear of the raw fruit.

Bubbled up into a compote they are incredible with yoghurt and granola, as they are scattered whole into a far less virtuous apple crumble, flecked in American muffins or simply spread as jam on hot buttered toast. Not bad for a plant that grows like a rampant weed hey?

Calamondin lime *Citrofortunella mitis*

The esteemed Asian condiment disguised as a common UK houseplant

Growing up in Asia, these little green marbles were what I knew simply as 'limes', sold in giant piles in local markets. In fact, the large, oval types we know in the West are almost completely unheard of in Asia. Any Asian recipe that calls for 'limes' is really referring to the fragrant, orange blossom-scented pulp of these pretty bushes, not the straightforward acidity of the giant Western supermarket specimens. Also known as: calamondin orange, calamansi lime, musk lime, limoncito.

Growing

Growing calamondin limes is dead easy, being cultivated in pretty much exactly the same way as any other citrus relative. But while orange or lemon trees cost a fortune in garden centres despite only producing a handful of cheap-to-buy fruit, calamondin limes are the exact opposite – being the cheapest of all citrus plants to buy, yet providing huge amounts of a rare and expensive crop in return.

Botanically speaking the calamondin isn't actually a lime at all, but a cross between a tangerine and a kumquat, inheriting the fragrance of tangerines with the fresh acidity (and surprising hardiness) of the kumquat, while being far more delicious than either one of its parents. You can easily find them in the houseplant section of every UK garden centre.

To get growing:

- Give them a bright, sunny spot and a gritty, ericaceous (acid) potting mix, such as the specialist citrus potting mix sold in all garden centres or simply regular rhododendron compost with an extra handful of grit added.

- A regular soaking every couple of weeks will allow the compost to dry out a little before dousing again (these plants like to rest a little between waterings).

- With full sun and plenty of dilute, high-potash fertiliser, such as an organic ericaceous or citrus feed, at every watering during the growing season your plants will reward you with little green fruit by the dozen.

Perfectly happy outside on a patio all summer long, the plants are usually brought under cover of a shady conservatory or porch in the winter, where they like to be kept cool and dry but with plenty of light. Having said this, if your bush has outgrown the living room and (crucially) you live in a particularly mild part of the country, you might just be able to get away with putting it outdoors, with the shelter of a south-facing wall and a draping of horticultural fleece in the winter. In fact, large, mature plants are some of the hardiest citrus relatives around and are even capable of handling short-lived freezes to −5°C given the right protection.

45 cm

2m

1m

Harvesting & eating

Treated to a spoilt spot in a warm conservatory, production can last a full 12 months of the year, flowering and fruiting at the same time in a constant cycle. To harvest, simply snip the little limes off the branches with a pair of sharp secateurs.

Most UK garden writers have unfairly labelled these plants as highly ornamental, but with fruit that is sour and not worth eating unless candied in tons of sugar. However, after much investigation, this appears to be all down to two key missing pieces of insider foodie knowledge:

1. The fruit in Asia is only ever eaten while the skin is still green, which is when they are at their most bright and fragrant tasting, yet almost all UK writers talk about eating the fruit when it ripens to its full orange hue, when they are long past their best.

2. As the ripe fruit looks pretty much identical to a mini mandarin, it seems that most Brits bite into these expecting a sweet, sugary flavour, instead of a refreshing, lime-like tartness.

The green spheres of fruit can be used in all the same ways as a lime – squeezed into Key lime pies, used in salad dressings or added to a rather special caipirinha (a Brazilian concoction of halved limes, bashed with sugar, ice and sugarcane rum, and topped up with soda).

Their unique fragrance and tang means that traditionally they are used more like a condiment, served sliced in half alongside a little dish of chilli sauce as a ubiquitous accompaniment to everything from sticky grilled chicken wings and pad Thai-style fried noodles to barbecued fish and a fiery nasi goreng – kind of like the South-East Asian version of the tabletop salt and pepper shakers.

Sea buckthorn *Hippophae rhamnoides*

Tangy micro-oranges, packed with vitamins and hardy to −30°C

Growing the sophisticated tang of Seville oranges might be an impossible dream on our cold and blustery island, but I think we can go one better. Blizzard proof, drought tolerant and packed with 15 times the vitamin C, these tiny 'micro-oranges' have all the flavour of the finest Seville marmalade with none of the fuss. Also known as: seaberry, sandthorn.

Growing

Spanning an enormous swath of territory, from Britain's Atlantic coast to the frozen wastes of Siberia, these little amber berries are famous for their adaptability to a huge range of climates. Hardy down to −30°C, tolerant of extreme drought, poor fertility, sub-zero freezes and salt-laden gales, there really is no excuse for not being able to grow this most hard-core of crops. Covered in silvery, willow-like leaves and decorated in thousands of golden orbs from late summer through the depths of winter, they also make a highly ornamental small garden tree. So what are you waiting for? To get growing:

- Site plants in full sun and dig in plenty of grit or horticultural (not builders') sand to ensure rapid drainage, water in well and you really can leave them to get on with it.

- They will even fertilise themselves, being one of the few non-bean-related species to fix nitrogen from the air into the soil, thereby bulking up their fertility.

They are a great candidate for an edible windbreak for blustery seaside gardens and, with their thorny disposition, make a burglar-proof hedge.

Harvesting & eating

The only downside I have yet to find is that the ripe berries are very soft-skinned and therefore squash extremely easily, making harvesting a bit of a messy operation. In Scandinavia and Eastern Europe where the berries are grown commercially, long sections of the fruiting branches are cut off, before being frozen whole. The rock-solid fruit can then easily be knocked off the stems and packed into plastic bags, destined for the freezer cabinets of local supermarkets. This method will significantly lower your yields for the following year though, so I prefer to brave getting stained fingers, picking and using them *au naturel*.

The berries have formed a much-loved part of the cuisine of Scandinavia, Eastern Europe and China for thousands of years. They are an astonishingly rich source of vitamin A, C and E – all major antioxidants – and as a result are increasingly becoming a staple on the shelves of health-food stores everywhere in juices, jams and cordials.

The berries have a distinct tart citrus flavour, like orange-flavoured ice lollies combined with a hint of tinned peaches, ending in a burnt caramel-like bitterness. This unusual amalgam of flavours creates an effect similar to Seville oranges, and just like these, they do require a sprinkling of sugar to bring out their best.

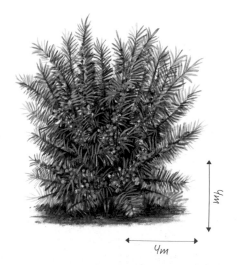

4m

4m

3m

Once sweetened they can be turned into everything from jams and juices to liqueurs and a particularly good glaze for rich meats like game.

To make a refreshing, food mile-free 'bitter orange' squash, bubble up the berries with an equal weight of sugar and just enough water to cover for 20 minutes. Strain through a sieve, reheat until bubbling, funnel the syrup into sterilised bottles while still very hot and seal. This will stay fresh for over a year if kept sealed and up to two weeks in the fridge once opened.

For a healthier version, swap the water and sugar for agave syrup (a lower GI sweetener available from health-food stores) and continue as per usual.

You can use the resulting syrup in just the same way as you would oranges, diluted and mixed with gelatine to make a golden jelly – flecked with a few of the fresh berries – or drizzled over a slice of breaded, deep-fried goat's cheese to offset the fruit's healthiness. The same syrup, spiked with a dash of Grand Marnier and a knob of butter, makes an indulgent, bittersweet take on duck á l'orange (or should that be duck *sans* l'orange?) dragging the dish into the 21st century.

Alpine 'snow' strawberries

Fragaria vesca 'White Soul'

Pineapple-flavoured, bonsai-sized strawberries

One of the easiest of all fruit crops to grow, these nouvelle cuisine-sized strawberries pack all the flavour of a ripe pineapple into a fruit the size of a raisin. Their unusual cream colour not only gives them a fun visual appeal, but means they are virtually invisible to marauding birds, so all the more for you. Also known as: wild white strawberries, white alpine strawberries.

Growing

Resistant to pests, hardy down to a chilly −20°C, with a season that runs from April to November you will wonder why you ever bothered with the supermarket versions. Here are my growing tips:

• Sow the seeds in April in trays of seed compost on a sunny windowsill.

• Once they have four to five leaves, prick these out with a fork into modular trays or individual little pots. Keep well fed and watered and these should soon become little rosettes.

• Each packet of seeds can provide you with up to 300 individual plants that will start bearing berries later that very summer, making them one of the cheapest fruit crops you can grow.

variety 'Regina'

variety 'White Soul'

• Plant these out in June in sunny beds, pots or window boxes at a spacing of 15cm. Unlike most fruit plants alpine strawberries can handle a little light shade, although their yields (and flavour) will not be as great on such sites.

• As the plants grow no more than 15cm high, try planting them in the bare soil under taller crops, packing in up to 50 plants per square metre to form a thick, weed-suppressing blanket. I like to plug plants into any gaps in beds, tubs and troughs, because as each fruit is so small you need to have a large number of plants to ensure a generous harvest.

Harvesting & eating

By using the above growing technique just two-square metres of ground (that would otherwise lay empty under taller crops) will give you regular fistful-sized harvests of little berries from early April right up until November.

They are fantastic in fruit salads, on muesli and scattered over trifles, stirred into white chocolate-chip cookie dough or folded into vanilla cheesecake mix. Simmered in a little sugar they can be used to flavour fancy vinegars.

15cm

15cm

15cm

Juneberries *Amelanchier alnifolia, A. canadensis*

The super-productive tree blueberry with almond-flavoured pips

It's not often you get a plant that combines a delicious rare crop with a low-maintenance disposition, beautiful flowers, fiery autumn colour and is available in every garden centre. Looking and tasting like a sweet, fragrant blueberry, with a texture more like a dessert apple, the flesh of this fruit is studded with little marzipan-flavoured seeds, creating a delicious two-toned flavour. Quite simply, if the word 'yum' could be defined, the juneberry would be it. Also known as: saskatoon, serviceberry.

Growing

There isn't a great deal to say about growing juneberries, primarily because this is just so easy to do.

Here's all you need to know:

• The plants will fruit well in both sun and part shade. Having said that, the higher the light levels the sweeter the berries and more intense the colour.

• Water well while establishing and ensure maximum harvest by giving the plants a good few doses of high-potash liquid feed throughout the summer.

• There is no need for pruning apart from snipping off any diseased or damaged stems as they appear.

• Hailing from the prairies of North America they are super-cold hardy and resistant to all kinds of pests and diseases.

Varieties to try

These are extremely popular garden plants and can be picked up at any nursery, hiding innocuously in the ornamental tree section rather than among the apples and pears. I would go for the species grown commercially for its fruit in Canada, *Amelanchier alnifolia*, as this has the largest, tastiest berries. Failing that, the slightly more common garden ornamental, *A. canadensis*, is a perfectly reasonable runner-up.

Harvesting & eating

The fruit is absolutely delicious straight off the tree in June (hence its name). Don't let them hang around too long though, as the one downside to juneberries is that they are loved by birds who will denude the branches in just a couple of days after the fruit become fully ripe.

Scatter the raw berries over Greek-style yoghurt drizzled in honey, chuck into a smoothie or sprinkle them over your muesli in the morning. For me, the fresh fruit are so delicious that it is a shame to overcook them, as I feel they lose a bit of their intensity and complex flavour if boiled up beyond recognition. But studded into muffins, tossed into an apple crumble, scattered between the layers of a bread and butter pudding or made into a pie, they are simply stunning.

Their bright sweetness works well with tart fruit like blackcurrants, gooseberries and rhubarb – or with all three, to make a quirky 'jumbleberry' pie.

The Native Americans prized the fruit above all other wild berries for their intense sweetness and lack of grainy seeds or astringency, adding them to all manner of dishes including pemmican, a traditional beef jerky made from bison meat. For a quirky (albeit wildly inauthentic) take on this, I simmer the crushed berries with a tablespoon of brown sugar, and add this to a sprinkle of lemon juice, dash of soy sauce and a grating of wasabi. Strips of sirloin are then marinated in this mixture overnight. The strips are charred for a few seconds on each side in a searing-hot pan, before deglazing with a dash of rum, these are wonderful in a crusty white baguette with caramelised onions and leafy salad.

3m

2.5m

4m

Oregon grape *Mahonia aquifolium*

The Native American forest fruit that grows in supermarket car parks

Once prized by Native Americans, these powder blue bunches of blackcurrant-flavoured berries from the Pacific North West are more likely to be found on our side of the Atlantic looking pretty in your supermarket car park than on your dinner plate. Yet with their delicious tart flavour and sky-high vitamin content, you might already have a hidden bounty of these growing at the bottom of your garden, cleverly disguised as highly ornamental, super low-maintenance garden shrubs. Go on get up and have a look! Also known as: Oregon grape-holly, Oregon holly-grape.

Growing

Council roundabouts and supermarket car parks just wouldn't be the same without the evergreen architectural leaves and fragrant yellow spring blossom of Oregon grapes, where they are enormously popular for their ability to put up with nearly anything that is thrown at them. Here's what you need to know:

• These are incredibly forgiving plants – tolerant of drought, poor soil and will fruit in both scorching sun and deep shade.

1.2m
50cm

• For the biggest crops treat them to a sunny site on soil high in organic matter and liberal showerings of high-potash liquid fertiliser in the summer.

Being slightly prickly (their species name 'aquifolium' means 'needle leaf') these plants are often employed as a dense hedging plant to keep out unwanted visitors – particularly useful, say, planted under a ground-floor window.

Conveniently, they are great for wildlife too, coming into flower from January to April to provide a vital nectar bar for emerging insects long before the main flush of spring blossom arrives.

Harvesting & eating

The bunches of berries are ready to harvest in the early autumn, when they turn from hard green bullets to deep navy blue bunches of mini grapes. Use sharp scissors or secateurs to snip off bunches whole, as this is far easier and cleaner to harvest than picking off each tiny berry by hand.

Much like gooseberries or redcurrants, the fruit really need the assistance of a sprinkling of sugar and a gentle bubble in a saucepan to bring out their true flavour. When raw they have a distinct sharpness and curious pea-like flavour, which somehow miraculously turns into a delicious fusion of grape and blackcurrant upon cooking.

Their only real drawback is quite a large seed, which is, however, very easily removed by simply pushing the cooked fruit through a sieve with the back of a spoon to isolate the delicious jammy pulp. In the States this deseeded pulp is simmered into a rather wonderful jelly (see *A recipe idea*, page 250). Try slaking the jelly over a shop-bought vanilla cheesecake or bubble up the pulp with maple syrup to make a tangy sauce for pancakes and waffles.

A touch of ginger, chilli and a splash of cider vinegar turns the same mix into a fruity relish, great as an alternative to redcurrant jelly with roast lamb, duck or chicken. Simmered in water until the berries burst and give up their juicy contents, Oregon grapes make a delicious cordial and can even be brewed to make a really pleasant dry, fruity wine. Be careful though, as the juice leaves almost indelible stains on fingers and clothes.

Medical marvel
Oregon grape bark and roots contain high levels of an antibacterial substance known as berberine, which has been used for centuries in the traditional medicine of America's indigenous peoples to treat all manner of infections. This is far from being a historical anecdote, as it was recently discovered that berberine's complex method of action makes it effective at treating certain new, drug-resistant strains of bacteria, including MRSA.

Oregon grape jelly & peanut butter sandwich

The rich blackcurrant grape flavour of these powder-blue berries makes for a grown-up twist on an old-school kid's favourite.

Ingredients
1 large Bramley apple
150g Oregon grapes
220g caster sugar
finely grated zest and juice of ½ a lemon

Roughly chop the whole apple – core, skin and all – into small cubes. Don't worry, these fibrous bits will be sieved out later and the large amounts of pectin they contain will actually help create a smooth set to the finished jelly.

Tip the apple into a medium saucepan with the Oregon grapes, sugar, lime zest and juice. Gently simmer on a low heat for 30 minutes, stirring occasionally.

While still steaming hot, press the mixture through a metal sieve using the back of a spoon and pour the strained liquid into sterilised jars (see *My ten commandments*, page 35).

Serve by spreading generous helpings of the jelly in a peanut butter sandwich for a classic all-American favourite, made even more 'American' by frying in butter on both sides until crisp, golden and oozing.

Fuchsia berries *Fuchsia sp.*

Discover an exotic Andean berry lurking in your flower borders

Once prized by the Incas for their delicious, jumbleberry-flavoured fruit, the stunning pendant flowers of this ubiquitous pub hanging-basket have somehow distracted us from the incredible edible potential of their shiny purple berries. To me they're easily the best-kept South American secret since the map to Eldorado.

Growing

Hardy, quick growing and highly ornamental, pick the right variety of fuchsia and you will be rewarded with a spectacular annual display of flowers, followed by a bumper crop of Andean berries that'll ask for very little in return.

There is a huge range of different fuchsia species spanning the tropical Amazonian rainforest right down to the wintery fjords at the very tip of southern Chile. By some remarkable stroke of luck for gardeners in chilly old Blighty the species with the tastiest fruit are generally the more southerly ones, making them able to withstand anything our winters can throw at them.

This is really good news as although all fuchsia berries are edible, flavour quality is highly variable between varieties – some richly jammy and fragrant, others watery and tasting of virtually nothing. For this reason, I would say that picking the right variety is the most important part in growing fuchsias.

Varieties to try

• *Fuchsia regia* subsp. *regia* – my definite top runner in the flavour stakes, after having taste tested nearly 60 varieties. From the highlands of southern Brazil it has masses of black, very sweet berries on long trailing stems.

• *Fuchsia magellanica* – if *Fuchsia regia* ssp. *regia* isn't available, try this closely related species (the regular purple-flowered variety, not the white form), the berries of which are is still sold today at indigenous markets in Chile.

• *Fuchsia* 'Genii' – makes a nice neat hedge with a good sweet flavour.

• *Fuchsia* 'Jingle Bells' – produces enormous spherical fruit almost identical to a black cherry.

Known as *chilca*, meaning literally 'grows by water' to the Mapuche people of Chile, these hardy fuchsia berries will grow best if you do the following:

• Pick a bright sunny area that gets a little shade for at least part of the day, on moist, yet well-drained soil.

• Plant the plants about 5cm deeper than the depth of the pot to help protect the roots from severe frost, while also encouraging lateral rooting from the branches below ground level.

• Water these moisture lovers liberally throughout the summer, applying a potash-rich feed such as comfrey tea to encourage maximum flowering and fruiting.

Once planted the only additional care the plants will need is a hard pruning back each spring after all risk of frost has passed, trimming

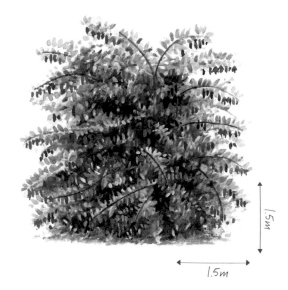

1.5m

1.5m

them down to about 20cm above ground level. This will not only ensure maximum flower production, which occurs on the new season's growth, but will also help contain the plant's size, as these can reach up to 4m high in sheltered locations.

Harvesting & eating

Gather the berries when they are soft to the touch and as darkly coloured as possible. Don't let a bright pink hue fool you; their flavours don't fully develop until they turn a deep black cherry tone. The easiest way to harvest these without squishing them is to pick them by the stalks, like cherries – you can always remove these later in the kitchen.

The flavour of the fruit comes in two successive waves: at first sweet and berry-like, somewhere between a fig and a black cherry; later a spicy, dry aftertaste reminiscent of freshly ground black pepper.

Fuchsia berries are wonderful fresh, scattered over Greek-style yoghurt drizzled in honey. The berries' flavour develops a marked intensity upon cooking, making a fantastic jam laced with a dash of vanilla. Try them dotted through muffins like blueberries, cooked up with ginger and chilli as a tangy relish or in my all-time favourite – fuchsia berry and cream cheese empanadas (opposite).

Fuchsia flower & leaf remedies
The flowers too are edible, making an interesting garnish, and despite not possessing much noticeable flavour are believed to be a remedy for broken-heartedness in Chilean folk medicine. The leaves, brewed into a tea are traditionally used as a treatment for menstrual disorders and fevers, and are said to possess diuretic properties.

a recipe idea

Sticky fuchsia berry & cream cheese empanadas

One of my favourite street-food snacks while doing research in Andean markets, these crisp fruity pastries are pure heaven with a big pot of strong black coffee.

Serves 4

Ingredients
1 tbsp cornflour
1 tbsp water
juice of 1 lemon
200g fuchsia berries, destalked and washed
200g caster sugar
1 tbsp soft light brown sugar
75g cream cheese
1 pack of ready-rolled shortcrust pastry
2 tbsp butter, melted
icing sugar to dust

Preheat the oven to 180°C. Combine the cornflour, water and lemon juice with a spoon until you have smooth paste.

Scoop the paste into a saucepan and add the fuchsia berries and caster sugar. Stir well. Heat for 15 minutes over a medium flame, stirring occasionally, until the fruit begins to burst and the liquid thickens.

Take the saucepan off the heat and leave to cool, then refrigerate for 30 minutes, after which point, you should have a thick, jammy consistency.

Blend the brown sugar with the cream cheese until you have a smooth mix.

Cut the pastry into 15cm rounds. Fill the centres of these with 2 tablespoons of the fuchsia berry mix and 1 tsp of cream cheese mix, leaving a thin border all around the pastry rounds. Brush around the edges with the melted butter and fold the pastry over to seal it like a fruity Cornish pasty. Brush the top of your empanadas with the remaining melted butter.

Bake in the oven for 10–15 minutes or until golden brown. For a truly indulgent treat, these can be deep-fried for 5 minutes, until crisp and golden. Sift over a light dusting of icing sugar. Serve simply as is or with a good quality vanilla ice cream.

Barberries *Berberis thunbergii*

Fistfuls of Persian 'redcurrants' borne on stunning garden bushes

Imagine a long-lost, giant redcurrant bush, producing so many berries that birds can barely dent its harvest, so tough it can be completely ignored for years and beautiful enough to hold its own in any Chelsea Flower Show garden. If your imagination has failed you there is a picture of it right here. These cranberry-flavoured berries are enormously popular in Persian cuisine and tricky to track down outside of Iranian delis – all the more reason to grow them yourself! Also known as *zereshk*.

Growing

Grown as a much-loved fruit in Britain until the late 19th century, barberry bushes can be picked up in even the most ordinary garden centre for bumper harvests for decades to come. At this point I should make a confession. The species once grown here and that the Iranians are so mad about is actually the European species *Berberis vulgaris*, not the Japanese one I recommend here, *B. thunbergii*. However, as its flavour is virtually identical and the plants are far more readily available, I reckon the Japanese form is a far better option to go for.

Beloved by council landscapers everywhere, once established these are ultra-resilient, low-maintenance shrubs. Simply:

• Plant the shrubs in rich, well-drained soil in full sun – although they will thrive in any soil type apart from those that are waterlogged in winter – and keep well irrigated in their first year or two while they establish.

Then promptly forget about them – apart for the occasional admiring glance and berry-picking raid come autumn.

Varieties to try

Variety-wise my top picks would be:

• *Berberis thunbergii* **'Atropurpurea'** – for its burgundy leaves that beautifully set off the ruby red berries.

• **'Georgii'** – a hybrid that is believed to include the 'proper' Iranian species as one of its parents, is super-productive and has stunning, salmon-pink jewel-like bunches.

Both these have the side benefit of bearing great bunches of pretty scented blossom in spring. Producing some rather spiky thorns, the plants make an impressive intruder-proof fence and can even be grown against a wall to eliminate any chance of an accidental prickle while walking past.

Harvesting & eating

The berries come into season in autumn and will keep fresh on the plant right into mid winter, so you can harvest them as and when you need them throughout the coldest months of the year by snipping them off with secateurs. Mind the sharp thorns though!

Like redcurrants, the berries are very tart and fruity, somewhat like pre-sweetened cranberry juice, and are used to add a fresh acidity to a huge range of Middle Eastern dishes. They're lovely in jams and jellies, scattered into pies and tossed into fruit salads to add a brightness to other much sweeter fruit like bananas or grapes.

In Iran barberries are sun-dried like raisins and tossed into a buttery saffron pilaf with toasted pistachios, looking like ruby and jade Christmas baubles among the golden rice. Given our rather sunless autumns, we Brits can mimic the effect by scattering them on a metal tray and popping them in a very low oven for a few hours.

If you don't fancy rice, the same principle works great in couscous or tossed with caramelised onions, black olives, roasted red peppers and plenty of parsley to make a cold cracked-wheat salad like tabbouleh.

These 'barberaisins' are used similarly scattered over baked chicken, marinated in saffron, butter, cloves and cardamom in a simple but wholly exotic dish guaranteed to chase away the autumnal chills. Of course barberries can also be used straight off the plant too – indeed this is apparently how they are preferred by rural Iranians who have access to the garden-fresh unprocessed type – where they are used exactly as their urban and expat cousins would use the dried form.

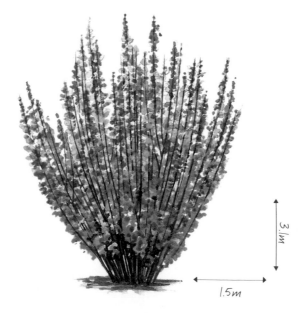

3.1m

1.5m

American cranberry bush *Viburnum trilobum*

The cranberry imposter that produces double the crops on pretty garden shrubs

Found in every supermarket, but almost no allotments, cranberry plants are notoriously fussy to grow, not to mention stingy on the production front. But swap the finicky true cranberry for this easy-going imposter and you will get double the crop for half the effort and a flavour that even the most avid cosmopolitan drinker would be hard-pressed to tell apart. **Also known as: American highbush cranberry, cranberry viburnum.**

Growing

Despite sharing a virtually identical flavour, these plants are not actually related to true cranberries at all, being a far closer cousin of our native 'Guelder Rose' *Viburnum opulus*, from which it is in fact rather tricky to tell it apart. It is rather important that you pick the right species however (look for the Latin name '*Viburnum trilobum*' clearly printed on the label), as the fruit of *Viburnum opulus* will give you the runs if you eat too many! Not a mistake you will make twice at least ...

Forming highly ornamental bushes that burst into clusters of stunning white lacy flowers in the spring, these slowly turn into bunches of bright red faux 'cranberries' towards the end of summer.

To get growing simply:

• Pick a sunny site, dig plenty of organic matter into the planting hole and water in well.

• Give them generous applications of high-potash liquid feed throughout the growing season to maximise your harvest.

After that they really will be perfectly happy to go it alone.

Harvesting & eating

The bunches of berries are ripe and ready to eat when they turn bright scarlet and translucent in the early autumn, at which point they can be simply snipped off with a pair of secateurs.

The tart red berries should be cooked and eaten as a direct substitute for cranberries in any recipe with the only real difference being that they have small, but rather stony seeds in their centres, so they need to be strained through a sieve before serving.

To make a great mock cranberry jelly, simmer 500g of the berries with 250ml of water and bubble away for 20 minutes or so until the fruit have burst and gone soft. Pour this mix into a sieve above a mixing bowl and leave overnight night for the juice to drip through. You can do this infinitely quicker by pushing the pulp through the sieve with the back of a spoon but this won't result in a crystal-clear jelly, more a translucent red slush. Measure out the strained juice – for every 600ml you will have to add 450g of jam sugar (from the baking aisle) and simmer for 15–20minutes on a low heat. Pour

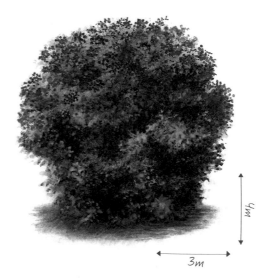

3m

4m

into scrupulously clean jars while still hot, seal and you are done.

Alternatively try making cranberry-bush juice – the basis of a great cosmopolitan. Simply simmer the berries in an equal amount of water for 15 minutes, churn up the whole mix with a stick blender, strain and sweeten to taste. For this, you will need a rather scary amount of sugar, which gives you a bit on an insight into just how much goes into supermarket cranberry juice, although much of this could be replaced using a natural sweetening agent (see *Experimental herbs, spices and flavours*, page 206) such as sugar leaves or sweet cicely, added during the simmering stage. Add a shot of this juice to two of vodka, one of Cointreau and a twist of lime juice, and you won't care how much sugar is in it.

Please don't risk the temptation of chewing on a raw one as just like regular cranberries, what begins as intense sourness soon turns into an all-encompassing bitterness making you far less inclined to experiment with them. However, with a good stewing in an avalache of sugar, they miraculously turn into that crisp, deliciousness we all know and love.

Chilean guavas *Myrtus ugni (aka Ugni molinae)*

Slacker-proof strawberry-flavoured 'blueberries' with a hint of eucalyptus

Reputed to have been Queen Victoria's favourite fruit, the berries of this guava plant look like blueberries yet taste like wild strawberries, creating a plant with a rather wonderful identity crisis. They even come with sweetly scented, powder-pink lily-of-the-valley type flowers which adds to the confusion. Also known as: strawberry myrtle, tazziberry, New Zealand cranberry.

Growing

Hardy down to a bitter −10C, these little evergreen shrubs from the rainforests of Chile should prove hardy in all but the coldest regions, particularly when given a nice sheltered site. Here's what you need to know:

• Start your collection by buying young plants, at least 50cm high, from specialist nurseries or even in the ornamentals section of larger garden centres and you will have fruit from the very first year.

• Although they will fruit well partial shade they will offer up the largest and sweetest crops in full sunshine.

• They prefer to have their roots in an acidic soil, preferably with great heaps of organic matter dug in to mimic their woodland home. If you are gardening on a chalky area, it is best to plant these in pots of ericaceous soil-based potting mix sat on a sunny patio, which also gives you the benefit of being able to bring these in during particularly harsh winters in the coldest northern districts.

• Keep them well watered with an organic ericaceous liquid feed throughout the summer, although at a pinch the plants will survive short periods of drought.

Chilean guavas won't need any special pruning, are totally self-fertile and can be enormously productive so you won't need to plant enormous tracts of them to get a very respectable harvest.

Harvesting & eating

The berries start coming into season in midsummer and they generally take on a pinkish hue before they reach their full size or ripeness. Wait for them to get to the size of a blueberry, when they should be similarly just soft to the touch and a deep rich red, then just gently pull them off with your fingers.

> **Tazziberry**
> Marketed by enterprising Tasmanian growers as the 'Tazziberry', punnets of these sell for a small fortune in fancy London department store food halls.

Chilean guavas can be used in all the same ways as you would a blueberry. They are sugary enough to be eaten fresh off the shrub, adding an intoxicating fragrance to fruit salads, scattered over your morning cereal, tumbled over cakes or blitzed up in a strawberry smoothie. Stewed in sugar and a tablespoon of water, they can be added to all manner of sweet treats like hot cakes, crêpes or atop steaming hot porridge oats.

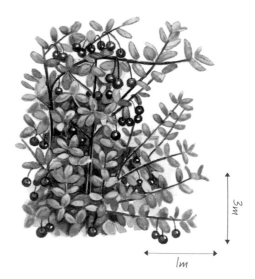

3m

1m

a recipe idea

Chilean guava hot cakes with spiced syrup & vanilla ricotta

Studded through crisp, chewy hot cakes, like little flavour bombs, these fragrant berries are the key ingredient in my favourite autumn treat.

Makes 12 pancakes

Ingredients

For the spiced syrup
150g Chilean guavas, rinsed
  and dried
250ml maple syrup
¼ tsp allspice
1tbsp butter

For the vanilla ricotta
200g ricotta
2 tbsp icing sugar
finely grated zest of ½ a lemon
1 tsp lemon juice
2 tsp vanilla extract

For the batter
100g plain flour
4 tbsp sugar
½ tsp salt
1 tsp baking powder
60g melted butter, plus
  extra for greasing
2 large eggs
finely grated zest of ½
  a lemon
1 tsp vanilla essence
50ml milk
250ml plain yoghurt

Combine all the ingredients for the syrup in a saucepan and simmer for 5 minutes over a low heat. Strain the stewed berries out with a slotted spoon and leave to one side (these will be used in the hot cake batter). Keep the infused syrup to serve with the hot cakes.

Now make the vanilla ricotta by mixing the ricotta, icing sugar, lemon zest, juice and vanilla extract in a bowl and mix until thoroughly combined. Set aside.

For the batter, combine flour, sugar, salt and baking powder in a small bowl and set aside. Whisk the melted butter, eggs, lemon zest, vanilla essence, milk and yoghurt together in a large bowl. Add the dry batter ingredients and stir in slowly – you should have a relatively thick mixture.

Generously grease a large frying pan and place over a low heat. Add tablespoons of the batter into the pan. Scatter a few of the stewed Chilean guavas over the hot cakes and press into the batter using the back of a spoon. Flip over once and cook until golden brown on both sides. Serve drizzled with the spiced syrup and a generous helping of vanilla ricotta.

Garden Essentials

Your garden kit

Walk into a garden centre and you're soon confronted by an array of shiny tools, gaudy bottles of sprays and potions and a huge variety of gadgets and gizmos – which can understandably be daunting. The good news is that you don't need the vast majority of the stuff on the shelves to achieve bumper crops. So dodge the gimmicks and invest in just a few pieces of really good quality gardening kit and save yourself a fortune – and the nightmare of having a garage full of unused gadgets.

Metal tools

For the average domestic-sized vegetable garden you will only really need five key tools: a **spade**, **fork**, **hoe**, **trowel** and **secateurs**. For the spade, fork and hoe, I would go for a set of forged models (made from a single piece of metal), which are so durable they almost always come with a lifetime guarantee. For the trowel and secateurs, go for ones with a carbon-steel blade. Pick up a sharpening stone to keep all your tools in mint condition – remember, the sharper the tool the quicker and less effort all your work will be.

All of the above should come to about £100, which despite being quite an initial outlay should last you a good 50 years.

Watering cans & hoses

Watering cans

If you are only gardening in a small space you might only need a largish watering can, meaning you won't need to battle with a tangled hose. Pick a can of a minimum of 9 litres to save you dozens of trips back and forth to the tap. Personally for me, the best ones come with a detachable rose (the part on the end of the nozzle with the tiny holes) and a single 'wrap around' handle that arcs over the back and top of the main vessel for easy pouring. I would go for a galvanised metal model, as although these are much pricier to begin with, they will last decades rather than just a year or two like the flimsy plastic ones. In small spaces a metal model also makes a stunning garden feature in its own right.

Hoses

If it is a hose you are after it is **always** worth spending a little extra on getting the best quality you can afford. A decent set-up will last years and save you water, time, and an enormous amount of frustration. In the long run it will be far cheaper than buying a new 'value' reel, washer, spray head and so on every couple of months. So here are a couple of tips:

• Get a spray-gun attachment to ensure your hose is only spewing water exactly when you need it. The best ones come on 'lances' so water can be directed to reach tricky places like hanging baskets or pots at an arm's length.

• Get a hose with a self-winding reel – they really do make tidying it away a breeze.

Soil-based compost

Apart from when sowing seeds, striking cuttings or potting on very small plants, it is always best to use a soil-based potting compost for growing edible crops. Using soil-based composts generally require less frequent watering, make sturdier specimens and are likely to have a better flavour due to the levels of micronutrients found in soil that traditional peat-based blends lack. In fact, as peat-based potting composts (which make up the vast majority of what is sold in garden centres) contain almost no naturally occurring nutrients of their own and hold added nutrients extremely poorly, you become locked into a cycle of needing to also fork out on fertilisers to ensure healthy plant growth.

You can even make your own soil-based blend virtually for free by using a blend of soil from your plot combined with organic matter such as homemade composted garden waste or the municipal compost that many councils give away at your local tip. For more information on how to do this see *My ten commandments*, page 19).

Fertilisers

If you are growing in a soil-based compost enriched with plenty of organic matter you will automatically need to use far less fertiliser than you otherwise would. Although I make much of my own liquid feed from nettles and comfrey (see *Tips & tricks*, page 51) I find an application of blood, fish and bone or pelleted chicken manure sprinkled over the beds and lightly worked in or scattered into planting holes a invaluable nutritional boost. Both of these are highly concentrated, relatively inexpensive fertilisers that you can pick up at any decent garden centre.

Pots & containers

Generally, it is better to have a few larger containers rather than loads of little runty pots knocking around your garden. Larger volumes of compost tend to dry out less quickly in summer and protect plant roots against the wide fluctuations of temperature that can occur in smaller containers.

Propagation lamps

These are the one bit of gardening kit that I am totally in love with. Propagation lamps have a unique ability to greatly extend the growing season (effectively moving your garden several hundred miles further south) and to pep up weak or sickly plants after just a couple of days basking in their rays.

They might look like regular fluorescent light tubes, but they are specially designed to emit a spectrum which supercharges plant growth. Propagation lamps allow you to sow seeds far earlier in the year than you would normally be able to do, in dark, cold winter days, and get your new plants off to a head start. With many species that need a long growing season, this can effectively double your yields over the year. Cuttings planted out under one of these lights also have an enormously increased chance of rooting well and resisting the dreaded infections they so often suffer from.

For best results site your seeds on a windowsill during the day and under the propagation lamp by night, as plants don't need sleep. 24-hour light means 24-hour growth!

Buying a propagation lamp

One tricky aspect of propagation lamps is tracking down a domestic-sized, affordable version. Look for models described as 'propagation lamps' rather than 'grow lamps' as these are generally the best suited to the homegrower. They might be pricey (typically about £60–£70) but the difference they make is dramatic – and of course they're cheaper than moving to warmer climes!

A budget lamp
If you really are on a tight budget, you can create a homemade propagation lamp by simply screwing ordinary 'daylight' bulbs (available in every hardware store) into a regular desk lamp and shining this directly over (about 20cm above) your seed trays.

Geek-speak glossary

Jargon getting all a bit too much? Here's my attempt to translate geek speak into pure, simple English.

Acid/Alkaline soil – Soil with a pH lower than 6.5 is described as acid by us plant geeks; also known as 'bitter' by some old boys. Although these soils are generally not ideal for the majority of crops, some species like blueberries, cranberries and Chilean guavas have specifically evolved to thrive in these conditions.

Soils with a pH above 7.5 are considered alkaline (or, to older folks, 'sweet') and are the type preferred by plants in the cabbage family like broccoli, pak choi, Brussels sprouts and so on. Soils in the neutral zone between pH 6.5 and 7.5 are generally the most versatile growing media, able to support the widest range of plant species.

Annual – A plant that normally lives for no more than one growing season, capable of sprouting, maturing and producing seed all within one year. Because at the end of the growing season annuals die, they need resowing each year if you plan on growing them more than once.

Bedding plants – Tender or half-hardy plants grown outdoors only during the frost-free months of the year (usually mid May to mid-October).

Cloche – Essentially a portable mini greenhouse, usually no more than 30–40cm high, that can be laid over plants to raise the soil and air temperature around them by a few degrees. Uses: to protect young or tender plants from frost in winter, to help extend the growing season or to spoil heat-loving plants in summer.

Croziers – The unfurling baby fronds of a fern, which still resemble a spiral.

Cutting – A small section of a plant, usually no more than 15cm long, used to propagate new specimens. Generally the freshly cut material from young shoots or roots is inserted into gritty, free-draining compost and kept warm, moist and humid.

Ericaceous – **In plants:** a species that thrives only when grown on acid soil. **In composts:** a growing medium with a pH of less than 6.5, specially formulated for growing ericaceous plants.

Germination – The process of sprouting in seeds.

Gourds – Fruits in the pumpkin family that are large and have a hard skin. This includes melons, pumpkins, squashes and the like.

Grafting – A horticultural 'cut and pasting' process, where the shoots or branches of one plant is joined or 'grafted' onto the roots or lower half of another. This makes a plant that combines the desirable characteristics of two plants into one – for example, grafting tomato leaves onto potato roots will produce a plant that produces both tomato fruit and potato tubers. This can generally only be done with plants that are closely related.

Growbag – Bags of specially formulated compost designed for crops to be planted straight into, omitting the need for a pot or other form of container. These are sold in all good garden centres and are usually marketed for growing tomatoes or other greenhouse crops, but can essentially be used for any shallow-rooted species (i.e. not root veg). Holes are sliced through the plastic and the young plants planted into (and watered through) these slits.

Half-hardy – Able to withstand short periods of sub-zero temperatures down to a few minus degrees (no less than −5°C), especially if given some form of protection such as an insulating blanket of horticultural fleece, straw or mulch.

Hardening off – For cosseted indoor-grown plants, the gradual acclimatisation to life outdoors. Generally this involves placing them outside in a sheltered, shady spot during the day and bringing them back indoors each evening for five days to one week, before finally planting them in their permanent positions.

Hardy – A plant able to survive prolonged sub-zero (less than 0°C) temperatures, happily growing outdoors all year round.

Horticultural fleece – A light specialist fabric sold by the roll in all good garden centres that can be laid over or wrapped around plants to create an insulating blanket to seal in warmth in the summer or shield against cold in winter.

High-potash fertiliser (see 'Potash')

Mulch – A soil covering made from organic matter like compost, bark chippings, leaf mould or even more exotic materials like cocoa shells and wool. This is laid on in a layer between 5–15cm to suppress weeds from springing up, seal in vital moisture and keep roots cool in the summer and shielded from frost in the winter.

Overwinter – To successfully care for a tender plant over the winter months to allow it to survive until the next spring.

Perennial – A plant that lives for more than one growing season. As these will return year after year, they do not need to be sown each spring.

Pinching out – Removing the growing point at the very tips of branches to induce denser, bushier growth, which in many cases also improves flower/fruit production. This is done by literally pinching off the last 0.5–1cm off these tips with your thumb and forefinger.

Pollination – This is basically the plant equivalent of conception in humans. Pollen is transferred from male flower parts to female ones, initiating the process of fruit and seed formation. Without successful pollination by wind or the actions of visiting bees and other animals, the flowers will simply fall off without producing any fruit at all. Improved pollination levels are therefore often directly proportional to yield in fruit or seed crops, creating a spike in the amount you'll harvest if you get it right.

Potash – A naturally occurring chemical necessary for the healthy production of flowers and fruit in plants. In fertilisers, formulas containing higher concentrations of potash are specifically designed for use on flowering and fruiting plants, such as rose and tomato feeds to stimulate higher yields.

Pricking out – Lifting out newly sprouted seedlings when they have developed their two first true leaves and transplanting them into small pots of compost to grow on. This is usually easiest to do using a regular table fork instead of a trowel, as the plants are so tiny. Handle the delicate seedlings by their leaves and not the stem, as these are least prone to damage.

Propagate – To increase your stock of plants by sowing the seeds of or taking cuttings from your existing specimens.

Pruning – The removal of leaves, branches or roots of plants to manipulate their growth in some way. This can be to remove dead or diseased tissue, induce bushier growth, improve the quality or size of fruit or flowers, dictate a plant's shape, or simply to control its size.

Tender – Used to describe a tropical or sub-tropical plant that is incapable of surviving temperatures of below 0°C for any considerable amount of time.

Transplanting – The moving of a plant from one site to another by uprooting it and replanting it in new growing media. As transplanting almost always causes some damage to the roots it is usually a good idea to prune off some of the leaves too. This helps reduce the loss of water from the plant via its foliage while its ability to replace this loss by absorption through the roots is compromised. For this same reason give newly transplanted specimens a good old soak and keep them moist and in the shade while settling in to their new site.

Places to inspire

Fancy pinching a couple of ideas from the pros? Here's my hand-picked batch of top-notch gardens that are like botanical Disneylands for 'grow your own' geeks.

Royal Botanic Gardens, Kew, Surrey – The place where I did much of my training and a worldwide authority on cool stuff to grow. I've been obsessed with scanning the grounds for new ideas and plants since I was about 8 years old.
www.kew.org

Chelsea Physic Garden, London – Hands down my favourite garden of all time. A tiny 3-acre patch of Central London entirely dedicated to weird and wonderful edible, medicinal and historical plants, including Britain's largest outdoor olive tree and the world's most northerly outdoor grapefruit – covered in fruit each summer. Also a source of London's best tea and cake!
www.chelseaphysicgarden.co.uk

Eden Project, Cornwall – Space-age architecture meets primeval rainforest and all packed with unusual edibles to boot. Check out the Malaysian rainforest vegetable garden and the edible beds that wrap around their beautiful alfresco café.
www.edenproject.com

Garden Organic, Coventry – The only place I know in the UK with a whole garden entirely dedicated to exotic crops from all over the world. Part of an ongoing project working with immigrant communities, many of whom were the first to try growing these crops on our shores over 40 years ago, this is really somewhere you should not miss.
www.sowingnewseeds.org.uk

The University of Oxford Botanic Garden, Oxford – A stunning oasis in this beautiful city, packed full of exotic edibles. A great place to get inspired, lay on the lawn in the sun and eat cake.
www.botanic-garden.ox.ac.uk

The Royal Botanic Garden Edinburgh – Pioneers in growing, researching and teaching about edible and medicinal plants. They have stunning glasshouses and unique collections of fascinating east Asian plants that are the next best thing to a flight to the Himalayas. Check out the herbology course, which I've had the pleasure of teaching on.
www.rbge.org.uk

Royal Horticultural Society's Garden at Wisley, Surrey – With model fruit and veg gardens that make me green with envy, this is one of the best places in the country to see horticulture at its very finest. Spend a couple of hours drooling over all it has to offer and try and keep your jealousy under control.
www.rhs.org.uk/Gardens/Wisley/About-Wisley

Supplier directory

The sources of a good horticultural fix are constantly adding to and updating their wares each season. For the latest information on who sells what go to www.jameswong.co.uk/homegrownrevolution

Agroforestry Research Trust
46 Hunters Moon
Dartington
Totnes
Devon TQ9 6JT
01803 840776
www.agrofrestry.co.uk

Burgon and Ball
La Plata Works
Holme Lane
Sheffield, S6 4JY
0114 2338262
www.burgonandball.co.uk

Chiltern Seeds
Bortree Stile, Ulverston
Cumbria LA12 7PB
01229 581137
www.chilternseeds.co.uk

D.T. Brown Seeds
Bury Road, Newmarket
CB8 7PQ
0845 3710532
www.dtbrownseeds.co.uk

Edulis
The Walled Garden
Bere Court Farm
Tidmarsh Lane, Pangbourne
Reading
Berkshire RG8 8HT
07802 812781
www.edulis.co.uk

Otter Farm
1 Weston Cottages
Honiton
Devon EX14 3PA
www.otterfarm.co.uk

Pomona Fruits
Pomona House
12 Third Avenue
Walton on the Naze
Essex CO14 8JU
0845 6760607
www.pomonafruits.co.uk

Poyntzfield Herb Nursery
Black Isle
By Dingwall
Ross and Cromarty IV7 8LV
Scotland
www. poyntzfieldherbs.co.uk

Real Seeds
PO Box 18, Newport near
Fishguard
Pembrokeshire SA65 0AA
www.realseeds.co.uk

Sutton Seeds
Woodview Road, Paignton
Devon TQ4 7NG
0844 922899
www.suttons.co.uk

Thompson and Morgan
Poplar Lane, Ipswich
Suffolk IP8 3BU
0844 2485383
www.thompson-morgan.com

Index